TOWARD RESPONSIBILITY
IN THE NEW WORLD DISORDER

Also in this series

Warriors in Peacetime:
The Military and Democracy in Latin America
edited by Gabriel Marcella

Defence and the Media in Time of Limited War
edited by Peter R. Young

TOWARD RESPONSIBILITY IN THE NEW WORLD DISORDER

Challenges and Lessons of Peace Operations

Edited by

MAX G. MANWARING

(Colonel, US Army, Retired)

JOHN T. FISHEL

(Professor of National Security Policy, US National Defense University)

FRANK CASS
LONDON • PORTLAND, OR

First published in 1998 in Great Britain by
FRANK CASS PUBLISHERS
2 Park Square, Milton Park,
Abingdon, Oxon, OX14 4RN

and in the United States of America by
FRANK CASS PUBLISHERS
270 Madison Ave,
New York NY 10016

Transferred to Digital Printing 2005

Website: http://www.frankcass.com

British Library Cataloguing in Publication Data

Toward responsibility in the new world disorder :
    challenges and lessons of peace operations. - (Small wars
    and insurgencies)
    1. Peace 2. Conflict management
    I. Manwaring, Max G. II. Fishel, John T.
    327.1'72

ISBN 0 7146 4901 5 (cloth)
ISBN 0 7146 4456 0 (paper)

Library of Congress Cataloging in Publication Data
has been applied for.

This group of studies first appeared in a Special Issue on 'Toward Responsibility in the New
World Disorder: Challenges and Lessons of Peace Operations'
of *Small Wars & Insurgencies* (ISSN 0956-2318) 9/1 (Spring 1998) published by Frank Cass

Contents

Preface   **Editors**   vii

An Interview with General John R. Galvin,
US Army (Ret.), Dean, Fletcher School of
Law and Diplomacy, 6 August 1997   **Max G. Manwaring**   1

Tragedy in the Balkans: A Conflict
Ended – Or Interrupted?   **Michael Moodie**   12

From Peace Making to Peace Building
in Central America: The Illusion
versus the Reality of Peace   **Kimbra L. Fishel**   32

The Challenge of Haiti's Future   **Donald E. Schulz**   50

Waiting for 'The Big One': Confronting
Complex Humanitarian Emergencies and
State Collapse in Central Africa   **Walter S. Clarke**   72

Normative Implications of 'The Savage
Wars of Peace'   **John T. Fishel**   102

Beyond the Logjam: A Doctrine
for Complex Emergencies   **John Mackinlay**   114

Policing the New World Disorder:
Addressing Gaps in Public Security
during Peace Operations   **Michael J. Dziedzic**   132

The Future of Peace Support
Operations   **Robert H. Dorff**   160

Facing the Choice Among Bad Options in
Complex Humanitarian Emergencies   **Dayton L. Maxwell**   179

The 'Almost Obvious' Lessons of   **Max G. Manwaring and**
Peace Operations   **Edwin G. Corr**   192
Abstracts   200

About the Contributors   204

Index   209

Editors' Preface

The driving concept behind this special issue of *Small Wars & Insurgencies* is found in our title, 'Toward Responsibility in the New World Disorder'. It has been our experience and perception that the major failing of the various civil-military peacekeeping operations beginning in the last days of the Cold War and continuing through the present has been the unwillingness of the major participants and the international community to accept fully their responsibility for the long-term outcomes of the interventions they undertake.

We lead off the volume with an extensive interview with retired US General John R. Galvin. He was Supreme Allied Commander in Europe culminating a distinguished military career which provided more than a passing acquaintance with recent peace and stability operations in the former Yugoslavia, the former Soviet Union, and Africa. His career also included tenure as Commander-in-Chief, US Southern Command and an intimate involvement in the conflicts in Central America during the 1980s. While at Southern Command, General Galvin published a seminal article entitled, 'Uncomfortable Wars'. His extensive experience and that article provide continuity with our theme.

The second part of this special edition analyses four peacekeeping cases involving varying degrees of success and failure. Michael Moodie enters and leaves the Balkans with a cogent question as to whether traditional United Nations and NATO (North Atlantic Treaty Organization) peacekeeping approaches are sufficient to combat new challenges that could well become more familiar in future conflicts. Thus, he also wonders whether the conflict in the former Yugoslavia has been ended or merely interrupted. Kimbra Fishel looks at the Central American cases and stresses the fact that despite success in establishing peace in the region, the root causes of the conflicts there have yet to be addressed. The related question she asks is whether the current Central American peace is reality or illusion. This problem is repeated in Donald Schulz's analysis of the Haitian case. His concern is based on the fact that the intervening international community has been unwilling to make available the resources necessary seriously to address the central political and economic causes of conflict in and the refugee flow out of that unhappy place. Walter Clarke looks at the tragedies in central Africa over the past several years and the high probability of recurring complex humanitarian emergencies and state collapse in that part of the world. He argues that the implementation of a holistic and totally-integrated international civil-military campaign planning process is absolutely essential to help bring failed and failing states closer to peace and stability.

John Fishel's contribution marks a transition to the next part of this special edition. Using as a point of departure, his recently published "*The Savage Wars of Peace*", he discusses the normative implications of peacekeeping cases ranging from the Congo in the 1960s to Bosnia in the 1990s. Thus, his study sets the stage for John Mackinlay's argument that current doctrine is inadequate to the requirements of contemporary multilateral and multi-organizational political-military peacekeeping. Michael Dziedzic focuses on identifying gaps in public security typically confronted during peace operations, and recommending measures intended to increase proficiency in providing that fundamental human right. Robin Dorff follows with a discussion of the ambiguous and subtle political nature of future peace operations. In turn, Dayton Maxwell challenges us all to address the difficult questions surrounding these kinds of collective security actions. Finally, Max Manwaring and Edwin Corr suggest that the lessons which should have been learned over the past several years of peacekeeping fall into a category that might best be described as 'almost obvious'. That is, they are the kinds of lessons that had we kept our eyes open as we reviewed past peace operations and planned new ones, we might never have made the mistakes that these contributors illustrate.

Separately and collectively, those writing here argue that responsible peace operations take us beyond protecting a people from another group of people or from a government. They take us beyond compelling one or more parties to a conflict to cease human rights violations and other morally repugnant activities. They take us beyond repelling simple aggression. They take us beyond providing some form of humanitarian or refugee assistance in cases of misery and need. The amorphous contemporary peacekeeping task is to create internal conditions within failed or failing states that can lead to the mandated peace and stability – with justice. The intent is to ensure that an internationally supported government does not revert to the unstable status quo ante and initiate another threat to the interdependent international community.

This volume, then, commends itself to the reader to provoke thought about what governments and international organizations ought to do when faced with the responsibilities of a given peace operation. Equally important, it suggests what we as citizens in the world community ought to demand of our governments and that community in the current world disorder. In that context, we commend this special edition of *Small Wars & Insurgencies* to you – the reader – with the hope that you will make effective use of the insights of the contributors.

An Interview with General John R. Galvin, US Army (Ret.), Dean of the Fletcher School of Law and Diplomacy, 6 August 1997

MAX G. MANWARING

John R. Galvin served as Supreme Allied Commander, Europe (SACEUR); and as Commander-in-Chief of the US European Command (CINCEUR) from 1987 to 1992. Prior to that, he served for two years as Commander-in-Chief of the US Southern Command in Panama (CINCSOUTH). General Galvin has also served in several academic positions both during his more than 40 years in the Army and since. He is the author of many articles and several books, including *The Minute Men*, a study of the first battle of the American Revolution, *Three Men of Boston* a study of the political events preceding the Revolution, and 'Uncomfortable Wars: Toward a New Paradigm'. John R. Galvin is currently Dean of the Fletcher School of Law and Diplomacy.

Since the end of the Cold War, the international security system has undergone fundamental changes. In place of the relatively stable and predictable Cold War structure, the new world disorder generates ambiguous and dangerous instabilities. The spillover effects of intranational, national, and regional instability place demands on the international community to take control aggressively of a situation from those who have been profiting from chaos, establish law and order, feed and harbor victims, and ensure a secure environment for the reestablishment of responsible civil authority. Increasingly, these international 'peacekeepers' are expected to support and protect that civil authority and a subsequent political reconciliation process. The senior editor of this special issue of *Small Wars and Insurgencies* discussed these and other issues and their implications with John R. Galvin on 6 August 1997.[1]

As the North Atlantic Treaty Organization (NATO) expands physically and in terms of role and missions, how will it deal with out-of-area concerns and threats?

NATO is already dealing with some out-of-area concerns and threats – especially Bosnia. I think that Bosnia will be the prime example of

NATO acting in a different role from what was considered when NATO was formed back in the latter 1940s and early 1950s. Clearly, there will be some differences of views, especially depending on where an out-of-area event is taking place. For example, there is a difference between how Italy considers the questions of Bosnia and how Iceland might consider these same questions.

There is a real question in my mind as to whether we need to have unanimity in the North Atlantic Council regarding NATO taking part in some kind of out-of-area operation. I think it might be better to allow countries to pass, if they wish, on whether or not they themselves are willing to be specifically committed. They could still allow NATO resources to be used such as bases, ports and pipelines, communications, intelligence, and so forth.

Thus, in terms of new roles and missions, I think NATO is flexible. Obviously, there would be plenty of discussion about all that, but I do not see that NATO has had a problem up to now adapting itself to new roles and missions, and I doubt that it would in the future.

Finally, the United Nations cannot control 15 or 20 or 30 different operations all over the world at the same time. It needs help from regional and subregional structures for peace and security, and I mean by that political and military structures. Those will only come about through time. Until then, NATO can play a role.

Please elaborate on the changing model for intervention and security in failing and failed states.

The question of responsible governance and nation-state stability is really something we are going to have to deal with in the near future. The writings of Bob Kaplan and others who are really experiencing these things out in the world tell us that there are ways in which disintegration is taking place – especially in states that are being affected by weak national administrations, corruption and mismanagement, historic problems of disfranchisement for large parts of the citizenry, economic stagnation, and the technological and communications explosions.

Moreover, many nations in transition today that are dedicated to achieving political pluralism, rule of law, minority rights, and the other principles and aims of liberal democracy are also hounded by the challenges of change and are vulnerable to every kind of instability. The lack of political infrastructure, rapid population growth, environmental decline, and poverty generate further economic decline, violent internal conflicts, mushrooming demands by various groups for political autonomy, and, sometimes, state collapse.

Sooner or later, the spillover effects of these kinds of instabilities place demands on the international community, if not to solve the problems, at least to take care of the victims. As a matter of fact, the nearly 100 armed conflicts since the end of the Cold War have virtually all been the result of internal disintegration.

When these things happen, I think that intervention needs a mandate. We already have in international law ways that we can address the problems of failing and failed states. Within current law, it is possible for nations to intervene in a case where another nation is clearly incapable of handling a specific problem. It is important not to have to rely only on international law, however. It is also important to gain the support of the international community through the United Nations (UN) and its Security Council so that there will be a solid legal and legitimized basis for action.

So, is there a changing model for security and intervention in failed and failing states? Yes, indeed.

Analysis of the problems of governance and stability takes us beyond providing some form of humanitarian assistance or refugee assistance in cases of human misery and need, as in the case of the Kurds. It takes us beyond traditional monitoring of bilateral agreements, as in the Sinai. It takes us beyond protecting a people from another group of people or from repressive warlords, as in the case of Somalia. It takes us beyond compelling one or more parties to a conflict to cease human rights violations and other morally repugnant activities, or repelling simple aggression, as in the case of Bosnia and the former Yugoslavia.

These crises of governance and stability require the UN, NATO, or other responsible international or regional bodies to mount a coordinated humanitarian-political-economic-psychological-military effort. The purpose of such an effort would be to create internal conditions within failed or failing states that can lead to responsible governance that will deal with the problems that brought on the disaster in the first place.

The assertion of an international obligation to intervene in failed or failing states to achieve a desired level of stability redefines the purposes and means by which contemporary stability operations might take place. The key issue, in this context, is the role of the military in this environment. The logical role of a military deployment in such situations is to support the lead humanitarian and political elements in the intervention and create a security environment in which humanitarian and political efforts can proceed.

In this connection, there are so many roles for the military in complex human emergencies that if you were to try to establish a different structure for each role you would create an enormous hodgepodge. What we will see in the future are events in which the military is performing almost every role and mission in the portfolio – all at the same time. We will be ranging from one end of the spectrum to another and be involved in just about every conceivable action. For example, military stability operations are increasingly expected to support and protect emerging democratic political processes. We have seen much of that in those responses that we have taken already.

Interestingly, we used to talk about tooth to tail in the Army – meaning that the ability to fight was important and support to the combat elements was not. So, we created this military alligator that is all tooth and a little bob-tail. I think we are going to find ourselves talking about tail to tooth. It will take a lot of logistical, engineer, military police, civil affairs, psychological operations, and other support to help resolve the kind of long-term problems we are taking about.

Please comment on the changing concept of national sovereignty.

Because of the interventions we have just been talking about, the fact is that sovereignty has already changed. Since 1990, the Security Council has declared a formal threat to international peace and security over 60 times. These actions challenge and diminish the sovereignty of those states in which the political or humanitarian situation has demanded some sort of multilateral action. The change is already here.

Regional structures, such as OSCE (Organization for European Security and Cooperation), ASEAN (Association of South East Asian Nations), OAU (Organization of African Unity), OAS (Organization of American States), and others are also involved. For example, the OAU has strengthened and has proven itself practical. It has been able to take on some activities in Africa that people pretty much predicted would not happen.

Subregional organizations – NATO being one – are, I think, showing a lot of promise. I believe that we need a strong international structure for peace and stability on this shrinking planet on which we live. Until we can achieve this, let us support the international and regional stability structures we have. I hope that NATO will play a role in that. The primary importance of NATO is as a regional aggregation of collective international military power completely subordinate to collective civilian political decision-making. Political control of the military is essential for ensuring stability and peace. NATO is a prime example of that.

NGOs (non-governmental organizations), PVOs (private voluntary organizations), and transnational corporations are diluting national sovereignty, as well, and in different ways. These kinds of organizations work as collectives to influence the global media, reach behind national frontiers to mobilize internal public opinion, and lobby governments to make decisions they otherwise would not make. This is not all bad. Some positive change has been accelerated tremendously.

There is growing recognition that, in interdependency, national problems such as the environment, terrorism, the drug scene, or something else must be handled cooperatively. All the major challenges out there show the necessity to rely on others for help. For example, global warming has got to be dealt with as a collective issue. By the same token, national security cannot be achieved by one country acting by itself, alone. The collectives, I think, are going to be strengthened. Whether they are governmental or non-governmental or whether they are private, these transnational organizations are going to be strengthened. What is not going to be strengthened, in relation to these, are the national governments.

Thus, there are other things that are challenging traditional ideas of sovereignty besides Iraq or Yugoslavia, Rwanda or Bosnia, or anything like that. In addition to NGOs, PVOs, and other collectives I have already mentioned, these things include forces such as international finance, banking, trade, business, and communications. All these things are crossing borders in an uncontrolled manner. Borders have never been less protected than they are right now, and they probably should not be. In fact, some of the major improvements of the past century have been due to communications and other things crossing national frontiers. We are seeing a weakening of the classical notion of sovereignty. Those nations that hold onto it will be antique, and more and more irrelevant in our interdependent world.

Are our present peacekeeping 'models' adequate to the tasks of dealing with complex humanitarian emergencies?

I do not know that we have a peacekeeping model. We have had a lot of stabs at making a model, and, as you know, there are different ways of looking at this. I do not think they are adequate to an understanding and an ability to act in complex humanitarian emergencies.

The concept of peacekeeping has gone from monitoring agreements between a relatively few absolutely sovereign, consenting, and responsible parties to a considerably larger number of more difficult and ambiguous tasks outlined in Chapters VI and VII of the UN Charter. These kinds of situations are intensely political-psychological and involve intra-state and/or transnational factions attempting to gain control of a government, attempting to dismember a nation-state for their own purposes, or simply trying to escape chaos and injustice.

In any case, peacekeepers will probably find no totally legitimate government with which to work, no single part of society on which to concentrate, no specific territory to control, and no definable military force to neutralize. Nevertheless, they must relieve human suffering, deter the escalation of violence, and facilitate a secure environment that allows progress toward some form of conflict resolution. Without effective political-diplomatic conflict resolution measures, peace operations risk becoming limited military occupations. Again, enforced peace is intended to provide a point of departure from which to begin a reconciliation process.

What does it take to accomplish all this?

First, there is an operational need to be able to respond worldwide. Most humanitarian crises occur in the most inaccessible places. So, first of all, it is a question of getting to the place, geographically. And, then, there is the problem for which the military is a good answer. That is simply existing in the place, and operating in a very difficult environment – either in a jungle, or a desert, or someplace else where there is not the usual infrastructure. This has been a problem each time we have become involved in a complex humanitarian emergency.

Civilian governmental and NGOs go to a remote place and find that they are not prepared to exist under the conditions they find there. They do not have personal security, they do not have shelter, they do not have water, food, or electric power – to say nothing of intelligence, communications, and so forth. These are the kinds of things that the military can provide. That is, it tends to have tents and blankets, transportation, things that dig, things that purify water, and things that provide power. The military also has the ability to provide security. The military is one of the very few organizations in the world that is ready to provide these things. Later, there can be a substitution of non-military means to accomplish these tasks.

Second, there is the strategic need to plan, organize, and implement the ways and means of achieving an agreed definition of success. The enormity and logic of the peace-building solutions required for the achievement of responsible governance and stability in a given situation demand a carefully thought-out, phased, long-term planning and implementation process. This, too, has been a challenge each time we have become involved in a complex peacekeeping operation.

In these kinds of operations, long-term success is achieved at the strategic level by coming to a mutually agreed definition of success and integrating international military, multi-organizational (e.g., IO – International Organization – /NGO/PVO), and unilateral (e.g., US and other national interagency) civil-military planning and implementation efforts. To achieve this synergy, representatives from the various national and international agencies must collaborate from the outset on an overarching plan that will become the source for developing subordinate operational-level plans that will make direct contributions to the achievement of the mutually agreed end-state.

So, what does all this mean? It means that IOs, NGOs, GOs

(Government/Interagency Organizations), and military organizations, which are GOs, must practice what it is they are expected to do. They have to model their operational and strategic efforts and get together with a lot of computer support to understand what kind of responses they should make, given a set of realistic scenarios.

Thus, they will be able to prepare themselves for future complex humanitarian emergencies by establishing what they must do and how they are going to accomplish it.

There have been complaints that there was 'strategic clarity' in the 1991 Persian Gulf War, but that there is 'strategic ambiguity' in the effort to bring peace to the former Yugoslavia. Is there a way to provide strategic clarity in situations similar to that in the Balkans?

I agree that in the case of the former Yugoslavia there was a question from the beginning regarding strategic clarity. I would say that there was no strategic clarity because there were different approaches, or a lack of strategic approaches. Nations took their own individual approaches and allowed the former Yugoslavia to fall apart and break into different states. Now, if you ask if there was an overall strategic concept or mutual agreement that the disintegration of that country was the desired end-state, I am not sure.

In any case, unlike conventional military operations such as Operation 'Desert Storm' in the Persian Gulf War, the lack of strategic clarity in the Balkans has created operational and tactical confusion, unclear civil-military responsibilities, and multinational *inoperability*. This, in turn, has caused leaders to react *ad hoc* and piecemeal to crises – rather than proactively moving toward an agreed end-state through integrated, well developed plans.

Is there a way to generate agreed end-states and integrated planning and implementation, and thus achieve strategic clarity?

I would like to think that we can develop that, but I think it will take an effort on three different levels.

First, we must strengthen the structures for stability in the world so they can and will develop reasonable and responsible end-states for the peace operations they conduct. We must strengthen the UN and the regional structures for the same purposes, and to allow them to anticipate problems and deal with them collectively and decisively. At present, we tend to struggle along through a crisis until it becomes so painful that we have to act in collective ways. We struggle along until we are eventually forced to build a forward-looking strategy for dealing conclusively with a complex human emergency, or until we are forced to give up the project and come home.

Second, in the context of strengthening stability structures, we must develop executive-level management structures that are capable of ensuring an integrated civil-military planning and implementation effort. The key to strategic clarity (i.e., shared goals and objectives, a common understanding of constraints, and a broad understanding of what must be done or not done or changed in the process to achieve the mutually agreed definition of success) is unity of effort. All this is time consuming, frustrating, and often requires complex negotiations between and among the major players, but it is necessary.

Third, we must get people who are, or who will be, involved in large, complex emergency responses to think strategically. In that connection, leaders at all levels must understand the complete political-strategic nature of their tactical and operational actions. They must understand ways force can be employed to achieve political and psychological – rather than military – ends. They must understand ways political considerations affect the use of force. They must understand how to communicate and deal with a diversity of peoples and cultures. They must understand and deal with GOs, IOs, NGOs, PVOs, and other military organizations. All this facilitates the ability of commanders and staffs to develop plans that promote operational synergy for the achievement of the common vision of success.

To me, these are the things that have to happen to provide for strategic clarity. Otherwise, we are going to struggle along on the margins of intranational and international peace and security crises until we reach a point where we understand that we cannot really deal with them at all.

How has the validity of your thoughts on 'uncomfortable wars' fared over the years?

Very well indeed! Very valid, of course.

As you know, the central theme in my comments on uncomfortable wars was that we, as a military and perhaps as a political-military entity, tend to conceive of future wars as the ones we would be most comfortable dealing with. ['Uncomfortable Wars: Toward a New Paradigm', was the subject of General Galvin's 1986 Kermit Roosevelt Lecture. It was published in *Parameters: US Army War College Quarterly* 15/4 (December 1986), pp.2–8; and subsequently also in Max G. Manwaring (ed.), *Uncomfortable Wars* (Boulder, CO: Westview Press, 1991), pp.9–18.] What we like, and the United States is not unique in this, is a war that we as a nation are prepared to win, and are configured to win, and are psychologically ready to fight. We like to build organizations that satisfy that concept. We thus feel safe and comfortable. We say we have a big air force, and a big navy, and a big army, and therefore we are all right. But, there are lots of things a big air force, a big navy, and a big army cannot handle.

It might be that we cannot handle it because it is like Saddam Hussein. We did not fight his war. We fought our war. He would have been comfortable in a war that was soldier-to-soldier, slugging it out with lots of casualties on each side, because he felt he could take the losses and we could not. We would have liked to have had a stand-off war where we had no casualties, and through our high technology, we destroyed the enemy without many casualties. As it turned out, we fought a comfortable war in that sense. However, if as a high-technology nation you try to fight a low-technology war – and you are down in the weeds where it is one-on-one as we fought in Vietnam – it is an uncomfortable war.

We do not like to think about the types of conflict we really would not want to deal with. For example, we still do not like to think much about Vietnam. We do not like to think about terrorism as a type of war in which cyberspace becomes a battlefield, or chemical and biological weapons are used. Surrogate wars, general violence, subversive activity, numerous small wars, multiplication of intra-state conflicts, and complex humanitarian emergencies have also intruded on our vision of war. So, we search for ways to categorize and then dismiss conflicts that do not fit into our image of war. We relegate those conflicts 'short of war' to theoretical pigeonholes where they can be dealt with – preferably by someone else – while we wait to fight the large, relatively conventional wars.

We have not realized that internal conflict – in which the societal dimension takes on crucial importance – has become a dominant form of conflict throughout the world. Of the 125 to 150 conflicts that have taken place in the past four decades, 90 per cent have occurred in developing regions and are best characterized as intra-state wars, or as complex humanitarian crises. In these struggles, violence is less an instrument of power than a psychological tool to influence the attitudes and perceptions of specific – controlling – sectors of population. The conflict becomes a form of political education that forces a reluctant, basically neutral civilian populace to take a stand in support of the government or its illegal challengers.

We need to sense the thrust of the future, the directions of change, and especially the possibilities of inherent instabilities and conflicts that vast transitions have brought since the ending of the Cold War. We can hedge against the risks involved by developing an architecture of security institutions – concentrating on ways to manage contemporary crises and building the broad coordinating mechanisms necessary for a responsive mix of political-military capabilities to deal with all eventualities. Balancing all civil-military capabilities and levels ensures the full range of options essential for appropriate and responsible action in peace, crisis, and war.

As we prepare for the future, therefore, we must learn about the various types of conflict we are likely to face. And, we must fashion new paradigms that address all the dimensions of the conflicts that may lie ahead.

What are the great successes in the peacekeeping lexicon?

I do not think that we necessarily understand the nature of the problem. I guess that is the way I would start an answer to that question. We Americans – in our collective psyche – think that a crisis is something to be addressed, and in a snap of the fingers, resolved. We do not think of a crisis as a long, drawn-out, complex, agonizing situation – such as Northern Ireland, North and South Korea, even the Cold War, but definitely the Middle East, Cyprus, parts of central and west Africa, and all over the place. We have kept a US battalion in the Sinai now for well over a dozen years. The situation goes back to the 1950s in Cyprus, the 1960s in Northern Ireland, and the 1970s in the Congo.

We, therefore, feel that somehow we have missed the key to success – meaning the key to quick success. Is it lots of military force? Is it a small military force? Is it better intelligence? Is it this or that? I think that what we have to understand is that if we have a big, amorphous, complex problem like the kinds of crises we see around the world that involve governance and stability – and actually go back hundreds and hundreds of years – you are going to have to have a multifaceted, long-term, costly approach to resolve them. There is not any way to wave a magic wand and make these crises go away. There has not been a crisis that has gone away, in that sense.

These conflicts become uncomfortable wars, and they tend to smolder for long periods of time with occasional spikes of violence. If the violence gets bad enough or if international norms are seriously violated, we go into a situation and create an enforced peace, and then – most of the time – we leave. Later, when there is another spike of violence, we do not seem to understand that the problem that created the conflict in the first place was never really addressed.

That is why the only real answer is to prevent the crisis from occurring in the first place. If you cannot prevent the crisis, then you must engage in a long-term conflict resolution process. That is the way to a more stable world.

How to do that? I would say the answer is in recognizing international interdependency, recognizing the need for collective action, and recognizing the need for collective long-term strategy and agreements on how to do these things. That is not going to be easy.

As a result, there will have to be some substitutes for this solution for a long time to come. Those substitutes will be the leadership of the most powerful nations, and the influence of those nations to move other nations collectively in response to crises. That response must be a responsible, long-term, integrated, humanitarian-political-economic-psychological-military effort to deal with the problems that caused the disaster in the first place. In that connection, something has to happen in terms of creating social leadership – the kind we usually call government. When things fall apart, they often fall apart because there is a lack of responsible leadership.

I wish we were able to develop our social sensibilities to the same extent that we have been able to develop our technology. If we could, we probably would not have the problems we have today.

What in your opinion is the future of peacekeeping?

Peacekeeping has a big future, because there is not going to be much peace. People who can operate to restore peace are going to be much in demand. Political-military organizations need to think about this on the national, international, and transnational levels because most of our time will not be occupied in large or medium sized conventional – comfortable – wars. Most of the time, we will be occupied with these uncomfortable peace operations that we have been talking about.

Now, does it mean that we should do away with the forces that can conduct large-scale conventional war? No. What it means is that we have to build flexibility and versatility into the forces we have. The real thing has to be versatility. Contemporary military forces, in conjunction with IOs, GOs, NGOs, and PVOs, must be able to deal with all eventualities. Any alternative to this is unthinkable.

Tragedy in the Balkans:
A Conflict Ended – or Interrupted?

MICHAEL MOODIE

The intervention of the international community in the conflicts in the former Yugoslavia has been the focus of world attention. This is so, at least in part, because of the sense that the tragedy in the Balkans reflects the kind of challenges that will typify the post-Cold War security environment. It poses in a dramatic fashion tough questions regarding the role of external actors in local conflicts and the complex interaction of diplomatic and political efforts and military power to achieve, in the first instance, an end to the fighting and, ultimately, a resolution of the conflict. In the Balkans, traditional approaches, including well-known peacekeeping operational practices, were insufficient in combating the novel challenges confronting external actors. Those challenges that were new in the Balkan context, however, could well become more familiar in conflicts in the future.

This essay will examine the role of external actors in the former Yugoslavia, particularly in Bosnia-Herzegovina. It will argue that while much of a positive nature has been accomplished, the influence of the international community ultimately is not decisive in determining whether a lasting peace can or will be achieved. Only the parties themselves will determine that outcome. The international community can go a long way in creating the conditions – both internal and external – in which the local parties can decide in favor of peace. In Bosnia-Herzegovina, it has done so, although much work to improve those conditions also remains. The fundamental issues that gave rise to conflict in Bosnia, however, especially the dilemma between the pursuit of partition by some actors and the desire for integration of others, can be resolved only by agreement among the local actors. Until such a resolution is achieved, the international community confronts the unattractive choice of leaving its military forces in place to maintain the fragile peace or to depart in the knowledge that conflict is likely to erupt again.

Origins of the Conflict and External Involvement

The current conflict in the Balkans is the product of developments both deeply rooted in history and as immediate as television news reports.[1] Its historical roots date back centuries to the settlement of the Ottoman Turks in Europe and their millet system of government for the region that divided populations into semi-autonomous religious groups. As a consequence of this system, religion became a major element in the national identity of the people living under Turkish rule in the Balkans. The result was that 'subjects [of the Ottoman Turks] identified themselves not by place of residence but as members of communities of faith: Muslims, who, of course had primacy; Orthodox Christians; Catholics; Jews, etc. These communities existed as sets of islands often widely separated.'[2] In the nineteenth century the emergence of the concept of nationalism linked territorial claims and this religious identification in such a way that it helped to create the powder keg in the Balkans that served to ignite World War I.

Following autocratic rule in the interwar years, the Serb, Croatian, and Muslim ethnic groups populating the central Balkans were held together in the country of Yugoslavia largely by the force of personality of war hero, resistance leader, and communist, Tito (Josip Broz). Following Tito's death, and particularly after the fall of communism in the Soviet Union and Eastern Europe, Yugoslavia lost any semblance of cohesiveness. In the absence of effective democratic institutions, ethnic nationalism came to be regarded as the best way to provide both economic and physical security for self-defined peoples. A propensity to nationalist extremism and demagogy were intensified and exploited by nationalist leaders – such as Slobodan Milosevic in Serbia and Franjo Tudjman of Croatia – for the expansion of their own political power bases. The coming to power of Milosevic in Serbia in 1987, in particular, served as 'the critical mass' for instability in the Balkans that lit the fuse erupting in conflict in the early 1990s.[3]

Although the initial fighting involved the newly self-proclaimed countries of Serbia, Croatia, and Slovenia, those conflicts were brought to a halt relatively quickly. It was in Bosnia-Herzegovina – split among its Muslim, Serbian, and Croatian populations – that the conflict became the most severe and prolonged. Fighting among Bosnian ethnic groups began in March 1992. Participants took part in an intricate dance of ever changing partners through intermittent clashes and constantly collapsing ceasefires. Bosnian Serb forces enjoyed the advantages of better equipment and training as well as the (often unspoken) support of Serbia itself. Bosnian Croats benefited from similar external support from neighboring Croatia. The Bosnian Muslims forces, while larger, were underequipped and poorly trained, at least initially. The war was prosecuted with a particular ferocity, and the international community confronted both a humanitarian disaster and the prospect of the dismemberment of a newly-recognized independent country through the use of military power. It was hardly a comforting, or acceptable, precedent.

International involvement in the Balkans passed through several phases reflecting the lead of different international organizations at different times. Initially, the European Community (EC), viewing this first post-Cold War crisis as an opportunity to exercise leadership on a security problem in its own backyard, sought to broker a peace. It became clear, however, that 'Europe' would not be able to halt the fighting through its diplomatic efforts. By September 1991, Milosevic was looking to stop the war but retain his territorial gains, and he turned to the United Nations (UN) and the introduction of UN peacekeepers to help achieve that objective.[4] Advance parties of UN troops entered the former Yugoslavia in March 1992. NATO's involvement in the region developed piecemeal, starting in July 1992 with maritime operations to monitor and then enforce the UN mandated arms embargo. Its activity then shifted to air operations in support of UN forces on the ground, and it culminated in 1996 with the deployment of a NATO-led peace Implementation Force (IFOR) to ensure the implementation of the 1995 Dayton Accords. Through this transition 'NATO has shifted from the role of a subcontractor responding to UN requirements to a more active participant in seeking to stop the fighting and in defining its own missions and mandates.'[5]

Throughout the various stages of international involvement in the Balkans, the leading powers shared three basic goals: prevention of a humanitarian catastrophe; containment of the conflict; and creation of conditions for a long-term settlement. Of course, the problem with achieving the last of these objectives made the first two more difficult to secure as well. External powers also shared a central misgiving about their involvement in the conflicts: the increasing costs and risks of military operations and the fear that even a small commitment would escalate into a 'quagmire' from which it would be difficult to extricate themselves. Throughout their involvement, then, external powers confronted a dilemma: on one hand, there has been a strong desire and some public pressure to do something to bring the conflict to a halt. On the other, external powers felt the constraint of not doing so much as to assume an open-ended commitment that would not only be expensive in financial terms but costly in terms of casualties to military forces.

The nature of external involvement supported by military forces in the Balkans and their efforts at conflict resolution can be divided into two phases: before the 1995 Dayton Accords and after. Differences between the two periods relate not only to the institutional framework within which external involvement was expressed but also by different conceptions of the use of military power in pursuit of conflict resolution.

Pre-Dayton: The UN and the Contact Group

The fighting in the Balkans, and in Bosnia-Herzegovina in particular, was especially brutal. A particularly heinous practice was ethnic cleansing, or the forcible expulsion of people of the wrong ethnic background from a given territory through violence and terror including murder, rape, arson, robbery, and beatings. The goal was to create such a feeling of threat in the population that they would want to leave and never return. All sides engaged in the practice, although the Serbs are held to have pursued it most widely. Beyond ethnic cleansing, the conflict in Bosnia also involved the systematic bombardment of civilian targets as well as the blockade of humanitarian relief efforts. The initial involvement of the United Nations was largely in response to the brutality of the conflict and the humanitarian tragedy, and the mandates given to UN forces were expressed largely in terms of ensuring the delivery of humanitarian aid.

In February 1992 the UN Security Council voted to dispatch 14,000 peacekeepers to the Balkans for 12 months and further support was given in April. By July the UN had also authorized a 1,100-strong contingent to take control of Sarajevo airport in hopes of facilitating delivery of relief supplies. As the fighting showed no signs of abating, even as diplomatic efforts to negotiate an end to the conflict proceeded in London and Geneva, in September 1992 the Security Council authorized the enlargement of the UN presence to escort relief convoys. In March 1993, the mission of these UN forces (the UN Protection Force, or UNPROFOR) was extended to include the creation of a 'no-fly zone' over Bosnia-Herzegovina from which aircraft and helicopters of the contending parties were barred. In mid-1993, France led an effort to declare certain areas 'safe havens' under UN security, and the Security Council subsequently accorded such status to Sarajevo, Zepa, Srebrenica, Gorazde, and Bihac. As events were to prove, they were anything but safe.

The insertion of UN forces into Bosnia-Herzegovina represented something the United Nations had never before encountered—the introduction of peacekeepers into the middle of an ongoing conflict. Analyst Adam Roberts notes that past UN operations had been essentially of two kinds: 'enforcement (war by another name) against overt aggression on the one hand and peacekeeping (often seen as permitting only very restricted uses of force) on the other'.[6] The first category includes UN-sanctioned operations in Korea and Iraq. In the second case, UN peacekeepers traditionally had been deployed only after a ceasefire had been achieved between the warring parties and both sides agreed to the UN presence, often as a means of separating opposing forces. In the case of Bosnia, although the various contending parties accepted the presence of UN forces, they did not stop fighting. The result was a major problem described by Roberts: 'how the UN and its members can react in those relatively few situations where agreed ceasefires are violated; where there are massive atrocities; when the situation demands, or UN mandates seem to require, more forceful military action than peacekeeping on its own can provide; or when the credibility and impartiality of a UN peacekeeping force may be as much at risk from military inaction as from use of military force.'[7]

In part because the UN confronted novel requirements that were perhaps not understood, and in part because of concerns among key Security Council members regarding the risks of deeper involvement, the role of UNPROFOR was consistently kept limited. The Clinton administration, for example – chastened by its experience in Somalia – repeatedly made clear that while it was willing to supply troops once peace had been achieved, Washington would not send ground forces to the war zone until the fighting stopped. Similarly the United Kingdom 'opposed any tendency of the UN effort to slide from peacekeeping to peacemaking'. London also resisted NATO involvement and was skeptical of the value of air strikes despite Security Council authorization of the use of NATO air power to protect the 'safe havens' and humanitarian convoys.[8]

Part of the concern in London related to the security of humanitarian relief efforts. The UN needed the cooperation of the parties, particularly the Bosnian Serbs, for delivery of humanitarian assistance. Moreover, such a mission, by its very nature, requires troops that are dispersed and, hence, vulnerable. London worried that any escalation would create risks of retaliation against those efforts or the forces (particularly British) protecting them. Given the priority that London and others gave to the humanitarian relief efforts, anything that jeopardized them was to be avoided if at all possible.

This concern did prove warranted. In 1995, for example, after NATO aircraft attacked Bosnian Serb military infrastructure targets, they retaliated – at the direction of local Bosnian Serb leaders Radovan Karadzic and Ratko Mladic – by taking more than 300 UN peacekeepers hostage.

The result of the caution of key UN Security Council actors was the creation of a situation in which UN forces were not given the tools to do their job properly. This shortcoming became apparent particularly as the Security Council imposed new requirements such as the creation of 'no-fly zones' that had to be enforced and safe areas that had to be protected. At the time the UN was considering the creation of the safe areas, UN Secretary-General Boutros Boutros-Ghali estimated that as many as 34,000 additional troops would be needed, but no commitments to provide either supplementary forces or money to support the forces of others were made by any UN member.[9] Given the inherent limitations of air power in performing such a mission, as well as the reluctance of UNPROFOR commanders to authorize the use of air power, the absence of ground forces probably doomed that mission to failure. To some extent, UNPROFOR confronted difficulties over which it had no control. Stable ceasefires were extremely difficult to establish, particularly in light of the intense animosities, mutual suspicions, broken commitments, and personal agendas of the leaders of the various ethnic groups. Different interests of the states composing UNPROFOR also made coordination and command and control difficult, as did the fact that key states saw the nature of the conflict quite differently. Some analysts also criticize the United States for failing to assume leadership. But the United States was not alone in its caution. Indeed, the case can be made that the UN became the vehicle for external efforts precisely because going the UN route meant that individual countries – including those in Europe – would then not have to shoulder the burden directly (as the EC tried to do early in the conflict with such a notable lack of success). The UN is a creature of its members. It is clearly not capable of decisive action if its members do not want it to be. To some extent, therefore, although UNPROFOR is widely perceived to have failed, such a view is too simple.

This is not to suggest that the UN is not without responsibility in UNPROFOR's less than rousing success. Clearly, the UN effort in the former Yugoslavia lacked a unity of strategic command. Officers in the field, for example, were known to complain that they simply could not carry out the wide range of mandates they were given. The absence of strategic direction itself reflected the lack of a shared view among the UN members and international staff about what the ultimate objective of the UN's involvement should have been. This dilemma was highlighted following the hostage incident mentioned earlier. That event prompted the British government to promise an immediate increase in its forces of 1,200 troops with another 5,500 to come later. NATO defense ministers agreed to create two Rapid Reaction Forces under UN command that would be outfitted with heavier equipment, including helicopters, armored combat vehicles, and artillery. At a time when these efforts to reinforce UNPROFOR were underway, however, the UN leadership began openly to advise the opposite course of action. In his May 1995 report to the Security Council, Secretary-General Boutros-Ghali favored the option of UNPROFOR returning to a classic peacekeeping mission rather than shifting to more assertive peace enforcement efforts or even maintaining the status quo.[10]

In that May 1995 report, Secretary-General Boutros-Ghali argued that peacekeeping and peace enforcement were incompatible missions. Although the Security Council rejected this view, it is not clear that the United Nations ever fully understood the nature of the adaptations that were necessary in the unique situation Bosnia presented. Certainly, traditional peacekeeping operations in Bosnia were ineffective as long as the fighting continued. This was particularly the case with the peacekeeping principle that UN forces should be neutral with respect to the adversaries. Since the military forces of hostile adversaries were not separated (as they had been in earlier UN peacekeeping operations) but engaged in day-to-day conflict, almost any action taken by UNPROFOR would be interpreted by one side or the other as favoring its adversary, leading, not surprisingly, to reprisals against UN troops. The Bosnian Serbs, for example, accused the UN of using its mandate to create 'safe havens' for protecting bases for assaults by Bosnian government forces against Serb positions, although the UN had no ability to control government forces in such 'safe areas' as Bihac and Srebrenica.

Finally, as Bosnian Serb attacks against 'safe areas' mounted and they eventually overran the havens of Srebrenica and Zepa, the inability or unwillingness of the UN to take action to protect the threatened communities as their mandate suggested was inexplicable. As Adam Roberts points out, 'The fall of these towns – to the accompaniment of official claims that the UN forces were only there to deter attacks, not to defend against them – exposed the UN, and in some measure NATO, as incoherent, impotent and untrustworthy.'[11]

The Contact Group

As mentioned, UN efforts were seriously hampered by differences among key UN players who also became members of the Contact Group, established in April 1994 to promote a diplomatic solution to the conflict. These countries – France, Germany, Russia, the United Kingdom, and the United States – viewed the nature of the conflict differently, had different interests at stake, shaped their approaches to respond to unique domestic political dynamics, and promoted alternative approaches to managing the conflict. These differences were to complicate international efforts whether in the UN, the Contact Group itself, or NATO.

The Contact Group did maintain its cohesion in its early days, producing a set of conflict resolution proposals that took the form of a map assigning portions of territory that were to be controlled by the warring ethnic groups. The plan, which gave 51 per cent of the territory to a Muslim-Croat federation and 49 per cent to the Bosnian Serbs, was effectively rejected in mid-1994, after which the splits among the members of the Contact Group became more evident.

The United States (to an extent tacitly supported by Germany) viewed the conflict as the product largely of Serbian aggression and stressed continually that such aggression should not be rewarded. Presidential candidate Bill Clinton argued that the United States should support the Bosnian Muslims more assertively than he believed the Bush administration was doing, while rejecting any role for US forces on the ground. This policy became the basic approach of his administration, and it included efforts to secure allied agreement to lift the arms embargo on the Muslims, something the Europeans consistently rejected. After the 1994 US elections gave control of the Congress to the Republicans, Washington announced that it would pull its ships out of the naval task force in the Adriatic enforcing the arms embargo. The decision was decried by allies as a unilateral US measure that would injure allied cohesiveness and set an unhelpful precedent.

The refusal of the United States to commit ground forces in the Balkans – other than a small contingent of 300 observers on the Serbian-Macedonian border – was also a major sore spot. As the situation deteriorated in late 1994, for example, US-European tension heightened considerably, with the Europeans carping that the Americans were 'willing to support the Bosnian government down to the last French or UK soldier' and that 'even though the Americans don't have troops in Bosnia, that hasn't prevented them from telling the Europeans what to do'.[12]

A related source of tension was US preference for relying on air power, particularly against the Serbs. Britain, France, and Russia all felt such an approach would unduly threaten the humanitarian mission of the troops on the ground and draw the alliance further into the conflict. This difference emerged particularly after Serbian forces overran the 'safe haven' of Zepa in July 1995, which resulted in further atrocities. The United States called for air strikes as central to a 'decisive response' by the UN and NATO that the Contact Group had agreed would be forthcoming if the Serbs conducted a similar attack against the safe haven of Gorazde. The Russians, however, rejected large-scale air operations, a position consistent with long-standing and open Russian criticism of NATO's air strike policy that Moscow viewed as favoring one party to the conflict. Similarly, a month later, in late August 1995 after a Bosnian Serb mortar attack on a Sarajevo market killed 37 people, NATO initiated Operation 'Deliberate Force', a three week graduated campaign of air strikes against Bosnian Serb military targets that included 300 sorties in the first 12 hours. In response, Moscow 'raised particularly strong reservations'.[13]

Russia's role in the wars in the Balkans has been complicated. On one hand, some analysts have felt that given its identification with the Serbs who are fellow Slavs, Moscow has always supported, and to some extent, protected them. Some reports even speculated that Russia provided the anti-aircraft batteries that began to appear in Bosnian Serb inventories in late 1994, which had the impact of curtailing NATO air operations. But Russia's role has not been completely negative. In February 1994, for example, following a NATO ultimatum to the Bosnian Serbs after attacks on civilian targets around Sarajevo, Russian special envoy Vitaliy Churkin convinced the Bosnian Serbs in Pale (the Bosnian Serb 'capital') to withdraw from the 'exclusion zones' around Sarajevo, thereby removing the need for NATO air strikes and defusing the situation.

Russia is also one of the non-NATO nations to contribute troops – an airborne brigade – to the NATO-led Implementation Force (IFOR) and Stabilization Force (SFOR) deployed after the Dayton Accords were agreed. According to one analyst, 'Russian participation in IFOR and SFOR has helped to maintain military stability in the sensitive area around Brcko and to mitigate Bosnian Serb concerns about NATO's balance in helping to implement the peace agreement.'[14]

NATO Before Dayton

As previously mentioned, NATO's role in the Balkans conflict evolved through a series of stages that witnessed progressively increasing military action. All of its activity has been authorized by UN Security Council resolutions, and throughout its involvement NATO's mandate has been carefully limited. NATO's view of its role has been one of creating conditions in which the parties themselves would seek, first, an end to the conflict, and second, the creation of a viable, stable political system. The ceasefire has held for two years; to that extent, the first goal has been achieved. The second goal, however, remains elusive, and recognition is now widespread that creating the political conditions for peace under the Dayton Agreement will require much more time than originally envisioned. How long NATO troops should stay and help shape the environment in which that can be done is now a policy debate among the Clinton administration, the US Congress, and European allies.

Prior to the Dayton Accord, NATO's role was to support UNPROFOR. The first form of that support came with Operation 'Maritime Monitor', designed to monitor the arms embargo on the region in the Adriatic. This mission was transformed into Operation 'Maritime Guard', which gave NATO the authority to enforce the embargo through stopping, inspecting, and diverting ships in the region.[15] These operations constituted NATO's first out-of-area operations in the history of the alliance.

After the UN Security Council authorized the 'no-fly zones' over Bosnia in March 1993, designed to neutralize the Bosnian Serbs' advantage in fixed wing aircraft, NATO was given the responsibility for enforcing the UNSC decision. A major test for NATO in this role occurred in February 1994 when Bosnian Serb aircraft attempted to evade the restrictions. Four of the six Serb aircraft were shot down in NATO's first combat action in its 45-

year history. Despite this success, NATO did encounter problems in fully meeting this mission in light of the difficulties of preventing the use of helicopters which were more difficult to detect and could land quickly if identified. Civilian helicopters or those involved in medical evacuations were also difficult to distinguish from military aircraft.

In June 1993 the UN Security Council authorized NATO to provide close air support to UNPROFOR on the ground. This development, while seemingly logical, created enormous difficulties for the entire international mission in Bosnia. First, it became apparent that there was a significant mismatch between the humanitarian and traditional peacekeeping mission of the UN troops on the ground and the peace enforcement operations NATO was conducting in the air. The vulnerability of ground troops conducting those operations diluted the deterrent impact of NATO's air power. So, too, did the UN's need for the parties' cooperation, which was undermined by the NATO air attacks, especially against the Bosnian Serbs. This mismatch in the mission of the two forces made it extremely difficult to develop and conduct a concerted, coherent approach to the challenges the UN/NATO force encountered, particularly the Bosnian Serbs' attacks on the 'safe areas'.

Second, command arrangements were difficult to arrange and complicated once established. Following the creation of the safe areas, the UN Secretary-General delegated the power to authorize air strikes to his Special Representative in the theater, Yasushi Akashi. Given UN sensitivities to the priority of the humanitarian mission and the potential vulnerability of ground forces, which Mr Akashi shared, this arrangement was no guarantee that UN forces, if put under military pressure, would receive immediate self-defense. It was only in late 1993 that the UN and NATO reached an agreement, endorsed at the January 1994 NATO Summit, to establish a 'dual key' over the authorization of air strikes as a way to manage the problem of who would decide when to bomb in the former Yugoslavia. The agreement provided that the UN commander on the ground and NATO's Commander in Chief of the Allied Command-South (CINCSOUTH) would decide jointly on targeting, once they had received the necessary political authorization from the respective organizations.

The 'dual key' arrangement meant that several people had to agree on the decision and its execution, people who did not always see the problem in the same terms or accept air strikes as an appropriate solution. This arrangement often prevented immediate and effective responses when they were promised to such action as deployments into the 'exclusion zones' around Sarajevo which were to be free of heavy weapons. Recognizing the difficulties in command arrangements between the UN and NATO, the warring parties in the field often went right ahead and engaged in such practices as the shelling of Sarajevo with heavy artillery from within the zone from which the international force was to ensure they were excluded. NATO commanders obviously chafed under the 'dual key' arrangement. It was not until after the fall of Zepa in 1995, however, that UN Secretary-General Boutros-Ghali agreed to any change in the arrangement. Following that disaster, final authority was shifted from the civilian Special Representative to the UN military commander in the field. Because this move was portrayed as a shift within the existing UN mission, it did not require a new Security Council resolution which the Russians were expected to veto.

A third source of tension between the UN and NATO was their institutional perspective on the use of military power. As described by NATO official, Gregory Schulte, NATO stressed 'the effective application of military power, even when used in a limited fashion', while the UN sought 'to protect the traditional peacekeeping principles of impartiality, consent and the use of force only in self-defense. The difference in philosophy was not bridged ...'[16]

Despite these differences, relations between the two international organizations were not so bad as to prevent the creation of practical arrangements that provided important mechanisms for bringing pressure to bear on the antagonists in the conflict. NATO did conduct air strikes with UN authorization that increased in severity over time. Efforts such as Operation 'Deliberate Force' combined with other developments to generate enough pressure to bring the antagonists to the negotiating table which led to what became known as the Dayton Accords. The relations and procedures that the two organizations developed also facilitated the transition from UNPROFOR to IFOR as the lead military organization responsible for implementing the Accords.

The Dayton Accords

The NATO air strikes against the Serbs in September 1995 clearly shook the Bosnian Serb leadership. As a result, the Serbs in Pale agreed to join a 'joint team' with Serbian President Milosevic for purposes of conducting diplomatic negotiations being pushed by the United States. The pressures for negotiation were intensified by a large-scale offensive in September and October 1995 by Bosnian Croats and Muslims that retook almost 20 per cent of the territory held by the Serbs, who had been psychologically and materially weakened by the NATO air attacks. The resulting situation on the ground came close to the 51–49 split in control of territory envisioned in the first Contact Group proposal and subsequently agreed as part of the basic principles of a peace accord achieved in Geneva under the auspices of US

Assistant Secretary of State Richard Holbrooke. A 60-day ceasefire was agreed among the parties on 12 October 1995, and the parties conducted proximity talks at a US air base near Dayton, Ohio that produced an agreement initialed there on 21 November.

The Dayton Accords were formally established as a General Framework Agreement for Peace in Bosnia-Herzegovina and signed by Bosnian President Alija Izetbegovic, Croatian President Tudjman, and Serbian President Milosevic in Paris on 14 December 1995. The agreement called for Bosnia-Herzegovina to retain legal status as a single state, albeit composed of two distinct entities: a Bosnian-Croat Federation that would control 51 per cent of the territory and the Republika Srpska with 49 per cent. The agreement further provided for federal institutions in which the three ethnic groups are represented, including a rotating presidency, a bicameral national parliament, a constitutional court, and a central bank. The agreement also included measures to repatriate refugees and reunify Sarajevo.

The Dayton Accords also contained important military provisions. These included the shut-down of all early-warning, air defense, and fire-control radars; disarming of all civilian groups, except police; the withdrawal of all foreign forces; withdrawal behind a two-kilometer zone of separation on either side of the ceasefire line; release of all prisoners; departure of forces from areas to be transferred to another entity; the withdrawal of all heavy weapons to barracks or cantonments and the demobilization of all forces that could not be cantoned; and negotiation of arms control agreements governing the size of the holdings of key weapons categories not only of the entities in Bosnia itself but also throughout the region.

With the entry into force of the Dayton Accords, UNPROFOR's mission came to an end, and the NATO-led Implementation Force (IFOR) replaced it. Indeed, much of the enthusiasm for Dayton and the hope for its success were generated by the fact that NATO was assuming a key role in its implementation. NATO stressed, however, and the United States in particular, that IFOR's mandate would be to monitor and enforce compliance with the military aspects of the Dayton Accords, including

- maintenance of the cessation of hostilities;
- separation of the armed forces of the warring sides;
- transfer of territory between the two entities;
- movement of forces and heavy weapons to approved sites; and,
- creation of a secure environment for the implementation of the civil aspects of the agreement.

US and other NATO spokesmen made clear that IFOR would not have major responsibility for resettling refugees or other civilian and human rights missions. The irony of the description of IFOR's mission should not be lost on those examining post-Cold War peacekeeping. On one hand, the United Nations – usually responsible for peacekeeping operations – sought to secure a peace for more than three years amid a continuing conflict. NATO, whose strength lies in its military capabilities, was being asked to implement an agreement among parties, based on their strategic consent and to engage in a variety of peace support tasks. NATO, however, was quick to point out that it would not necessarily abide by the 'neutrality' often adhered to by UN peacekeepers which entailed a reluctance to single out one faction for fear of compromising its mandate. IFOR, on the other hand, would act even-handed, treating any party that violated the agreement in a similar manner.

Post-Dayton: What is Peacekeeping?

Since the signing of the Dayton Accords implementation of the agreement has met with mixed success. The military aspects of the accord, for example, were implemented relatively smoothly. Reconstruction of the national infrastructure has also begun, including road and rail repair. In contrast, less success has been achieved in securing the agreement's civilian dimensions. Freedom of movement and return of refugees are two areas, in particular, in which obligations have not been met.

Responsibility for this lack of progress rests first and foremost with the Bosnian leaders themselves who have displayed a lack of determination to honor their commitments made in Dayton. At the same time, given the slow progress and the continuing tenuous nature of the dynamics within Bosnia-Herzegovina, there has also been some criticism of IFOR and its successor SFOR for interpreting their mandate too narrowly and not providing adequate support to those responsible for civilian implementation.[17]

Subtle changes crept into the IFOR approach in the spring of 1996 largely as a result of such criticism. At that time, the sense that it must do more on the civilian side led IFOR troops to arrest arsonists and other troublemakers after the turnover of territory in Sarajevo by the Serbs to the Bosnian Muslims. NATO also promised that IFOR would assist more directly in protecting mass gravesites that were being discovered. Despite these new duties, IFOR remained sensitive to the prospect of 'mission creep' and keeping its activities limited. NATO spokesmen at the time, for example, argued that IFOR had the authority but not the obligation to detain indicted war criminals.

The slow progress in implementing civilian aspects of Dayton and mounting criticism of NATO's contribution to that process led US Secretary of State Madeleine Albright to announce in May 1997 that SFOR would assume new roles. According to Secretary Albright, the force would 'build on its past accomplishments by actively supporting crucial civil implementation tasks ... These include helping create a secure environment for managed refugee returns and the installation of elected officials in targeted areas and specific economic reconstruction projects, which could include inter-entity telecommunications and restoring civil aviation.'[18] The Pentagon reportedly resisted these calls for becoming more involved in non-traditional operations, but other officials argued that the troops could and should do more.

Beyond recasting SFOR's role, Secretary Albright's statement also indicated other lines that US diplomacy was pursuing to push implementation of Dayton. On one hand, the Secretary criticized leaders whose commitments to the peace process were questionable. For example, she scolded the Croatian Foreign Minister for mistreating Serbs and other violations of the accords, and warned that Washington would oppose Croatia's bid for membership in the NATO Partnership for Peace program and other institutions unless Zagreb improved its record. On the other hand, the United States announced an economic initiative to demonstrate that communities meeting their obligations, such as allowing the return of displaced persons, would receive international aid. Four municipalities were selected to participate in an 'open cities' project that would provide $3.6 million in assistance with another $5 million available to help repair buildings, provide agricultural support, and train workers in eligible communities.[19]

The shift in emphasis on the role of international forces in Bosnia reflected in large measure changing circumstances on the ground. As the *New York Times* reported in July 1997, 'with the antagonistic armies under control, NATO officers have begun saying that the real threat to peace was instability caused by the continued political power of the hardline nationalists and the anger of the refugees kept from home.'[20] The rate of settlement of displaced persons was very low. By early 1997, only some 220,000 of 2.4 million refugees and displaced persons had returned since the Dayton Agreements were signed, and a further 100,000 (mostly Serb residents of Sarajevo) had become displaced.[21]

Moreover, nationalist leaders in each of the communities had little interest in seeing the Dayton agreements work. Their hardline nationalist stance in many ways provided the bases for their political power, and an effective agreement would undermine the reasons for their appeal.

At the political level, throughout the summer of 1997, the United States and others continued their efforts to confront the leaders in Bosnia with the consequences of not living up to their promises. An international aid conference in July 1997, for example, singled out the Bosnian Serbs in particular for continuing to flout their obligations. The result was to make it impossible for the international community to offer them greater financial support. Hans Van den Broek, the European Union's Foreign Affairs Commissioner, argued that humanitarian assistance would continue to be provided, but as long as indicted war crimes suspects such as Bosnian Serb leader Radovan Karadzic remained at large, 'It would be irresponsible to continue spending public funds for reconstruction purposes.' As a result, the Serb-held part of Bosnia has received only a trickle of the available international funds, some $8 million of roughly $800 million (or 1 per cent). At the same time, conference participants pledged another $1.2 billion over five years.[22] In early August 1997 the United States warned Yugoslavia that it might seek the renewal of economic sanctions and other punitive measures against it if President Milosevic did not become more active in handing over indicted war crimes suspects at a time when Bosnian Serb leaders such as Karadzic and Ratko Mladic were reported to be moving freely through its territory.

The US threat was part of increased diplomatic pressure that preceded the visit to the region of Richard Holbrooke, who had brokered the Dayton Accords, seeking more rapid implementation of the agreement. While Holbrooke was able to secure progress on some issues, little progress was made on such basic issues as freedom of movement and the return of refugees. Holbrooke did secure a promise that Bosnian-Serb leader Karadzic would remove himself from the political scene, but many people doubted the sincerity of this promise, a doubt that proved justified in light of subsequent events.

The limited success of the Holbrooke visit occurred against a background of transatlantic bickering over who was to blame for the spotty implementation of the civilian aspects of the Dayton agreements. The US State Department criticized the international mediator for Bosnia, Carlos Westendorp of Spain who had replaced Sweden's Karl Bildt. This criticism led London's *Financial Times* to comment that 'the attempt by unnamed US officials to put the blame on the harassed international representative, Carlos Westendorp, hints at a return of the squabbling and scapegoat-seeking which have dogged NATO policy on Bosnia from its beginning.' A harsh article in the Italian newspaper *Corriere della Sera* stressed that 'Washington's takeover of the management of the Bosnian crisis is a slap in the face of the Europeans.'[23]

During his visit, Holbrooke made clear to Milosevic that the Clinton administration was prepared to arrest Karadzic, reflecting the assessment that his removal as a political force was essential for the success of the effort to bring peace to Bosnia.[24] At the time of the Dayton Accords, Karadzic had promised to take himself out of the political picture, but by mid-1997 he had emerged as the major political force in the Bosnian Serb leadership in Pale. That reemergence was a key factor in the growing debate over the role of SFOR in the apprehension of indicted war crimes suspects.

Under pressure to do something on this front, British troops conducted two operations in late July 1997 to arrest indicted Bosnian war criminals. One was captured, and the other was killed during the operation. The action seemed to contradict the statement made a day earlier at the summit in Madrid by President Clinton and other NATO leaders that arresting war criminals would remain the obligation of local officials rather than NATO forces. Russia strongly objected to the operations, saying that it did not 'correspond to the mandate of the international force deployed in Bosnia'. There were further newspaper reports of French opposition to additional raids as too risky. Although the reports were denied in Paris, unnamed NATO officials were cited as indicating that the alliance had serious disagreements about 'the who, the what, the scale, and the how' of operations to arrest war criminals.[25]

Holbrooke's visit intensified the spotlight on the war criminals issue and on Karadzic in particular. In October 1997, *The Economist* reported that 14 of the 18 Croats who have been charged with war crimes were in custody, and all three of the indicted Muslims were on trial. Only the Bosnian Serbs had failed to cooperate; one was tried and sentenced, while two more awaited trials, and three were thought dead. That still left 51 at large, of whom the most important was clearly Karadzic.

Despite his status as an indicted war crimes suspect, and the fact that he was stripped of formal office at the time of the Dayton Accords at US insistence, Karadzic remained the most powerful figure in the eastern part of the Serbian entity in Bosnia, a position that led him into a bitter power struggle with Biljana Plavsic, his successor as president of the Republika Srpska. Karadzic controlled most of the police and media, while Plavsic, suffering from a weaker base of domestic support depended on the support of the international community, despite her strong ultra-nationalist credentials. Pro-Karadzic Serbs clashed with NATO forces in late August 1997 in what was described as 'one of the sharpest confrontations' of the post-Dayton period. Although NATO troops had been subjected to low-level attacks from pro-Karadzic paramilitary units, it was also the first time they had ever been assaulted by a civilian mob. On the eve of municipal elections in September, Karadzic supporters plastered his picture throughout Pale. When the juridical arm of the Organization for Security and Cooperation in Europe which was overseeing the election decided that this activity was against the rules and disqualified the party from participating in the election, the decision was overturned by the OSCE's mission head, fearing reprisals. The result was that Karadzic's party won the vote in virtually all the eastern sector of the Bosnian Serb entity.

Pro-Karadzic media outlets were also responsible for spewing out virulent anti-Western propaganda that played a part in inciting the population against the NATO forces. As a result, NATO units seized four transmitters and turned them over to Plavsic. While this had a positive impact for a limited time, illicit transmitters under Karadzic's control began broadcasting again in strongly anti-Western terms.

Another aspect of the problem was the approximately 2,000 'special police' who surrounded Karadzic as a virtual bodyguard and constituted his main protection. Initially, police were outside the military aspects of the Dayton Accords and NATO forces were limited in how they could deal with them. Given the role of these pro-Karadzic special police units in fomenting continuing violence, however, NATO made the decision in August that the special police would be considered a military unit and therefore subject to control by NATO troops. NATO monitoring of these units is believed to have increased Karadzic's vulnerability, and at the time of writing there is increasing speculation that NATO is considering an operation to seize and arrest him.

It is not at all certain the Karadzic's demise would secure peace in Bosnia. The municipal elections produced a complex outcome throughout the country that suggests that ethnic animosities are as intense as ever and that the issues of displaced persons, the resettlement of refugees, and the seating of elected municipal councilors and administrators have combined to create an intricate, and potentially dangerous problem.

Conclusion

The West's increased attention to Karadzic and his ousting as a key to peace reflects pressure to leave Bosnia once the SFOR mandate expires in June 1998. In July 1997 the US Congress passed a non-binding amendment to the 1998 Defense Authorization Act Stating that 'US ground combat forces should not participate in a follow-on force in Bosnia' after 30 June 1998. Following the resolution's passage, President Clinton commented that he thought that the 'present operation will have run its course [by June 1998] and we'll have to discuss what, if any, involvement the United States should have there'.

Yet, the previous international mediator, Karl Bildt, argued before his departure that Bosnia could fall apart if SFOR is withdrawn after its mandate expires. Bildt contended that while he did not envision a 'massive troop presence for the long term ... nor a need for it', nevertheless 'there needs to be deterrent function so that when we say we are not going to tolerate a resumption of hostilities, people know that these words can be backed up ... with force.'[26] European allies have made it clear, however, that if the United States withdraws its ground troops from Bosnia, they will do the same. A US-led departure of NATO from Bosnia could do enormous harm to perceptions of US global leadership and relations in the Atlantic alliance.

Although the US State and Defense Departments have voiced different perspectives on the need for continuing SFOR's presence (with Defense preferring their departure by the June 1998 deadline), the Clinton administration now appears inclined to support continued deployment of NATO forces, including US troops. The argument for doing so is twofold: first, that such forces are needed to support the implementation of the Dayton Agreements as the only basis on which civil and political progress can be made; and second, that withdrawal now undoubtedly will spur a resumption of fighting. But will the administration make an open-ended commitment or set another deadline for departure? Two such deadlines will have passed. A third will be equally artificial. Establishing another deadline for departure would also provide a further opportunity for those determined to prevail in this conflict to outwait the international community before they resort again to violence to achieve a resolution on their terms.

It is also not clear whether the Congress will agree with the administration. Demanding an exit strategy, some members doubt that, whatever happens in Bosnia, the costs of staying involved in a conflict in a region of peripheral interest to the United States outweigh the costs of withdrawal. Other members have called for partition of Bosnia as the only basis for resolving the underlying tensions motivating the conflict and for moving to that status as soon as possible to ensure the departure of NATO and US forces.

The international community has been successful in silencing the guns in Bosnia. That was no mean feat, but it remains a fragile success. At best, the continued deployment of NATO forces will buy time – to engage in the construction of political and civil institutions that will facilitate a positive interaction among conflicting parties, an interaction based on the belief that such engagement is better than the conflict continued. But it is not clear that such a belief really exists among the local actors today or that it will emerge in the future.

The job of creating a stable and workable political situation in Bosnia remains enormous. At least three critical tasks are still to be done, including the peaceful resettlement of vast numbers of displaced persons and refugees, the end to the willful violation of minority rights such as continuing forceful expulsion of minorities from their homes, and the bringing to justice of indicted war criminals. These issues remain at the core of the problems in Bosnia; they address how, where, and with whom people want to live. They were what much of the fighting in Bosnia was about, and it is not at all certain that the modest progress that has been achieved toward ethnic reconciliation would survive the withdrawal of NATO troops. Indeed, most people believe otherwise.

Maybe the time bought by the presence of military forces of the international community will make a difference. But it is hard to be optimistic – unless reconciliation proceeds better than the recent record suggests we have reason to expect. The time required for such reconciliation is likely to be well beyond the time political masters will be willing to keep their military forces there (regardless of the outcome of the decision to extend past June). Despite the best efforts of the international community, therefore, the parties themselves are shaping the decisive options for Bosnia's future: either renewed conflict after the NATO troops leave or a political agreement that destroys the vision of a single, multi-ethnic country that was the foundation of the mission of the international forces in the first place.

NOTES

1. For more detail on the events that led to the fighting in the early 1990s, see Michael Moodie, 'The Balkan Tragedy', ANNALS, American Academy of Political and Social Science, No. 541 (Sept. 1995) pp.101–3.
2. Albert Wohlstetter, 'Why We're in It – Still', *Wall Street Journal*, 1 July 1993.
3. The phrase appears in 'Post-Communist Balkans: The First Phase', *Strategic Survey 1990–1991* (London: IISS 1991), p.165.
4. See 'Turmoil in the Balkans,' *Strategic Survey, 1991–1992* (London: IISS, 1992) p.36.
5. Gregory L. Schulte, 'Former Yugoslavia and the New NATO', *Survival* 39/1 (Spring 1997) p.20.
6. Adam Roberts, 'From San Francisco to Sarajevo: The UN and the Use of Force', *Survival*, 37/4 (Winter 1995–96) p.7. Editors' note: Roberts fails to recognize the precedent set by UN operations in the Congo from 1960 to 1964.
7. Ibid.
8. 'Another Destructive Year in the Balkans', *Strategic Survey, 1993–1994* (London: IISS, 1994) p.101.
9. Roberts, 'UN and the Use of Force' (note 6) p.37.
10. 'Bosnia: No Easy Options Left', *Strategic Comments*, IISS, Issue No.5 (June 1995) p.1.
11. Roberts (note 6) p.22.
12. Chrystia Freeland, 'New World Order Going Badly Wrong', *Financial Times*, 19 Nov. 1994.
13. Schulte, 'Former Yugoslavia and the New NATO' (note 5) p.32.
14. Ibid. p.33. Also see this article for details of the military and political arrangements relating to Russian participation in IFOR and SFOR.
15. According to Gregory Schulte, NATO forces stopped 74,000 ships, inspected 6,000, and diverted 1,400. Ibid. p.20.
16. Schulte (note 5) p.28.
17. The Stabilization Force (SFOR) was established in Dec. 1996 with the expiration of the

IFOR mandate. SFOR deployed about half the number of troops that IFOR had in the field.
It was given a mandate to run through May 1998.
18. 'Albright Says Troops to Have New Bosnia Role', Reuters News Service, 22 May 1997.
19. Ibid.
20. 'Bosnians Back Home, With Quiet U.S. Help,' *New York Times,* 29 July 1997.
21. 'Can Peace Last in Bosnia?' *Strategic Survey, 1996–1997* (London: IISS 1997) p.137.
22. 'Aid Donors Want Serb War Suspects', Associate Press, 23 July 1997.
23. Cited in SFOR News Summary and Analysis, 6 Aug. 1997, *www.shape.nato.int/ifor/
sa/sumaug06.*
24. 'Serb May Be Seized, U.S. Envoys Warn', *Washington Post,* 10 Aug. 1997.
25. 'France Objected to NATO Planning of 2nd Bosnia Raid', *New York Times*, 16 July 1997.
26. Quoted in *Balkan Watch*, Vol.4.22, The Balkan Institute, 9 June 1997.

From Peace Making to Peace Building in Central America: The Illusion versus the Reality of Peace

KIMBRA L. FISHEL

The Myth of Lasting Peace

The fall of the Soviet Union, the demise of Communism in Eastern Europe, and the end of the Cold War ushered in a new era of international politics. The bipolar sphere of East-West conflict ended without the dreaded nuclear exchange between the two superpowers. In the early 1990s, scholars and philosophers spoke of the promise of an 'end of history'[1] and a lasting 'democratic peace' as the global community embarked upon a 'new world order'.

Heading into the late 1990s, an examination of the globe suggests that the emerging 'new world order' is better described as a 'new world disorder'.[2] One must be cautioned that peace, not always democratic, is seldom lasting and that history has a way of reemerging at the most inopportune moments. Today's international politics are played out in a global arena fraught with ambiguity, instability, and dangers, both new and old. These ongoing challenges are either products of the new system that is in creation or are rooted in historical circumstance. It is essential to recognize these dangers, for they give challenge to the reality of peace and illustrate that what appears to be concrete is often illusory.

One of the most salient examples of this ambiguity is the Central American region. The end of the Cold War combined with internal and regional changes allowed for the historic signing of the peace accords in El Salvador, Nicaragua and Guatemala.[3] Elections are now considered the norm in Central America, as El Salvador and Nicaragua have both undergone democratic transitions of power and Guatemala's 36-year civil war officially ended in December 1996. Positive signs in Central America are voluminous and include the move toward democratization, the peace process and apparent end of guerrilla warfare, efforts at Central American cooperation and integration, reform of the security and military forces, and heightened macroeconomic growth.

But challenges underlay the Central American peace and democratization process, and new forms of conflict are emerging out of the recently negotiated peace. For every concrete procedure which signals advances in the peace process, an alternative reality underscores the illusion of peace in this volatile area. Thus, other portents are not so positive. Democratization is a fragile process and although the peace accords have solidified, the root causes of conflict must continually be addressed. The prospects for cooperation among Central American countries are conversely met with regional divisions and border disputes among the very states that seek integration. The necessary reform of the military and police forces throughout Central America has coincided with a power vacuum within the internal security forces, allowing the newly emerging crime threat to run effectively unchecked and become the primary security dilemma for the region. Widespread structural adjustment policy has resulted in micro-economic difficulties which exacerbate the initial social and economic causes of conflict. It is no wonder that a respected security specialist and Latin American expert began a conference presentation on security challenges in Latin America with the following question and eventual answer:

'Duck'. Is that a noun or an action verb?
In Latin America today, it is very much an action verb![4]

This study examines the relationship between the reality and the illusion of peace in Central America. It argues that the two must be reconciled before continued, long term advancement in democratization and development is possible. The analysis suggests that the means of reconciliation lies in the ability of the major players involved in the peace building process, the United States, the United Nations, and most importantly the Central American region, to take responsibility for their actions.

Building Peace: The Reality versus the Illusion of Peace

The 'reality of peace' is not meant to be all inclusive, merely illustrative of the significant progress the Central American region has made in its efforts toward democratization and development. As will be shown, strides made in these areas are quite real and hold great promise for long lasting progress. However, there is another reality which underscores the idea that lasting peace in the region is somewhat illusory. That concept suggests that the realities of peace are superimposed upon areas of conflict and instability, thus making that peace tenuous, that is, an illusion. The following discussion shows the interrelationships and antagonism encountered in the Central American quest for peace.

Democratization: Resiliency versus Fragility

The 1990s witnessed a rise of democracy in Central America. Central

American leaders are optimistic that this move toward democracy will help ensure continued peace and development in the region. According to Salvadoran President Armando Calderon Sol, the rise of democratic governments throughout Central America has already resulted in conditions which promote regional stability.[5]

Calderon Sol's own country is a striking example of this progress toward democratization. Whereas in the 1980s El Salvador was in the midst of civil war with the Farabundo Marti National Liberation Front (FMLN), it is now common to see political displays posted along the roads in San Salvador advertising the FMLN as a functioning political party operating within a constitutional system. '*VOTA FMLN*' underscores the end of El Salvador's civil war and illustrates Central America's democratic process. Once a main threat to the Salvadoran government, the FMLN is now provided security for its election campaign rallies by the Salvadoran police.[6] The 16 March 1997 legislative and municipal elections in El Salvador saw an FMLN climb from 14 to 27 seats in the 84-seat National Assembly and an FMLN rise from 13 to 52 town halls out of 262 in the country's mayoral races.[7] On election night, Calderon Sol contacted San Salvador's new FMLN mayor, Hector Silva, congratulating him and conveying the central government's desire to cooperate with Silva and all FMLN mayors. This election, which was unmarred by fraud or violence and included the participation of the governing ARENA party, the rightist National Conciliation Party (PCN) and the Christian Democratic Party (PDC), demonstrated El Salvador's commitment to the democratic process.

Nicaragua, also, is undergoing the same move toward democracy. In October 1990, Nicaraguan elections were held under the observation of the Organization of American States (OAS). Over 433 OAS observers took part in the mission. This monitoring aided legitimacy of the process in that it helped increase confidence in the fairness of the procedure and encouraged all parties to accept the final outcome:[8] the defeat of Sandinista President Daniel Ortega Saavedra by Violata Barrios de Chamorro's National Opposition Union. Substantial progress was made during Chamorro's years in office. Her government worked to consolidate democratic institutions, advance national reconciliation and stabilize the Nicaraguan economy. The October 1996 elections proved to be fair and free of corruption. Dr Arnoldo Aleman's presidential victory denoted a democratic transfer of power from one elected government to another. Both the Salvadoran and Nicaraguan progress in democratic development was tied to the end of the civil wars resulting from both internal and external conditions, the latter including the end of US-Soviet confrontation. It is now hoped that with the end of Guatemala's civil war, that country will be able to advance democracy and human rights as championed by its President, Alvaro Arzu Irigoyen.

The success or failure of a democratic state, like any other state, rests ultimately upon the legitimacy of the system. Legitimacy may be defined simply as 'the moral right of the government to govern'[9] combined with the capability of the government to carry out its programs and policies. The newly emerging democracies of Central America are particularly fragile systems. They have risen in regions torn by conflict and inundated with poor social, economic and political conditions. As a result, ongoing episodes challenge the stability of the peace accords. In Nicaragua, defeated Sandinista (FSLN) Presidential candidate Daniel Ortega alleged electoral fraud and commented that he accepted the 'legality but not the legitimacy' of the electoral system.[10] FSLN threats to renew 'coercive tactics' if the democratically-elected Aleman government refuses its demands question whether or not the FSLN is fully ready to participate within the democratic context or resort to its previous campaign of violence. Similarly in Guatemala violence continues and includes isolated incidents with renegade elements from the Guatemalan National Revolutionary Unity (URNG) as well as widespread incidents involving common criminals. The threat of terrorism remains acute and is a tactic used by URNG radical fringe elements as shown be their dispensing of bombs accompanied by URNG leaflets.[11] El Salvador seems to be the exception in that politically motivated violence is practically non-existent, but El Salvador's new threat in the form of gang violence has earned it the title of the world's most dangerous country.

When these young systems must confront new conflicts in the form of such things as criminal violence in addition to leftover threats from previous conflicts, terrorism, and drug trafficking they are particularly vulnerable. In Central America, gang violence is now the leading threat to peace and plays upon the declining economic, social and political conditions of the rural sectors of many societies. Because democratization is a process of legitimation of democratic government, attacks against the state greatly challenge the legitimacy of the newly-forming systems. These challenges rest on a social, economic and security front.[12] Newly democratizing countries often lack firm legitimacy within the eyes of the population, an established legal and judicial system to handle criminal problems, and effective intelligence and military operations to combat the threats. These problems are particularly evident in El Salvador, Nicaragua and Guatemala as are the challenges of creating military and police forces which are capable, effective and responsible to democratic rule.

The military and police present a special problem in newly evolving democracies because in order to have a viable democratic government, it is essential that the security forces be firmly placed under civilian control. The military in turn must view itself as an instrument of the established government. In newly evolving democracies, the military forces must often readjust to this new type of role, an adjustment which may prove difficult under normal circumstances and extremely precarious under emergency conditions. Democratic governments must retain their legitimacy among the population as well as with the military in order for democratic values and ideas to become fully inculcated, a process that may take at least a decade. The rising problem with crime in Central America challenges the democratization process and strikes at the heart of the capability of the security forces to meet the threat and stay responsive to the citizenry and civilian government.

The Peace Accords versus the Root Causes of Conflict

Advances in democracy were possible due to the peace accords agreed upon by Central American governments and the warring insurgent movements. The history leading to peace in the region may be traced back to the early 1980s in El Salvador when José Napoleon Duarte assumed the junta presidency and embarked upon a course of democratic evolution to combat revolutionary transformation. The United States, the United Nations and regional actors including Costa Rica and Honduras played key roles in the peace process. For the United States, it was imperative that Communism not be allowed a foothold near its borders, and US policy throughout the 1980s utilized a force/diplomacy strategy to protect its interests and bring peace to the region.[13]

United Nations operations in Central America became especially prominent in the 1990s. The UN Observer Mission in Central America (ONUCA), was headquartered in Tegucigalpa, Honduras, and ran from December 1989 through January 1992. This mission was designed to verify the compliance of Costa Rica, El Salvador, Guatemala, Honduras and Nicaragua in ceasing aid to guerrilla forces and insurrectionist movements in the region and to help ensure that the territory of these countries would not be used in attacks against other states. ONUCA aided the voluntary demobilization of the Nicaraguan Resistance through monitoring the ceasefire and separation of forces.

ONUCA served as a precursor to perhaps the UN's most ambitious operation in the region, the United Nations Observer Mission in El Salvador.[14] On 20 May 1991 Security Council Resolution 693 established ONUSAL which built upon the framework laid by Duarte in the 1980s but derived directly from a 1989 negotiation process between the Salvadoran government and the FMLN. These negotiations were conducted under the auspices of the UN Secretary-General, in which the objective was to 'achieve a series of political agreements aimed at resolving the prolonged armed conflict in El Salvador by political means as speedily as possible, promoting democratization in the country, guaranteeing unrestricted respect for human rights and reunifying Salvadoran society'.[15] Today, the United Nations has only a few observers remaining in El Salvador, and their next great challenge lies in facilitating the end to conflict in Guatemala.

On 29 December 1996, Guatemala's 36-year civil war ended after nearly six years of negotiations when the Guatemalan National Revolutionary Unity (URNG) and the government signed a peace accord. The accords resulted in the disarmament and demobilization of 3,000 former guerrillas under the auspices of approximately 145 UN military observers, the reduction of the Guatemalan military and the cessation of the military's role in internal security. With USAID assistance, former guerrillas are facilitated in their reincorporation into Guatemalan society through vocational and educational training.

In addition to the reincorporation of former guerrillas into Guatemalan society, the country is also embarking upon programs to bring all members of society into the political process. According to Arzu Irigoyen, the peace accords resulted in the most diversified structure of citizen participation in the history of Guatemala.[16] The accords signified the commitment of the government to full integration of Guatemala's indigenous population, about 55 per cent of society, into the social, political and economic realm. The peace accords established three commissions that are currently working on 'Officialization of Indigenous Languages, Educational Reforms, and Identification and Preservation of Sacred Sites'.[17] With this latest agreement, Guatemala has joined El Salvador and Nicaragua in the pursuit of democratization and development in the region.

The victories achieved through the peace accords are impressive, but the original causes of conflict must be understood in relation to the concept of government legitimacy. Loss of legitimacy by the government rested in the root cause of conflict: poor economic, social and political conditions. The governments' victories in the war for regaining its legitimacy during the 1980s crises translated into victories for the peace accords and for transformation of the system. Nevertheless, in many countries, the root causes of conflict still persist.

As of 1995, 52.4 per cent of the Salvadoran population was impoverished with 23.9 per cent living in extreme poverty in rural areas. The Salvadoran poor suffer an inequitable access to social services, and less attention is paid by the government to issues such as environmental factors affecting health.[18] One source of the exorbitant crime wave is the extreme poverty in rural areas, but crime itself threatens continued progress in areas of concern to the poor. El Salvador's growing economy has difficulty keeping pace with ex-guerrillas, returned refugees and young people who must be absorbed into the system. Moises Naim of the Carnegie

Endowment states that in order to avoid a violent backlash to government reform measures, it may be necessary to dampen public expectations that the reforms will lead to immediate widespread prosperity.[19]

In Guatemala there is ongoing, turmoil over land tenure issues and human rights violations. In September 1997, approximately 4,000 *campesinos* marched in Guatemala City to demand 'an immediate solution' to the country's land tenure problems. This march ended with a confrontation with police and illustrates the underlying causes of conflict still present in Guatemala. Land tenure problems combine with human rights abuses and continued economic difficulties to place new demands upon Guatemala's civilian government elected at the end of the civil war. Former rebels laid down their weapons, joining demobilization camps and, as indicated above, are given training to aid in their reintroduction into society. However, once these former guerrillas are reintroduced into society they are entering an economy where 80 per cent of the people live in poverty and 45 per cent are unemployed.[20] In emphasizing US support for the Guatemalan peace process, Thomas McLarty visited Camp Claudia in May 1997, promising $260 million and lauding foreign investment.[21] Nevertheless, the reintroduction of former combatants will severely strain an already overburdened economy. Ex-combatants reintroduced into Salvadoran society faced similar difficulties and a portion of these individuals, both former armed forces and guerrilla members, turned to gang violence or offered their services to the public in the form of private security organizations to combat the criminal problem – something the Salvadoran public no longer believed the government capable of effectively addressing.[22]

Regional Integration versus Regional Confrontation

Heightened efforts at integration of the Central American region are a by product of the peace process. Integration rests upon cooperation among the states, a fact the Clinton administration has recognized. At the December 1994 Summit of the Americas in Miami, the Clinton administration's policy of regional cooperation was established. President Clinton, along with 33 other democratic leaders, embarked on an ambitious agenda designed to advance regional cooperation within Central America as well as between the Central American states and the United States. The goal is to address common areas of concern to Central America and the United States. The effects of this framework greatly strengthen the move toward Central American integration, as the agenda calls for the establishment of a Free Trade Area of the Americas by 2005, alleviation of poverty, sustainable economic growth, respect for the environment, and cooperation on addressing transnational threats.[23]

Regional institutions already exist which ease the process of integration. The area of free trade is one in which the Central American countries have presented a particularly united front. This is evidenced by the negotiation process between the Central American Common Market (CACM) and Mexico for a free trade zone. Other institutions of importance include the System of Central American Integration, headquartered in San Salvador, which evolved out of the 1980 regional crises and the 1995 Central American Democratic Security Treaty which provides a framework 'for confidence building measures' among the security forces. In addition, Central Americans are working together to pool resources for the Central American Police Academy in San Salvador[24] in an effort to deal with regional conflict in the form of crime.

In addition to political and economic integration, military integration of the Central American armies is also under consideration. On 9 June 1997 the commanders of the armed forces and defense ministers of El Salvador, Guatemala, Honduras and Nicaragua met in Guatemala City to discuss efforts to integrate the regions' military forces. Guatemalan Defense Minister General Julio Balconi stated that in order to meet the new security challenges, in particular the explosion of non-political violence and crime, integration of the armies is vital.[25]

As a result of such movements, many Central American leaders view integration as an outcome soon to be realized. At the 52nd session of the United Nations, El Salvador's Calderon Sol maintained that Central America has reached an apex where the peoples' 'latent impulse' toward reunification can be realized to pursue regional political union.[26] In regard to the San José Conference and US-Central American relations, Calderon Sol described the Central American stance on free trade as clear and united, marking the event as historical in that 'Central America spoke up with one single voice for one single cause and following one single policy.'[27] Similarly, Guatemalan President Alvaro Arzu Irigoyen stated that extraordinary progress has occurred in the area of integration. Central American governments had agreed on the need for economic integration and had embarked on the establishment of a regional political union whose purpose would be to overcome poverty and other economic difficulties and promote democratization.[28]

Despite these moves toward regional integration, regional divisions remain. Some countries are more reluctant than others to carry out the process. Costa Rica, for example, one of the most democratically consolidated and developed states in the region, is quite hesitant in pursuing Central American regional integration. It is not a member of the Central American Parliament and is far more interested in fostering and solidifying economic ties with its fellow countries than in any sort of political union.[29]

Also, for any political union to exist, long-time border disputes must be resolved. The Salvadoran and Honduran border dispute, supposedly settled by a 1992 World Court decision, leaves open issues of human settlement and demarcation which remain uncertain today. A 130-year-old territorial despute between Guatemala and Belize remains unresolved, and the Guatemalans are in the process of creating six new military bases in the Peten department near the Mexican and Belize borders. These new forces are supposedly created in response to deforestation problems along the borders but will 'allow the military to fulfill its constitutional role of protecting national territory'.[30] Despite the very real moves toward integration, clearly the idea of the sovereign nation state has yet to be sacrificed in favor of a larger integrated political union.

Reform of the Security Forces versus New Threats to the State

An outgrowth of the peace accords was the demobilization, dismantling, and reform of the security forces. In El Salvador, this meant the creation of the new National Civil Police (PNC). The PNC rose out of the 1992 Salvadoran Peace Accords and was established through the guidance and monitoring of the United Nations. According to the Chapultepec Accords, the military would be excluded from a public security function, and the three security forces existing under the Ministry of Defense would be phased out with the simultaneous formation of the PNC. The PNC, under the Ministry of Interior and Public Security, would be composed of 20 per cent former militarized National Police, 20 per cent former FMLN guerrillas, and 60 per cent new recruits. A new police training academy was also to be established.

Simultaneously, the Salvadoran Armed Forces would undergo reform and a major reduction. The Salvadoran Constitution was amended to prohibit the military from playing a role in internal security except under extreme conditions. The Treasury Police and the National Guard were both abolished, and a purge of the Armed Forces occurred in 1993 of those persons accused of human rights abuses and corruption. As of 1996, military personnel had been reduced to less than 20,000 personnel.[31]

Advances were also made in Nicaragua on reform of the security forces. In 1994 a new Military Code was enacted by General Joaquin Cuadra in the hopes of professionalizing the Army of Nicaragua. As a consequence, Sandinista Popular Army Commander General Humberto Ortega was replaced in 1995. In August 1996, the National Assembly legislated a new police organization law which 'further codified both civilian control of the police and the professionalization of that law enforcement agency'.[32] Chamorro's successor, President Aleman, has since named the first civilian Defense Minister.

In Guatemala, the internal security unit, the Mobile Military Police, which was established in 1958 was demobilized based on a 1996 agreement between the government and the URNG. In February 1997, legislation was passed in Guatemala which would create a unified National Civilian Police. Guatemala's new police force would include elements of the former treasury and national police. Dismissal of corrupt and abusive members of the security forces and the disbanding of paramilitary patrols are part of the reform process. In addition, legislation allows for the trying of military personnel in civilian courts for non military offenses.

Finally, in Honduras, the last country in Central America in which the police force remains under the military, President Reina committed to a restructuring of the security forces including the abolition of the position of the armed forces chief of staff and a transformation of the national police from military to civilian control. The Honduran Public Security Force will be reformed under the Organic Law of the Civilian Police which will define the structure and mechanisms of the new organization.

The reform in the military and police is essential for the continuing development and democratization of Central America. However, there are new problems associated with reforms, including a power vacuum during the period of the demobilization of the old security forces and creation of the new civilian units, that challenge the legitimacy of the state. This lack of effective security organizations weakens the state in its ability to combat ongoing crises such as the drug problem, a threat which undermines the legitimacy of the new system and spreads corruption throughout the hemisphere.[33]

Despite these ongoing threats to the state, the main challenge in the security arena lies in how to deal with non-political violence. El Salvador has a murder rate of 140 per 100,000 people,[34] and certain areas of the country are extremely perilous. In parts of eastern San Salvador, the gang warfare is so bad that the police reportedly leave the area at night, turning it over to the criminals, only to return in daylight to 'clean up the bodies'.[35] The Salvadoran police suffer from problems compounded by an inefficient and corrupt judiciary. This combination of the lack of professionalism by the police and a corrupt judiciary include 'occasional use of excessive force by police, denial of due process, lengthy pretrial detention, and long delays in trials...'.[36] In addition, PNC members have been arrested in high profile crimes. Many view the PNC as ineffective against its primary target – gang violence.

Crimes such as kidnappings and murder which are non-political in nature are threats which have more than substituted for the violence associated with revolutionary warfare. In Guatemala, it is estimated that in 1994 three or four wealthy individuals were kidnapped every month and that kidnappers secured approximately \$35 million.[37] As does El Salvador, Guatemala lacks a reliable and effective civilian police and faces an inefficient judicial system; 'The weakness of the police as an institution together with an antiquated, legalistic, and overburdened justice system, created a situation of de facto impunity that is only now, under the Arzu government, beginning to yield to the rule of law.'[38] But the Arzu government has a long way to go before reform of both the police and the military translates into democratic progress.

The Guatemalan military's human rights record continues to be of concern. US military assistance to the Guatemalan government was suspended in 1990 after the murder of American citizen Michael Devine by the Guatemalan armed forces. Concern over human rights cases resulted in the 1995 suspension of the only remaining element of US military assistance, the International Military Education and Training program.[39] United States aid to Guatemala for training in civil/military relations may resume in support of the peace accords, although military units have protested their disbandment as called for by the agreements.

The problem of crime is so bad that Guatemala is considering declaring a state of emergency which would place military anti-crime patrols throughout the country. These patrols could arrest suspects, and suspension of certain rights including due process would coincide with this state of emergency. The resort to this option apparently rests on the ability of the National Civilian Police to handle the problem, a force which has so far proved incapable of meeting the crisis.

Finally, President Reina's decisions to reform the military have not gone unchallenged in Honduras. In particular, there has been great criticism by the military high command of Reina's decision to abolish the armed forces chief of staff. The abolition of this position is a critical element of democratic government for Honduras, as the armed forces chief of staff is the supreme Commander-in-Chief of the nation's military. The theory of democratic government dictates that only an elective representative of the people can hold the position of Commander-in-Chief.

Macroeconomic Development versus Microlevel Crises

Overall, macroeconomic indicators are high in Central America. US Deputy Assistant Secretary for Inter-American Affairs John Hamilton reported that Central America is experiencing solid economic growth:

> Inflation appears to be largely under control, at about 12 per cent on average. Debt service burdens have been reduced through a combination of outward-looking, market based economic policies, reschedulings and occasional forgiveness. Parastatals have been

privatized and public sector employment rolls trimmed. The Central Americans have greatly liberalized their financial sectors. This is reducing capital flight and resulting in a more efficient allocation of resources. Central America's average external tariff level has been reduced by about two thirds since the 1980s. Our exports to the region in 1996 totaled $7.8 billion, double that of 1990. In turn, Central American exports... continue to show strong growth. In recent years, non-traditional exports from Central America have expanded at an annual rate of 12 per cent.[40]

With the signing of the 1992 Peace Accords, El Salvador experienced a post-war economic boom. In July 1995, an abrupt shift in monetary policy resulted in an economic downturn yielding a larger than expected government deficit,[41] but by the end of 1996 the outlook for the Salvadoran economy had improved. Throughout this decade, El Salvador has grown at an average annual rate of 6 per cent and is the Central American leader in trade liberalization. Internal trade and exports are currently growing at rates of nearly 25 per cent per year.[42] Similarly, Nicaragua is in its fourth consecutive year of economic growth. It is currently undergoing an export boom from both traditional and non-traditional exports. In 1996 the economy grew at a rate of 5.5 per cent, its best performance since 1977. No fewer than 351 state enterprises have been privatized, inflation has been reduced from 13,500 to 12 per cent, and Nicaragua is now 'poised for rapid economic growth'.[43]

Despite these strong macroeconomic indicators, microlevel difficulties remain. Poverty continues to be prevalent in the region. Except for Costa Rica, high infant mortality rates, low life expectancies, and illiteracy adversely influence the economy. Some 40 per cent of Guatemalans and Nicaraguans are illiterate.[44] El Salvador remains hampered by poverty irrespective of its broad macroeconomic success. Nicaragua is one of the poorest nations in the Hemisphere. It is second only to Haiti, and has a per capita GDP of $452. Nicaragua continues to suffer from unemployment and underemployment, persistent trade and budget deficits, and a high reliance on foreign assistance which consisted of 22 per cent of Nicaragua's 1996 GDP.[45]

Reconciliation of the Illusion and the Reality of Peace

It has been demonstrated here that the process of building peace in Central America is one which rests on a multitude of underlying challenges that must be addressed. As derived from this study, these challenges are manifest in five factors which illustrate the reality versus the illusion of peace.

REALITY	ILLUSION
Rise of Democracy	Fragility of Legitimacy
Peace Accords	Root Causes of Conflict
Regional Integration	Regional Divisions
Reform of Security Forces	New Threats to State
Macroeconomic Success	Microlevel Crises

Figure 1 graphically displays the reality factors superimposed upon elements which accentuate the illusion of the peace process. The fragile peace which is superimposed upon those conditions creating the illusion of peace gives rise to a highly unstable environment in which the major actors involved in the peace process seek to build a lasting peace in the region. The threat of this instability is a possible breakdown of the democratization process in the region and a return to military rule or civil war. The peace building process must work toward stabilizing this threat.

FIGURE 1

THE CENTRAL AMERICAN PEACEBUILDING ENVIRONMENT

PEACEBUILDING ENVIRONMENT

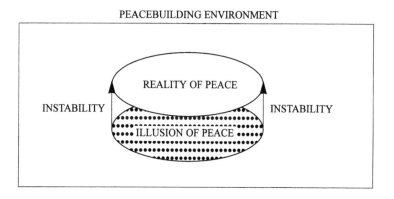

Building peace includes promoting and developing those institutions that further the democratization and development of the region and mitigate those factors which seek to destroy such progress. Long-term peace consolidation rests upon the legitimacy of the governments in question and that of the outside organizations seeking to facilitate the process. For legitimacy to endure, the peace building environment must be stabilized through reconciliation of these two contradictory spheres: the reality and the illusion of peace. This is not an easy task and requires a commitment of all actors involved, including the United States and the United Nations but most importantly the Central American players, to take responsibility for the consequences of the actions they have already embarked upon in the peace process.

The development strategies which Central American nations have advanced backed by the United States and the United Nations focus upon broad macroeconomic policies and privatization. However, economic development alone does not ensure overall development of a country, and structural adjustment policies have fundamental internal ramifications on society as a whole and may act to retard other areas of reform.[46] Safety measures are crucial to counteract the negative impacts of macroeconomic reforms. Macroeconomic policies do not address problems of equity and justice which are fundamental to continued development.[47] The need for continued reform of the Central American justice systems, improvement in education and human rights, and continuing reform of the security forces were and remain today crucial issues facing the countries.

These societal and political issues are fundamentally tied to continued economic advancement and fulfillment of the peace accords. The Central American nations and their supporters have a responsibility to fuse programs of economic, social and political development and recognize the interconnection among the three. Calderon Sol's attempt at creation of a 'Culture of Peace'[48] is a good illustration of this point as it requires social changes in values and attitudes of Salvadorans. The Salvadoran government has created a series of programs geared toward this effort including the Democratic Citizenship and Human Development, Recovery and Development of National Identity in a Culture Of Peace, and Learning and Living a Culture of Peace. Financial strains are tight in El Salvador as well as other Central American countries, and it is in the interest of the United States and the international community to attempt to find ways to ease the financial burden placed upon Central American countries in their quest for building peace. Otherwise the peace process will surely fail.

Several types of violence threaten the Central American region and include a breakdown of the peace process leading to a return to civil war, border disputes leading to an outbreak of interstate warfare, drug trafficking and terrorism. Commitment, coordination and cooperation among the US, UN and Central American states are key to offsetting many of these problems. It is imperative that the US and UN continue their efforts in support of peacebuilding and not disengage since the peace accords have been signed and the peacemaking stage has supposedly ended.

However, the new threat, that of criminal violence in the form of gang warfare, is the greatest security challenge facing the Central America region. The skyrocketing of criminal violence is an outgrowth of the end of the civil wars and the peace process. But, this issue is not only regional. The internationalization of gangs is a significant problem. As gangs originating in the United States are exported to Latin American countries, ethnic gangs originating from foreign countries are imported into the United States. Combating gangs on both an international and a regional level suffers from a lack of intelligence sharing among the countries involved: 'Although the sharing of intelligence on drug trafficking and terrorism has increased, there is very little data available on many of the gangs involved in a variety of more traditional criminal activities....'[49]

In El Salvador and other Central American countries, US policy is a key area of concern because a large portion of gang members have been imported from the streets of Los Angeles. This is an area in which it is vital for the US to take responsibility for its actions. Salvadorans fled their country during the civil war, hoping to find refuge in the United States. Today, many children of the people who fled the country during the war years are now returning as street gang members.[50] Salvadoran street gangs such as *Mara Salvatrucha* and the 18th Street Gang were originally founded in Los Angeles and then imported to El Salvador. Gangs are particularly threatening to newly forming democracy, and US policy toward legal and illegal aliens is expediting the return of gang members to Central America.

US policy dictates the deportation of legal or illegal immigrants at the end of prison sentences who have been convicted of felonies. This procedure was mandated by Congress nearly a decade ago in hopes that its effect would be to reduce the US crime rate, thereby saving the US taxpayer money. In 1996, Congress passed a new law which broadened the definition of 'aggravated felony' and vastly increased the number of crimes which were deportable offenses. The results of US policy have run counter productive to not only Salvadoran interests but US interests as well. A 'boomerang effect' has resulted in a fast return of criminals to the US who were only recently deported,[51] and the Salvadorans are currently unable to try criminals for crimes they committed on foreign ground. President Calderon Sol recently asked the US for an extradition treaty agreement so that Salvadorans accused of crimes in the US could be tried in El Salvador,[52] although it is questionable whether or not the Salvadoran justice system could handle such a process in its current state.

Resolution of these security issues are directly connected to political, social and economic advancement and vice versa. The responsibility of the United States, the United Nations and the Central American countries lies in the ability to recognize that the peace process, democratization and development are much needed and welcome achievements, but that they are also double edged swords. New challenges arise from the peace process and combine with the old. Only through taking responsibility for the actions which led to both the achievements and the challenges of the new peace building environment can major actors hope to retain legitimacy long enough to stabilize that environment, thereby furthering democratization and development of the region. Failure to reconcile the realities with the illusion of peace could have disastrous consequences, plunging Central America into further violence and destruction.

NOTES

1. See Francis Fukuyama, *The End of History and The Last Man* (NY: Avon Books 1992).
2. For a coining of the phrase, 'new world disorder', see Max G. Manwaring, *Gray Area Phenomena Confronting the New World Disorder* (Boulder, CO: Westview Press 1993).
3. For a detailed discussion of the complexity of events which led to the Salvadoran Peace Process, see Kimbra L. Fishel and Edwin G. Corr, 'UN Peace Operations in El Salvador: The Manwaring Paradigm in a Traditional Setting', in John T. Fishel (ed.) *"The Savage Wars of Peace": Toward a New Paradigm of Peace Operations* (Boulder, CO: Westview Press 1997).
4. This was a question and answer given by Dennis Caffrey at the 30 Oct.–1 Nov. 1997 Midwestern Association of Latin American Studies Conference in St Louis, Missouri. It refers to the explosion of criminal and gang violence that has gripped Latin America and its threat to the ordinary person on the street.
5. From Salvadoran President Armando Calderon Sol's address to the 52nd Session of the United Nations.
6. See, among others, Larry Rohter, 'Salvador's Ex-Rebels Expect Gains in Vote Today', *New York Times* Late Edition (East Coast), 16 March 1997, p.18.
7. John Hamilton, Deputy Assistant Secretary for Inter-American Affairs, 'Positive Trends in Central America', Statement before the subcommittee on the Western Hemisphere, House International Relations Committee, Washington DC, 25 June 1997.
8. See 'Background Notes: Organization of American States, May 1997', Bureau of Inter-American Affairs, US Department of State.
9. For a full discussion of this definition of legitimacy, see Max G. Manwaring, 'The Threat in the Contemporary Peace Environment', in Edwin G. Corr and Stephen Sloan (eds.), *Low Intensity Conflict: Old Threats in a New World* (Boulder, San Francisco, Oxford: Westview Press 1992) pp.53–4.
10. John Hamilton.
11. 'Patterns of Global Terrorism, 1996', US Department of State, Washington DC.
12. For a discussion of the impact of crime in El Salvador on the legitimacy of the system see Kimbra L. Fishel, 'From Revolutionary Warfare to Criminalization: The Transformation of Violence in El Salvador', *Low Intensity Conflict and Law Enforcement* 6/3 (Winter 1997) pp.48–63. Also see Kimbra L. Thompson Krueger, 'The Destabilization of Republican Regimes: The Effects of Terrorism on Democratic Societies', ibid. 5/2 (Autumn 1996) pp.253–77.
13. See Kimbra L. Krueger, 'Internal Struggle Over U.S. Foreign Policy Toward Central America: An Analysis of the Reagan Era', *Presidential Studies Quarterly* 26/4 (Fall 1996) pp.1034–46.
14. See Fishel and Corr (note 3).
15. 'United Nations Observer Mission In El Salvador', Program on Peacekeeping policy, The Institute of Public Policy, George Mason University on-line, June 1997.
16. From Guatemalan President Alvaro Arzu Irigoyen's address to the 52nd Session of the United Nations.
17. See Hamilton (note 7).
18. From USAID's 1997 Congressional Presentation on El Salvador. Washington DC.

19. 'Central America Open For Business' *The Economist*. London: Economist Newspaper Group, 21 June 1997.
20. Mark Potok, 'Guatemala, Guerrillas March Toward Peace', *USA Today*, p.10A, 20 March 1997.
21. Ibid.
22. Fishel, 'From Revolutionary Warfare to Criminalization (note 12).
23. Jeffrey Davidow, Assistant Secretary for Inter-American Affairs, Testimony before the House International relations Committee, Subcommittee on the Western Hemisphere, Washington DC, 19 March 1997.
24. See Hamilton (note 7).
25. 'Guatemala: Top Central American Military Leaders Discuss Integration', *Panama City ACAN*, 9 June 1997.
26. From Salvadoran President Armando Calderon Sol's address to the 52nd Session of the United Nations.
27. From a new conference by Salvadoran President Armando Calderon Sol, *San Salvador Radio Nacional de El Salvador Network*, 12 May 1997.
28. From Guatemalan President Alvaro Arzu Irigoyen's address to the 52nd Session of the United Nations.
29. See 'Background notes: Costa Rica, November 1996', Bureau of Inter-American Affairs, US Department of State.
30. See Adam Issacson's *Central American Weekly Update*, Center for International Policy, 20–26 Sept. 1997. Visit on-line at http://www.ciponline.org/caupdate.htm.
31. 'Background Notes: El Salvador, September 1997' Bureau of Inter-American Affairs, US Department of State, Washington DC.
32. 'Background Notes: Nicaragua, April 1997', ibid.
33. Davidow (note 23).
34. Figure reported in 'El Salvador: Take Out Life Insurance Before You Enter', *The Economist*, London, 8 March 1997, Vol.342, No.8007, p.44.
35. From a conversation the author had with a member of the US Military Group in El Salvador, July 1997.
36. 'El Salvador Country Report on Human Rights Practices for 1996', US Department of State, Bureau of Democracy, Human Rights, and Labor, 30 January 1997.
37. 'Growing Security Problems in Latin America', *CJ The Americas Online*, 1997.
38. Hamilton (note 7).
39. 'Background notes: Guatemala, May 1997', Bureau of Inter-American Affairs, Department of State, Washington DC.
40. Hamilton (note 7).
41. See *El Salvador:Economic and Trade Practices*, Department of State report submitted to the Senate Committees on Foreign Relations and on Finance and to the House Committees on Foreign Affairs and on Ways and Means, Washington DC, Jan. 1997.
42. 'Central America Open For Business'.
43. 'Background Notes: Nicaragua, April 1997' (note 32).
44. Hamilton (note 7).
45. 'Background Notes: Nicaragua, April 1997' (note 32).
46. See Moises Naim, 'Latin America: Post-Adjustment Blues', *Foreign Policy*, No.92 (Fall 1993) pp.133–51.
47. See Alvaro de la Ossa, 'Central America in The Global Economy', in Jolyne Melmed-Sanjak, Carlos E. Santiago, and Alvin Magid (eds.) *Recover or Relapse in the Global Economy Comparing Perspectives on Restructuring in Central America* (Westport CT: Praeger 1993).
48. Armando Calderon Sol, 'Message from El Salvador's President', Consultative Group Meeting For El Salvador. Paris, France, 1995.
49. Quoted by Jeff Builta, Director of Analytic studies in the Office of International Criminal Justice in Chicago. In James Pastor, 'Global Proliferation of Gang Activity', *CJ International Online*.
50. See Mike O'Connor, 'A New U.S. Import in El Salvador: Street Gangs', *New York Times*

Current Events Edition, 3 July 1994.

51. See Deborah Sontag, 'Boomerang Deportees: Faulty System and Shattered Lives', *New York Times Service*, 1997.

52. 'Calderon Sol Reiterates support for Illegals in the US', *El Diario de Hoy*, San Salvador, May 1997, p.7.

The Challenge of Haiti's Future

DONALD E. SCHULZ

> *The best lack all conviction, while the worst*
> *Are full of passionate intensity ...*
> *Things fall apart; the centre cannot hold.*
>
> William Butler Yeats

> *In our country, power is a sickness.*
>
> Prime Minister Rosny Smarth,
> upon submitting his resignation, 9 June 1997

Three years after the United States sent military forces into Haiti to depose the Cédras regime and restore President Jean-Bertrand Aristide, the situation is rapidly deteriorating. Perhaps, in view of Haiti's history, this should not be surprising.[1] Nevertheless, it raises major questions not only about the future of that troubled country, but also about peacekeeping operations in general. Few US military interventions have given rise to such heated debate over whether they were a success or a failure. In part, this has been a function of politics, but in part also it was because the extraordinary ease of the military operation created an optical illusion: military success led to triumphalism and complacence. It was assumed that, now that the dangerous part was over, it would be a relatively simple thing to foster democracy and socio-economic development.

In fact, the hard part was still to come. In perspective, it is clear that there was an inverse relationship between the ease of the Haitian military operation, on the one hand, and the difficulty of constructing stable and democratic political institutions and promoting socio-economic modernization, on the other. The very conditions that made the military part of the problem so easy make socio-economic and political challenges extremely hard. Put simply, there is almost nothing to build on. The pervading weaknesses of the Haitian political culture and institutions and the woeful lack of human and material resources – the very factors that made serious military resistance impossible – also make the construction of a new Haiti an enormous challenge.

This does not mean that the situation is hopeless. There have been very real accomplishments over the past three years.[2] A Haitian National Police force has been created which, in spite of inadequate manpower, training and resources, has performed about as well as one could reasonably have expected under the circumstances.[3] A new Congress and president have been elected. For the first time in Haitian history, power has been peacefully transferred from one democratically-elected president to another. At the same time, political violence has been greatly reduced. So far, at least, the country's political elites have mostly been willing to play by the rules of democracy.

Now, however, a new phase of crisis has begun, fueled by increasing political strife, criminal violence, and a failure to generate economic growth or improve living conditions. All this, moreover, is occurring as the United Nations peacekeeping mission is in its final phase-out stages. And so the question must be asked: will the center hold? Or will things fall apart?

This contribution will examine the challenges and prospects of Haiti's future. It will be partly based on a report written by Max Manwaring, Robert Maguire, Peter Hakim, Abigail Horn and myself on an extraordinary conference that took place on Capitol Hill in February 1997.[4] The focus of that meeting – which was jointly sponsored by the US Army War College, Georgetown University and the Inter-American Dialogue – was on the prospects of achieving socio-economic advancement, democracy and the rule of law, and on the role to be played by the United States and the international community. Perhaps the two most important messages that came out of the gathering concerned the need for realism and responsibility: not only must Haiti's foreign sponsors understand the full dimensions of the problem, but there also must be a willingness to do what is necessary to give the Haitian experiment a reasonable chance of success. A failure on either of these counts will doom the entire enterprise.

Realism, of course, is a two-edged sword. If one must be realistic about the situation in Haiti, one must also be realistic about political realities in Washington. The question is whether those two conditions can be synchronized. On this count, I must confess, I am not optimistic. Thus, beyond the conference report I will provide a brief history and analysis of what has gone wrong since that meeting was held. I will also suggest what needs to be done about it. Suffice it to say that the situation is unsettling, and the need for action is urgent. Unless Haitians and their foreign friends can rise to the challenge, there may well come a day when the UN mission in Haiti will be held up as a classic example of 'pre-chaos peacekeeping'.

The Challenge of Haiti's Future: The Conference

But first the report on the Capitol Hill conference. Among the participants at the gathering were two US congressmen and a senator, the Senior Director for Latin American Affairs on the National Security Council, the State Department's Special Coordinator for Haiti, the Director of Plans and Policy for the US Atlantic Command, the Senior Staffer for Inter-American Affairs on the Senate Foreign Relations Committee, an ex-US Ambassador to Haiti, a former Haitian Prime Minister and Foreign Minister, a former Haitian Justice Minister, a Haitian senator, the Haitian Ambassador, the Haitian representative at the World Bank, and the former head of the United Nations Civilian Police (CivPol) operation in Haiti. Other participants included representatives from the US Atlantic Command, the Departments of Defense, State, Commerce and Treasury, international financial institutions, the intelligence community, private enterprise, Congressional staffs, think tanks and universities, and human rights and other nongovernmental organizations.

The bitter struggles over US policy and Haitian political and socio-economic issues that had marked the preceding years were fresh in everyone's minds. Yet, despite this history and the considerable differences of opinion that continued to separate many of the participants, the tone of the conference was forward-looking, with a minimum of polemics or blame-placing. The following account captures the mood and substance of the discussions. Since there were significant differences among participants, an effort has been made to indicate where conflicts occurred. Since the meeting was held on a not-for-attribution basis, speakers are not identified.

Panel One: Social and Economic Advance – What Will It Take?

There was broad agreement that even though the primary historical obstacle to socio-economic development – the Predatory State and its military organization – is no more, the challenges remain enormous. Among other things, there are few functioning institutions, little human capital, and a long history of waste, corruption and mistrust. Thus, the challenge is not one of 'recovery' or 'restoration,' but rather of having to begin the development process virtually from scratch. A few speakers argued that the macro-economic reforms promoted by the international community may lead to even greater inequalities and hardships. They suggested that these measures are likely to generate more socio-economic and political conflict, undermine the legitimacy of the democratic government, and make sustainable development more difficult.

The panelists agreed that foreign aid is urgently needed, but also that it is important to avoid fostering dependency. Haitians must assume the primary responsibility for their country's development. Among other things, the Haitian government needs to:

- reaffirm its commitment to serious socio-economic reform at every possible opportunity;

- constantly demonstrate a commitment to the establishment of a professional police force capable of providing a secure environment in which socio-economic development can occur;

- revise or rewrite archaic laws, such as the 1827 Commercial Code, to encourage foreign and domestic investment;

- establish a competent and honest judicial system that can adjudicate the conflicts that will arise in a free-market economy;

- develop programs that will alleviate the crushing 70 per cent unemployment rate while formalizing the informal economy and bringing it into the mainstream;

- train a competent and honest civil bureaucracy that can manage public enterprise, protect and improve the degraded environment, and help implement socio-economic reform;

- generate the ways and means through which the Haitian educational and public health systems can develop a healthy, literate, skilled, and educated populace that can participate fully in the country's political, economic and social modernization;

- enhance revenue-generation through the development and implementation of equitable taxation;

- decentralize socio-economic development so that all Haitians can understand, participate in, and contribute to local, regional and national decision-making processes;

- as a corollary, decentralize human and financial resources so they are shared at the local level;

- appropriately staff local agencies, while avoiding behavior that will foster clientelism, corruption and favoritism;

- better manage the expectations of the Haitian people with regard to the fruits of democracy and a free-market economy so that there will be less societal friction in the development process;

- improve the national image in order to attract foreign investment and tourism; and

- enlist the support of the Haitian people, including the diaspora, along with the United States and the rest of the international community, to accomplish these ends.

All this, of course, is easier said than done. Many of the reforms advocated by the United States and International Financial Institutions (IFIs) are controversial in Haiti. All too often, the politicization of economic development there has caused the delay or stoppage of important projects. At the same time, ideological and political considerations have also played a role in the international community's behavior, leading to periodic interruptions of foreign aid which have severely impeded economic recovery.

Many participants emphasized a need for the developed countries, and especially the IFIs, to be more flexible. They generally agreed that the United States and the other players of the international community must recognize that Haiti, like other Caribbean nations, has been hurt by the North American Free Trade Association, which has diverted trade and investment away from the region. Accordingly, it was argued, Haiti's foreign friends should help remove barriers to international trade and investment, and assist the country in joining Caribbean and other global/regional economic groupings with a view to gradually substituting trade for aid.

Along these same lines, one of the Haitian speakers characterized the relations between Haiti and the IFIs as being very harsh. The IFI strategy, he said, did not recognize a basic fact of life – namely, that all countries are not at the same stage of development and have very different needs. The IFI strategy, he complained, does not recognize social costs. IFIs must take into greater account the desires and needs of the people affected by their policies. If not, those policies and the programs they engender will not solve Haiti's social problems, but only aggravate them.

In general, the participants accepted the need for the international community to adjust its preconceptions, strategies and requirements to fit Haitian realities. It was suggested, for instance, that resources invested in human capital (education and public health), social safety nets and job generation are crucial to stability, self-sufficiency and long-term development. By the same token, the international community should seek consensus with its Haitian partners rather than impose requirements and solutions that rankle Haitian feelings of national sovereignty and dignity.

Finally, the speakers acknowledged that the current loosely coordinated, seemingly piecemeal and *ad hoc* approach to socio-economic development must change. Haiti's people and government, in conjunction with their international partners, were challenged to engage in a more cooperative, integrated, long-term planning and implementation process to achieve mutually beneficial ends. Unless the country's development problems are addressed on a more coherent and long-term basis, self-sustaining socio-economic advancement will remain an elusive objective.

The Discussion

Much of the discussion that followed the first panel centered on the Haitian government's structural adjustment program. The panelists, all Haitian, offered a series of specific criticisms. One noted that there was no effective social safety net for those who were hurt by the program. Another commented that policies not accepted by the populace will not work. Still another observed that information and communication are crucial. He said that the government had not adequately communicated its intentions and reasoning to the populace, and if that is inadequate there will not be an adequate response. One panelist said that the Préval administration needed to signal strongly its commitment to reform. Instead, it had sent mixed signals. Some of those appointed to government posts are not committed to reform, while others lack the necessary competence. A member of the audience noted that the structural adjustment program has had destructive as well as constructive effects. He cited its devastating impact on rice production. The imposition of new taxes, moreover, had hurt the ability of some legitimate businesses to survive and invest. Another participant indicated that aid for family planning had been drastically cut and that efforts to reverse deforestation had been similarly curtailed. Only a few million trees were being planted annually, a totally inadequate number considering Haiti's disasterous ecological situation. (About 30 million a year are being chopped down.) He also suggested that one way that the government could demonstrate its commitment to reform and rapidly enhance revenue was to privatize the customs service. This proposal fueled discussion and debate throughout the day.

Panel Two: Achieving Democracy and the Rule of Law – Problems and Prospects

All speakers agreed that while some progress has been made, crucial areas remained in which democratic consolidation and the rule of law have not been achieved. This is in part because priority has been given to immediate political, security and economic stabilization requirements over longer-term needs. Those long-range needs, in turn, have remained highly vulnerable to political subversion, corruption and popular alienation.

The panelists stressed that a failure to meet socio-economic development goals and aspirations can suffocate political development. Part of the popular appeal of democracy lies in the expectation that it will lead to an improvement in personal well-being. Thus, economic growth and an improved quality of life are critical issues. If democracy and political stability are to be maintained, poverty, illiteracy and disease must be alleviated and increased opportunities for upward mobility provided.

This said, a failure to maintain law, order and public security can also undermine democracy. Popular acceptance and support of Haiti's fragile democratic experiment has been based largely on the fact that it is credited with the demise of military repression and plunder. In addition, the Haitian people expected the new government to establish a peaceful and secure environment in which they could live and work without fear. Here a critical component has been the effort to create an apolitical professional police force sufficiently large and effective to combat crime, violence and abuses of power. Beyond this, however, the panelists emphasized two largely missing elements in the current situation – namely, the judicial and penal systems. Without functioning courts and prisons, they stressed, security would remain an illusion. And if democracy could not provide security, it would ultimately be discredited.

The panelists observed that, although the old Predatory State has been replaced by a more responsible and responsive government, deeply-engrained popular notions of the state linger on. Most Haitians still view politics with considerable cynicism and distrust. While this is entirely understandable given their historical experience, it raises a critical issue: can Haitians fundamentally change their political values, attitudes and behavior? How and to what degree can the Haitian political culture be transformed? Only when the country's new political leaders and institutions achieve real reform, measurable socio-economic development and palpable security will inroads be made against deep-seated proclivities toward authoritarianism, demagoguery, corruption, distrust and alienation.

The speakers made many recommendations, which taken together establish a basis for a holistic agenda for the achievement of responsive participatory democracy and the rule of law. In general, the Préval administration was urged to accelerate the reform process, while controlling government and police irregularities, and extending the presence of reformed institutions to the countryside where there is often no effective police or judicial presence. Recommendations emphasized the provision of benefits to Haiti's poor majority, who have been widely excluded in the past. Among specific measures proposed were the need to:

- introduce and implant international norms, including human rights, into the legal/judicial system;

- modernize antiquated and/or inadequate criminal, civil, labor, commercial and family codes (some of which date back to the early nineteenth century);

- continue to strengthen and professionalize the Haitian National Police;

- give priority to the heretofore neglected task of creating an honest and competent judicial system;

- construct and upgrade physical conditions in the courts, police stations and prisons;

- develop a technically well-trained judicial police that can conduct professional criminal investigations, thereby freeing judges and magistrates from the burden of having to also serve as investigators;

- continue and improve the programs at the Police Academy and School of Magistrates;

- professionalize the office of Inspector General of the Haitian National Police;

- confirm in law and the budgetary process the independence of the judicial branch of government;

- screen detainees awaiting trial and release those accused of relatively minor offenses not defined as infractions of the penal code (currently, the prisons are overflowing, with 80 per cent of the inmates – and 94 per cent in Port-au-Prince – being pre-trial detainees);

- introduce judicial reforms supporting more informal means of providing justice in commercial, labor and family disputes;

- provide more education, information, and exchange of views between/among various elements of Haitian society, the Haitian government and the international community in order to enhance understanding of the democratic process and the rule of law;

- institutionalize and regulate political parties and other organizations in order to promote democratic ideals, proper financing, accountability and transparency; and

- create a more comprehensive tax base that will provide the revenues that government needs to effectively govern.

Again, these recommendations, as with those made in the previous panel, are easier said than done. To take just one example, there are enormous challenges in creating a professional police force in a country lacking any tradition of professional policing, where the function of the police historically was to serve as an arm of a predatory state. Deeply engrained attitudes and behavior patterns are not changed overnight. The Haitian National Police (HNP) received only four months training; the most field experience any of them had at the time of the conference was 19 months. It takes years to develop a truly professional and competent police force and establish lasting trust between it and the populace it serves.

Compounding the challenge, there is a glaring lack of resources. One panelist pointed out that the 5,200 officers in the HNP are not nearly enough to cover the entire country effectively. As a result, numerous private security and para-police forces, often composed of untrained and unsupervised individuals prone to human rights abuses, have emerged. Thus, Haiti's *attaché* tradition continues in altered form. Yet, there are no resources to expand the HNP to a force capable of providing nationwide security. Indeed, there are questions as to whether even the current force can be maintained. Most of its funding comes from international sources, and no one knows what will happen when that money dries up.

In sum, meeting these challenges will require years of education, internalization and institutionalization. If Haiti is to achieve the political development envisaged by the panelists, the country will need a great deal of help over a long time. This is not a crisis-management type of situation. Past experiences, both in Haiti and elsewhere, suggest that crisis-management solutions lead to half-way, ineffective, and sometimes counterproductive results. The enormous and complex task of achieving democracy and the rule of law will require nothing less than a carefully thought-out, phased, long-term planning and implementation program for sustainable political development.

The Discussion

One of the panelists observed that the Haitian crime problem should not be overstated, noting that there is more crime in one large US city than in the entire country of Haiti. Another commented that one of the main reasons there are so few police in the countryside is that there is no infrastructure and thus no access. Still another speaker observed that sometimes the solutions to problems create new problems. He noted that the police are paid more than judges, who are required to have a higher education. He said that there was a need to strengthen the system of informal justice. This, in turn, brought a reply from another panelist that this might be fine for land disputes and commercial problems, but not for criminal cases.

The most provocative comment, however, came from a member of the audience, who claimed that mob violence (especially land seizures) was increasing and that the government was encouraging this. Two panelists responded that he had overstated the problem. There had certainly been land seizures, but this was not the same thing as mob violence.

Another participant noted the tendency of the United States to return Haitian criminals in the US to Haiti, where they can become a violent, destabilizing force.

**Panel Three: The United States and the International Community –
Staying the Course**

Panelists generally acknowledged that, due in no small part to the
involvement of the international community, much had been accomplished
in Haiti over the previous 30 months. Not only had the legitimate Haitian
government been restored, but a national police force had been created and
several rounds of elections held. Political power had been peacefully
transferred to a new administration and Congress, and the performances of
both branches had been fairly impressive. Painful but necessary economic
reforms had been passed into law, and hopefully this would serve to attract
investment and stimulate the economy in the months ahead. Under the
leadership of Presidents Aristide and Préval, moreover, there had been
considerable progress toward replacing the traditional centralized,
authoritarian, and exploitative state-society relationship with one based on
government responsiveness and accountability.

Nevertheless, as the preceding panels amply demonstrated, enormous
challenges were still ahead. Political institutions remain very weak, violent
crime and human rights violations are on the rise, and the economy is still
largely stagnant. Some 70 per cent of the work force is unemployed.
Consequently, the frustrations of ordinary Haitians are growing as popular
expectations, raised to enormous heights in the aftermath of the September
1994 UN/US intervention, remain largely unfulfilled. The panelists agreed
that if these trends continue they could lead to political turmoil and
undermine the democratic experiment. Thus, the critical importance of the
international community's willingness and ability to sustain its commitment
to Haiti. Would it 'stay the course'?

While there was a general consensus among the conference participants
that the United States and the international community had to stay engaged
in Haiti, varying perspectives emerged as to what this meant. One speaker
argued that, regardless of whether or not you agreed with the Clinton
administration's decision to intervene, once that decision was made the
United States had an overriding interest that the policy not fail.
Unfortunately, he noted, the policy had become a partisan football, with the
result that there had been repeated interruptions in the delivery of aid and a
consequent undermining of Haitian economic recovery.

Another speaker had a very different interpretation. He argued that the
Clinton administration, having basically received what it wanted from
Congress, lacked the will to press the Haitian government on human rights
issues. The administration, he complained, wanted to claim success for its
policies and had simply rationalized away or turned a blind eye to political
violence. US officials had been less than candid in their congressional

testimony and had redacted documents in a misleading way. In this interpretation, 'staying the course' meant continued impunity and obstruction of justice. While the United States must certainly stay engaged, he said that staying the course as it had been implemented thus far might actually jeopardize the gains that had been made.

Picking up from these perspectives, panelists generally agreed that a positive commitment to Haiti's future presupposed more than just 'staying the course'. One warned that the United States must not do what it had so often done in the past – namely, forget about the country as soon as the immediate crisis had passed. The US-Haitian relationship had to be a marriage rather than an affair. At the same time, international actors should not be naïve about the prospects for progress. There must be a long-term commitment. Moreover, the United States should not think of its involvement as a unilateral venture. It needed to involve other Western Hemisphere countries. Rather than encouraging Haitian politicians to come to Washington, he said, we should encourage them to go to places like Jamaica, which are more relevant to their situation and thus better models to learn from.

Given the international community's lead role in promoting 'sustainable development,' that issue was discussed at some length. One panelist defined it as the process by which a society changes to meet the basic human needs of its population, largely by its own efforts, over the long run. He emphasized that there is no universal model that can be applied to every society. The Marshall Plan worked well for Europe because the continent had strong institutions. Haiti, however, does not have that advantage. The paradox is that the more a society needs assistance, the more difficult it is to assist. This is the problem of absorptive capacity, a dilemma which affects both recipient and donor. The latter, in particular, must find effective approaches to this problem without riding roughshod over the intended beneficiaries.

The same panelist noted that the 'Washington consensus' on structural adjustment works best when an attempt to build up civil society is incorporated into the approach. This is a slow process, however, and there is always a danger that the society will reject it. He recommended the adoption of a minimalist approach toward structural adjustment. Whereas some components of the strategy are universal and undisputable, others are more ideological and subject to debate. In Haiti, emphasis must be placed on institution-building and expectations management. Like others, he stressed the long-term nature of the economic reform process.

The same panelist suggested five lessons learned from the Haiti experience: First, massive UN involvement created the impression that solutions were just around the corner. This was an illusion. Second, at least in the Haitian case, when the going gets tough it is the United States and Canada that are on the spot. Third, the most difficult part of international involvement may be cooperation in the justice area. Trying to coordinate different approaches favored by the key actors – the United States, France, and Canada – has been hard. Everyone believes their own system is best. Fourth, donor coordination is essential and must be improved. Fifth, the international community must be flexible enough to go to extraordinary lengths to meet Haitian needs, rather than always placing the burden on the Haitians to meet donor demands.

Another speaker, who addressed the US military role in Haiti, stated that the economy is the most critical factor in maintaining stability and hope for the future. He noted that the US military had made considerable contributions in this regard. Among other things, it had provided advisory teams in the Ministries of Justice, Public Works, and Finance. It was also training Haitian National Police mechanics and was confident that they would soon be able to provide an autonomous institutional capacity to maintain the force's motor pool. Through its humanitarian and engineering efforts, the US Military Support Group had helped jump-start the infrastructure and raise Haitian living standards. Seventy-five medical exercises had reached out to 10,000 people. In light of fiscal pressures and other priorities, however, it had been recommended that the Support Group's presence be terminated. The speaker stressed that this did not mean that the US military is abandoning Haiti. It will continue to stop by regularly and provide humanitarian assistance, as it does in other Caribbean nations.

In early June 1997, two days after the Military Support Group's scheduled departure, it was announced that the group would stay in Haiti through November. As this article is being written, however, US officials are once again considering whether to extend the presence of the roughly 500-troop mission. The catch is that UN forces may well be gone by December, taking with them the cover of international support for a foreign military presence in Haiti.

Panelists focused generally on the challenge of planning and implementing a feasible, cooperative, and coordinated strategy for political stability and sustainable development. They saw the requirements of 'constructive engagement' as going well beyond the past and current adhocracy, to include:

• the need for a unified definition and vision of what ultimate success in Haiti will look like;

• the need for a small, unobtrusive multilateral organization to guide that vision to fruition; and

- the need to develop Haitian political and technical competence to the point where they will be able to take full responsibility for the oversight of their country's socio-economic and political well-being.

Various speakers emphasized that Haiti's nascent and fragile democracy remains at risk. If international involvement is to make a difference, it must be appropriate to the country's needs and capacities, and adequate, consistent, and carefully designed in concert with Haitian involvement and a long-range vision. If the United States and the international community do not respond appropriately to the aspirations of Haitian citizens for legitimate, stable government, economic growth and domestic security, there are likely to be major setbacks to the consolidation of democracy, including a possible breakdown in public order.

The Discussion

During the ensuing discussion, one of the panelists asserted that the Clinton administration, in its determination to declare US policy a success, had politicized the Haiti issue. In the process, it had ignored very real problems, particularly in the area of human rights abuses, and withheld information from Congress. The speaker said that the United States should press the Haitian government to pursue the intellectual authors of the political killings that had occurred since the September 1994 intervention. In response, another panelist agreed that it was important to continue talking to the Haitian government about these matters, preferably in private, but in public if necessary.

One panelist said that remaining obstacles holding up international aid must be removed. Specifically, the Haitian government must begin to implement the reforms required by the IFIs. He added that the government must also pay its civil servants, many of whom have gone months without pay. A member of the audience observed that the Haitian government needed to make a dramatic signal that it was really committed to reform. That message, he said, had not yet got through. He commended a previous suggestion to privatize the Haitian customs service. In response, one of the panelists asked rhetorically: privatize with which capital and which management? He noted that such an initiative could be very dangerous politically for the Préval government. Another panel member quickly remarked that reforms must have popular support or they will fail.

During the continued discussion, various participants again stressed the lack of communications within Haiti, due in part to the lack of a national communications network, and the need to develop a state regulatory capacity, especially a body of commercial law. In a concluding comment, one audience member underscored the importance of prioritizing policies and initiatives. While everything in Haiti needs fixing, not everything can be fixed at the same time. You have to make choices. His first priority would be to address the food crisis. (Severe drought had produced famine in some areas.)

Closing Remarks

Recurring themes of the conference centered on the continuing need for almost universal reforms; the need to manage expectations among all actors; the need to assist Haitians to more effectively participate in political and economic decisionmaking processes; and the need for organized and integrated long-term outside involvement and support for sustainable development.

To address these needs, Haitian and international players must come to terms with significant challenges and as yet unanswered questions. Among those challenges are:

- the simultaneity of priorities that places suffocating pressures on Haiti's institutional capacities, stymies Haitian expectations, and overwhelms the international support system;

- the tensions between a development approach that advocates strengthening the central government versus an approach that advocates decentralizing power to heretofore nonexistent or weak local governments;

- the effective engagement of the private sector, especially as a complement to public sector efforts;

- the uncertainties surrounding the willingness and ability of the United States and the international community to sustain their involvement in the effort to achieve democracy, the rule of law, and socio-economic development into the near and distant future.

Unanswered questions include:

- How much time do Haiti, the United States, and the international community have before unfulfilled expectations turn into serious political violence?

- What are Haitians learning about democracy as they are experiencing its application and mentoring by the United States and the international community?

- Within the context of externally imposed neoliberal economic reforms and continuing Haitian dependence on foreign aid, to what extent is Haiti really sovereign?

The Challenge of Haiti's Future: Political Culture and Political Decay

Recently, Anthony Maingot published a sobering analysis of the prospects for transforming the Haitian political culture. In a nutshell, he argued that one could expect that culture to survive the present international 'occupation' virtually unchanged:

> ... [O]ne can expect only individualism, not coalitions and conciliation, and eventually the rise of another *caudillo*. Understanding the true nature of the game, this *caudillo* will preach democracy even as he prepares to fend off all pretenders, by whatever means necessary. Similarly, the opposition, splintered and multiplied into a truly absurd number of 'parties,' will continue to resist forming enduring alliances and coalitions to confront what is essentially a political juggernaut. They, after all, also partake in the country's political culture.[5]

Whether Maingot's 'prediction' comes true remains to be seen. It occurred to me, however, that for all the useful insights and recommendations generated during the Capitol Hill conference on Haiti, very little was said about the self-destructive nature of the Haitian political culture and the challenges it poses to political and socio-economic development. In a sense, the Haitian participants were too civilized, too constructive, and thus may have created an overly optimistic impression about the ability of Haitian political leaders to work together for the good of the nation as a whole.

This is a crucial issue. As Gabriel Marcella keeps reminding me, the primary responsibility for Haiti's destiny is – and must remain – in Haitian hands. Even if the United States and the international community respond effectively, it will be Haitians who will determine whether that response takes root. Neither the United States nor the international community has the intellectual or political capacity to 'fix' Haiti. Even if they provided all the necessary resources – planted all the trees, generated full employment, eliminated disease and hunger, and so on – none of this would last without Haitian leadership and responsibility.

Much has happened in Haiti in the months since the Capitol Hill conference was held, almost none of it good. No sooner had the meeting ended than Haiti was once again caught up in one of the periodic waves of violence that have afflicted it in recent years. And while that violence soon subsided, the overall situation continued to deteriorate.[6] Spring and summer brought increasing political conflict and paralysis, and growing economic stagnation: In January 1997, former President Aristide had formally registered his newly-created political organization, the Lavalas Family (*Fanmi Lavalas*), as a political party. Subsequently, he and his supporters became an increasingly disruptive force, as they sought to challenge the government's economic reform program and the political dominance of the pro-reform Lavalas Political Organization (OPL). In April, elections were held for 6,275 local offices, 9 Senate seats, and 2 vacant seats in the Chamber of Deputies. Only 5–10 per cent of the voters bothered to turn out for the balloting, which was marred by widespread chaos, fraud, and other irregularities. The primary beneficiary of all this was the Lavalas Family, which seemed on the verge of a decisive victory. Consequently, the OPL and other parties declined to participate in scheduled run-off elections. Under heavy foreign and domestic pressure, the government was forced to postpone that balloting indefinitely.[7]

At this point, Haiti plunged into a full-scale political crisis. Even before the elections, the government had virtually ground to a halt. The growing split within the Lavalas movement had immobilized both the executive and Congress. The latter had not met in weeks because neither the Senate nor the Chamber of Deputies could reach a quorum. Legislation needed to comply with international agreements and rebuild decrepit institutions was not being passed. The budget was seven months overdue. Ministries were strapped for cash; employees went unpaid. Crucial economic and development programs needed to create jobs and reduce mounting social tension remained stalled.

Préval himself seemed paralyzed, torn between his loyalty to and dependence on Aristide and his commitments to his international sponsors and the Lavalas Political Organization. Increasingly, indeed, he seemed isolated within his own administration. By June, all of his cabinet members except Prime Minister Rosny Smarth had gone over to Aristide's party, and on 9 June Préval lost Smarth as well. After months of vitriolic attacks from Aristide and his followers, Smarth, who had become a lightning rod for critics of the government's economic program, finally threw in the towel and resigned. Subsequently, Préval procrastinated in nominating a successor, and when he finally did his nominees were rejected by congress.

While Haitian politicians fiddled, the economy continued to stagnate. Some observers, indeed, believed it was increasingly becoming an economy of consumption rather than production. Unemployment was widely estimated at around 70 per cent. Even the traditional oligarchy was doing poorly. Meanwhile, over $100 million in vital foreign aid remained undistributed because of the paralysis in parliament. As popular frustration grew, so did disillusionment with the Préval administration, congress, the international community, and – most seriously – democracy itself.

The following results from a July 1997 US Information Agency survey of Haitian public opinion are suggestive of the depth and direction of the crisis: 54 per cent of the 1,351 urban Haitians interviewed voiced little or no confidence in the Préval government, 60 per cent believed it would be unable to make inroads on the country's most serious problems, 64 per cent had little or no confidence in Parliament, and 62 per cent felt the same about the justice system. Not surprisingly, the early public support for the president was crumbling. Whereas the previous November, 65 per cent of the respondents had said that Préval was doing a good job, in July only 36 per cent felt that way. As for their attitudes toward those officials who had run for office in April, over half of those polled doubted that senators/deputies (57 per cent) or local mayors (54 per cent) cared anything *at all* about the problems affecting their constituents. Only one in ten felt these officials were at least somewhat concerned about local problems. Significantly, more people now believed that Haiti was not a democracy than that it was (40 per cent to 25 per cent, a reversal of the 28 per cent – 42 per cent findings of the previous poll), and only two in ten still expected democracy to change things for the better. For many Haitians, indeed, the sole hope remained Aristide. Not only did the former president's popularity remain high (61 per cent had a favorable opinion of him, down from 68 per cent in November), but most felt he was a positive rather than a negative force on the national scene (54 per cent to 21 per cent).[8]

These findings, again, were for July. One anticipates the next USIA survey will paint an even drearier portrait.

In mid-October, US Secretary of State Madeleine Albright broke away from President Clinton's South American trip to make a brief visit to Haiti. There she urged her hosts to bury their differences for the common good: While disputes in parliament were the lifeblood of democracy, she said, Haiti had 'gone too long with its government at a standstill. All politicians, of all parties, must ask not what is best for themselves, but what is best for Haiti.'[9] This was good advice. Several months have now passed, however, and the country still does not have a prime minister. Slowly, Haiti continues to slide towards ungovernability.

What is to be Done? The International Community and the Lessons of the Manwaring Paradigm

Five years ago, Max Manwaring and John Fishel wrote an important article in this journal on 'Insurgency and Counter-Insurgency: Toward a New

Analytical Approach.' While the Haiti problem today is more one of peacekeeping and peacebuilding than insurgency/counterinsurgency, some of the insights of the 'Manwaring paradigm' are of vital importance for the tasks ahead. Haiti today seems to be tredding the road of a modified J-curve of revolution, where a period of rising expectation has given way to disappointment, frustration and, potentially, serious violence.[10] Much of the challenge of Haiti's future in the short and medium-run will be to defuse growing frustration that living conditions have not improved before those tensions lead to a social or political explosion.

Here the 'war against social, economic, and political injustice is fundamental. ... [T]he centre of gravity is the perception of poverty, lack of upward social mobility, and disenfranchisement.' At stake may be the single most important internal dimension in struggles against subversion – the legitimacy of the incumbent government. Just as the '[f]ailure of the Intervening Power to reinforce the Host Government's efforts to attain or enhance its legitimacy probably dooms the counterinsurgency to failure',[11] so insufficient or inconsistent efforts to cope with stagnant or declining living conditions will undermine – perhaps fatally – the Haitian government's legitimacy and its prospects for survival.

What is to be done? The participants in the Haiti conference identified much that has been wrong about the international community's efforts: The lack of will and consistency, the piecemeal approach to the problem, the politicization of US policy, the insistence on imposing further sacrifices on the Haitian people that can only undermine support for the Preval administration and its reforms – all this has combined with internal Haitian conflicts, incompetence, corruption and an overwhelming lack of resources to produce the political and socio-economic regression that we see today. With this in mind, I make the following suggestions:

• The United States and the international community are in serious need of reevaluating their minimalist approach toward Haiti. While there have been important accomplishments, much of what has been done has been piecemeal and inadequate. Thus, for instance, there were only limited efforts to carry out disarmament, though an effective program was of crucial importance to the country's prospects for stability. The newly created Haitian police were rushed onto the job with entirely insufficient training. Judicial reforms were neglected, though without them police reform could not ultimately succeed. Foreign aid was distributed in a stop-start pattern that undercut economic recovery. The UN peacekeeping force was limited to repeated short-term extensions, which gave hope to subversives that all they had to do was bide their time until the foreigners left. While one can understand the reasoning behind these and other policies,[12] the fact remains that half-way actions lead to half-way, ineffective results. Put simply, if you are going to engage in peacekeeping, do it right.

- A concerted international effort should be made to resolve the current impasse/crisis. This initiative should include all major Haitian actors, but especially Aristide. Whatever one thinks of the former president – and I am not an admirer[13] – he continues to have a huge base of popular support. As such, he is an essential and legitimate participant in the search for solutions to the crisis. Efforts to isolate him will likely be counterproductive, giving rise to a nationalistic backlash and further polarizing the Haitian political situation. If Aristide is not part of the solution, he will be part of the problem, and his potential for mischief is enormous.[14]

- Accordingly, a strategy of cooptation should be adopted. An effort should be made to obtain Aristide's cooperation with regard to economic reforms, new elections, and the appointment of a new prime minister in exchange for concessions that would satisfy his own political needs and those of his constituents. Specifically, his criticisms of the government's economic modernization program must be taken seriously. The concept of modernization should be broadened to include social modernization, including education, health care, and housing. Most important, ways must be found to alleviate the crushing 70 per cent jobless rate. It is simply not realistic to expect Haitians to accept more unemployment as the price for economic reform. What is needed is a temporary, large-scale public works program, similar to the US Works Progress Administration (under the Roosevelt administration), which would not only provide jobs but also address Haiti's critical infrastructural needs. The bottom line is that, unless living conditions improve, political and social turmoil are likely to increase, undermining economic recovery and democratization in a vicious spiral that could very well destroy everything that has been achieved so far.[15]

- A moment of truth will come when foreign peacekeepers leave Haiti. At this writing, the Haitian National Police is probably still not capable of maintaining law and order by itself. Until fairly recently, UN troops played an important role in patrolling Port-au-Prince and providing critical helicopter transportation for Haitian crowd-control units around the country. They still serve as an important psychological deterrent to troublemakers, and offer a backup capability in case of disturbances. UN personnel protect the National Palace and the residence of former President Aristide. Civilian police (CivPol) are deployed in the capital and provinces, accompanying Haitian National Police officers on patrols and providing crucial training.[16] These activities must continue. If the UN presence is not extended, then other multilateral or bilateral arrangements must be made.[17]

- An accelerated effort should be made to create a functioning judicial system. In comparison to the energy and resources that have gone into the police, this sector of law enforcement has been sorely neglected. Yet, without just and effective courts, attempts to institute the rule of law will be doomed. Put another way, the sooner Haiti has an effective judicial system to support the professional police force that is being constructed, the sooner foreign peacekeepers can go home.

- Much more attention needs to be given to the task of creating an ecologically viable Haiti. Deforestation, erosion, soil exhaustion, water depletion, desertification and rapid population growth cannot be allowed to continue or the country will become utterly uninhabitable. Of all the problems Haiti faces, this complex of maladies, with their built-in momentum, poses the greatest danger to the country's survival.

- The United States should extend its military support mission in Haiti for several years, so that its infrastructural and humanitarian operations can continue. One of the mistakes the United States made when it went into Haiti was imposing severe limits on nationbuilding operations. This was a golden opportunity lost. Haitians would have loved for the United States to have done more of this kind of thing, and most of them still would. Certainly, the need is there.

- Finally, there is a need to continue pressing the Haitian government with regard to human rights abuses. If allowed to continue, violence on the part of the police and other security personnel could undercut the government's legitimacy and destroy everything that has been accomplished. One should caution, though, that it makes little sense to cut off aid for the Haitian National Police, as has sometimes been proposed. Rather, the police need *more* officers, equipment and training, including continuing human rights instruction. One does not create a better police force by denying it the means to become a truly professional and competent organization. Quite the opposite.

NOTES

1. See especially Robert Debs Heinl Jr and Nancy Gordon Heinl, *Written in Blood: The Story of the Haitian People, 1942–1971* (Boston, MA: Houghton Mifflin 1978).
2. For a more detailed discussion, see Donald E. Schulz, 'Whither Haiti?', *Small Wars and*

Insurgencies 7/3 (Winter 1996) pp.324–59; and idem, *Haiti Update* (Carlisle, PA: Strategic Studies Inst., 1997).

3. See Rachel Neild *et al.*, *The Human Rights Record of the Haitian National Police* (Washington, DC: Human Rights Watch/Americas, National Coalition for Haitian Rights, and Washington Office on Latin America, Jan. 1997).

4. For the full text, see Max Manwaring, Donald E. Schulz, Robert Maguire, Peter Hakim and Abigail Horn, *The Challenge of Haiti's Future* (Carlisle, PA: Strategic Studies Inst. 1997).

5. Anthony P. Maingot, 'Haiti: Four Old and Two New Hypotheses', in Jorge Dominguez and Abraham Lowenthal (eds.), *Constructing Democratic Governance: Latin America and the Caribbean in the 1990s* (Baltimore, MD: Johns Hopkins Press 1996) Part IV, p.158.

6. For details, see Donald E. Schulz, 'Haiti: Will Things Fall Apart?', *Parameters*, 27/4, Winter 1997–98) pp.73–91.

7. For a detailed account of the elections, see International Republican Institute, *Haiti: Election Observation Report*, 6 April 1997.

8. US Information Agency, 'A New Level of Discouragement Among Urban Haitians: Confidence in Government and Democracy Is Seriously Diminished', Briefing Paper, B-54-97, 15 Aug. 1997.

9. Joint Press Conference by US Secretary of State Madeleine K. Albright and Haitian President René Préval at the National Palace, Port-au-Prince, Haiti, 17 Oct. 1997.

10. I say 'modified' J-curve because, unlike the conditions posited in the original theory, there has been no prolonged period of objective economic and social development that has produced rising expectations that living conditions will improve. Rather, in Haiti expectations rose sharply as a result of the US military intervention and the subsequent influx of international aid and advisors. Those expectations are now rapidly being deflated. For the original theory, see James C. Davies, 'Toward a Theory of Revolution', *American Sociological Review* 6/1 (Feb. 1962) pp.5–19.

11. Max G. Manwaring and John T. Fishel, 'Insurgency and Counter-Insurgency: Toward a New Analytical Approach', *Small Wars and Insurgencies* 3/3 (Winter 1992) pp.285–6, 291.

12. The decision to field the police so quickly, for instance, was dictated by the unwillingness of the international community – especially the United States – to provide the troops or police needed to maintain order on an ongoing basis. Similarly, political support did not exist for a more lengthy UN peacekeeping operation. The Security Council could only approve short-term extensions of the original mandate in the repeated hope that each new increment would be enough. And again, the unwillingness of the original US peacekeepers to undertake a more extensive disarmament program was dictated, in substantial part, by a reluctance to risk casualties that might have destroyed congressional and public support for their presence altogether.

13. Aristide's recent behavior, especially, reflects some of the most unfortunate features of the traditional political culture. Among other things, the creation of the Lavalas Family represents an attempt to create a highly-personal political organization, based on cronyism and spoils. It fosters neither honest government nor an institutionalized political party system. Nor can one be comfortable with some of the people around him. There are too many former military officers, with records of corruption or human rights abuses, among their ranks. For a recent critical view of the ex-president, see Charles Lane, 'Island of Disenchantment', *The New Republic*, 29 Sept. 1997.

14. Among the most serious concerns, for instance, is that Aristide and/or his supporters might try to politicize the Haitian National Police.

15. Thus Jean-Germain Gros may very well be correct when he writes that, in Haiti at least, 'there may ... be a basic incompatibility between democracy and rapid market reform ... To the extent that market reform leads to a temporary deterioration in living standards, especially for the poor, democracy and "hard times" may become associated in the popular mind. People may come to see democracy as a ploy to get them to support shock therapy; they may vote enthusiastically in the first free election, but sit the next one out in disgust.' In 'Haiti's Flagging Transition', *Journal of Democracy* 8/4 (Oct. 1997) p.108.

16. United Nations, *Report of the Secretary-General on the United Nations Support Mission in Haiti*, S/1997/564, 19 July 1997.

17. As this is being written, plans are underway to assign 50 civilian technical security advisors to the UN Development Program in Haiti for a period of 18 months. The United States is also pushing for a new and separate UN Mission, which would include an internal rapid reaction force. But the latter is dependent on a request from President Préval and would, in any case, have to be approved by the UN Security Council.

Waiting for 'The Big One': Confronting Complex Humanitarian Emergencies and State Collapse in Central Africa

WALTER S. CLARKE[1]

The complex crises which exist... in Africa require more meaningful political engagement from donor governments and international organizations than they presently receive... the substitution of humanitarian action for deeper political engagement allows symptoms of emergencies to be treated, leaving root and proximate causes relatively intact and allowing egregious violations of fundamental human rights to go unaddressed...

John Prendergast
Specialist on Humanitarian and African affairs, 1997[2]

In the Fall of 1996, the world again wrestled with seemingly intractable moral, political and military issues associated with deploying military force in support of another complex humanitarian emergency in the heart of Africa, this one involving Zaire, Rwanda and Burundi, and indirectly a dozen or more other countries.[3] Scarcely two and one-half years earlier, in the same area, a government-sanctioned campaign of genocide caused the deaths of between 500,000 and one million Rwandan citizens, while the world stood by, apparently transfixed by the immensity of the crime and immobilized by poorly-learned lessons from Somalia and other peace operations.[4] The lack of a meaningful response to the 1996 Zaire crisis demonstrated that the world community had learned little since 1994 on necessary procedures to rescue distressed populations and to create conditions for the development of civil society. The 1996 crisis in Zaire, and the subsequent overthrow of the corrupt regime of the late and unlamented Mobutu Sese Seko, took place in a policy void in which the world made desultory preparations to relieve certain immediate refugee issues but again avoided any recognition of underlying political issues.

This analysis is not intended to be so much a criticism of the policy decisions taken at the time by the US government and other interested parties, but rather it attempts to demonstrate a more comprehensive and coherent approach toward alleviating such complex problems. Using a planning process discussed below, the fundamental political, humanitarian and security issues which are intrinsic to all peace operations may be addressed and, hopefully, resolved.

The meager and tardy world response to the Zaire crisis in 1996, and the nearly instantaneous abandon of projected military operations, demonstrates a general poverty of imagination, courage and leadership at a time when such tragic phenomena as state collapse and genocide appear to be on the increase. Indeed, within the United States, at the present time, there is increasing reluctance to apply military force to defend any humanitarian principles or political imperatives other than the right to have access to food. On the matter of national interest, it is disingenuous to claim, as some do, that the US has no strategic interests in the Democratic Republic of Congo. The country remains a minerals storehouse, some quite vital for US industry, and bordering on eight other central African states, the former Zaire holds a geo-strategic position for which the US invested greatly during the Cold War.

On the moral level, the author believes that few Americans can feel comfortable with the stark assertions of Robert Kaplan who bemoans the 'holocaust mentality' of American foreign policy, maintaining that 'callously put, the murder of up to a million Tutsis in Rwanda did not affect the US'.[5] Given the moral imperatives which most Americans believe are at the foundation of US foreign policy, genocide in Rwanda, or in Congo/Zaire, should be matters of vital concern to US policymakers and elected officials.

Despite the 1994 genocide in Rwanda, the record clearly demonstrates that very few governments were eager to become involved in central Africa in 1996. For the sake of discussion, we will assume that one of the major reasons for this was that no government knew how to handle problems of such dimensions. In this essay, we will examine the process through which peacekeeping interventions are developed and offer an alternative process that offers a more meaningful way of developing policy for such emergencies.

A practical world response focusing on the underlying political issues might have prevented the subsequent widespread killing of non-combatants while protecting the vital efforts of the international humanitarian community and, at the same time, establishing a context in which conditions could have been attached to the successor regime in Kinshasa. The lack of international resolve or commitment in November 1996 produced serious effects which are already clearly identifiable: (1) The counter-genocide of a large community of innocent non-combatant Rwandan refugees continues a year later in the mountains and forests of the former Zaire;[6] (2) The struggle in eastern Zaire is not over; attacks on innocents continue; the international humanitarian community remains unprotected; its supplies continue to be stolen and used by all sides to support military actions; (3) One corrupt dictator was deposed, and power was passed, without any legitimizing actions, to an individual whose commitments to democracy, human rights and free expression remain quite ambiguous. Given the proliferation of failed and failing states in the world, the unwillingness of the international community to devise a system for the legitimization and regularization of leadership change in such states effectively leaves such matters to the whims of warlords.

While acknowledging that many of the tools described below did not exist at the time of the events, the 1996 emergency in central Africa provides a useful case study of the need for improved techniques for handling such crises. The November 1996 period in which the world teetered on the edge of launching what, unfortunately, would have been an inadequate response is examined in some detail. The reluctance of the US, UK and certain other principal actors to become meaningfully engaged in the crisis is symptomatic of a far greater problem: at present, there are no international standards for intervention which take into account the interaction of political, social and humanitarian factors underlying complex humanitarian emergencies. A comprehensive planning process for such emergencies, which has been the subject of provisional use in various US military peacekeeping exercises in Europe, Asia and Latin America, will be offered.[7]

The marriage of political, humanitarian and military agendas in peacekeeping and humanitarian operations is not an easy one. In traditional peacekeeping, that is, during the Cold War, most operations significant enough to require substantial numbers of foreign troops were developed to separate states, or, as in the case of Cyprus, to separate domestic factions sponsored by foreign states. The acceptance of the UN presence by all parties was required, and total neutrality and impartiality of the UN force presence ensured that the UN force had minimal difficulties. The relative simplicity of Cold War peace operations has been replaced by such complex emergencies as Somalia, Bosnia, Haiti and Zaire, in which states are torn apart by internal rivalries. In such situations, non-combatants become essentially the political cannon-fodder for factional leaders, who hope to develop credibility through demonstrations of cruelty and impunity. To be effective, the international community is forced to become more pro-active, and the potential risks and pitfalls are far greater. Yet, unless we decide to establish some kind of cordon sanitaire around certain failed countries or regions, tools must be developed to handle such situations.

Unfortunately, the United Nations Charter provides little guidance for authorization to intervene in complex emergencies with strong political overtones. Although an array of international treaties and conventions are available to halt and judge such crimes as genocide, mistreatment of war prisoners, non-combatants and refugees, etc., these are not applied in any systematic fashion. These elements of international law, if anything, are usually ignored in the development of Security Council mandates for peace operations. Clearly, the world community must develop procedures which will focus on both short-term and longer-term solutions to complex humanitarian disasters.

The Central African Crisis

The three states directly concerned with the continuing central African crisis have known little peace and tranquility since their respective independences in 1960 (The Democratic Republic of Congo [DROC]) and 1962 (the Republic of Rwanda and Burundi, a Kingdom until 1965). All three states shared a common colonial experience in having been governed by Belgium for several generations. All three have been the scenes of particularly vicious ethnic conflicts, and there is chronic disaffiliation of substantial portions of their populations from national political structures. The three countries are geographically contiguous, and ethnic associations transcend the political frontiers. Rwanda and Burundi share certain common demographics, with a predominant ethnic group, the Hutu, who claim 85 per cent of the population, the Tutsi, about 14 per cent of the population, and the Twa, a pygmy forest culture who compose less than one per cent of the total.[8] In the Kivu province of eastern Zaire/Congo, approximately one-half of the population owed its origins to Hutu and Tutsi family groups who immigrated from Rwanda and Burundi over the past 400 years.[9]

The Trust Territories of Rwanda and Burundi were the doubtful beneficiaries of a last-minute rush to establish viable governments. In 1959, the Belgian trusteeship administration supported a Hutu 'revolution' in Rwanda, which led immediately to widespread killing of Tutsi and the departure of substantial refugees into Uganda and other surrounding states. Two years later, majority self-government was further made concrete by a Belgian-managed 'coup' against itself prior to the arrival of a UN visiting team in late 1961.[10] The Kingdom of Belgium attempted to reverse its long-standing reinforcement of the traditional role of the 'Mwamis' (kings) who had reigned in the mountain kingdoms before the arrival of the Europeans. Power sharing is not a political concept familiar to either Rwandans or Barundi, although this remains probably the only long-term solution to the current turmoil.[11]

Rwandan Tutsi citizens exiles in Uganda watched helplessly for many years as a succession of Hutu-led regimes monopolized Rwandan state power and persecuted those Tutsi who remained behind. It was these Uganda-based Tutsi exile groups who launched an insurgency in October 1990 that eventually gained partial legitimacy during a lengthy process of

UN and OAU-sponsored conferences. A peace agreement between various Hutu and Tutsi factions, was signed at Arusha, Tanzania, in August 1993. A UN peace operation, UNAMIR, was deployed to Rwanda in October 1993 to facilitate the implementation of the Arusha accords, then on the verge of collapse.

During the whole of 1990–94, radical Hutu agitators in the Rwandan government and military preached hatred of the Tutsi and prepared for mass homicide rather than submit to a mixed political system. To emphasize the interest of regional states in the success of the Arusha process, Rwandan President Juvenal Habyarimana was invited to Dar-es-Salaam on 6 April 1994 to hear a lecture from his peers. On the return flight, his Burundi counterpart, President Cyprien Ntaryamira, begged a ride because the Burundi presidential propeller aircraft was slow and not nearly as comfortable as the Rwandan's impeccable Falcon 50 jet, a gift of the French government. The plane was to fly to Kigali, drop off the Rwandan, and to continue on for the short hop to Bujumbura. As the flight made its final approach into Kigali, it was downed by two shoulder-fired anti-aircraft missiles. All aboard were killed, and Rwanda 'fell off the cliff'.[12]

No one has claimed responsibility for the deaths of the two presidents, and no real evidence has ever been offered to explain this maniac act. French analyst Gerard Prunier examines many hypotheses, without choosing any, but he notes that within 45 minutes of the downing of the plane, there were roadblocks all over Kigali put up by the *Interhamwe* ('those who work together'), a youth movement created and controlled by the Hutu government of Rwanda which, with the Rwandan army, immediately launched a genocidal campaign against its Tutsi and moderate Hutu compatriots.

Between April and June 1994, an estimated 500,000–one million Tutsi and moderate Hutu persons were slaughtered in Rwanda, mostly by clubs and spears. The course of the tragedy is well documented; neither Adolf Hitler nor Pol Pot had so many people killed so quickly. The mass killings ended only after the arrival in Kigali of an exile Tutsi army led by Colonel (now Major-General) Paul Kagame.[13] Fear of revenge by the hated Tutsi caused a stampede of Hutu citizens, in which over one million men, women and children poured, sometimes at a rate of 15,000 per hour, through the border town of Goma into the Kivu province of Zaire.

The 1994 pandemonium sparked two unilateral Western military interventions: The first was *Opération Turquoise*, in which French troops established a protected perimeter in southwest Rwanda to shield the terrified Hutu population (and incidently to cover the departure of allies in the failed Rwandan administration) from onrushing Tutsi troops. The second was Operation 'Support Hope', in which US military units quickly flew in from Europe, established a logistical system and transported and assembled equipment and piping to provide clean water to the hoards in the Goma area, where dysentery and cholera threatened to decimate the refugee population.[14]

The verdant, picturesque and potentially rich Zairian Kivu province was the last Congolese province to succumb to the initial breakdown of authority which afflicted that country immediately after its independence on 30 June 1960. Since Christmas Eve in 1960, when the province was taken over by a truckload of Lumumbist insurgents, the Kivu has only nominally been under the control of the central Zairian government. It was the scene of the bloody political movements in the 1960s, in which thousands of 'intellectuals' (literate) and land-holding citizens were systematically exterminated in Maoist-style pogroms. In recent years, as President Mobutu Sese Seko's misrule led to the near extinction of the country's social, political and physical infrastructure, the Kivu became virtually cut off from the capital, except for unreliable air transport, and the national government's usually unpaid local civilian and military representation largely subsisted on corruption and crime. As elsewhere in Mobutu's Zaire, these authorities had no capacity to provide any state services, and what they did provide was of only the most marginal relevance to local populations. With the addition of over a million ethnic Hutus, including former members of the Rwandan army (FAR – Forces Armées du Rwanda) and *Interhamwe* from the mass exodus of 1994, to the population of the Kivu, a volatile mixture was created. In the immediate, FAR-*Interhamwe* killer teams launched a campaign against the ethnic Tutsi living in the Masisi area of north Kivu, killing hundreds and causing thousands to take refuge in Rwanda. The 1994 events in Masisi drew disparate Tutsi groups in north and south Kivu together. With assistance from Rwanda and Uganda, they provided the nucleus of the armed force which would soon sweep away the rotten Mobutu regime.

In a situation which has become strikingly common in the post-Cold War period, the refugees in Zaire effectively became hostages to their putative FAR and *Interhamwe* protectors. Initially dependent upon these forces for fear of retribution from the Tutsi, and later simply held to provide protective cover for the resurgence efforts of the former Hutu government, the refugees subsisted as wards of the international community. The dimensions of the Zairian refugee problem, indicated in Table 1 (p.78), were dramatic.[15]

These numbers are probably conservative, especially for Burundi refugees, and, in any case, their presence was exacerbated by the presence of hundreds of thousands of internal refugees, for example, displaced persons, who do not enter officially into UNHCR figures. In a region as

TABLE 1

REGISTERED REFUGEE NUMBERS

	May 1996	May 1997
Rwandan Refugees in		
Uganda	4,000*	16,000*
Burundi	90,636	2,000*
Tanzania	537,309	100,715
Zaire	1,088,437	294,463
Total Rwandan refugees	1,720,352	380,577
Burundi Refugees in		
Rwanda	3,260	7,000*
Tanzania	94,618	275,964
Zaire	109,119	44,000*
Total Burundi refugees	206,997	326,954

* = estimate

Source: UN High Commission for Refugees

poor as central Africa, there was no way that local economies could sustain the continued presence of hundreds of thousands of unemployable, landless immigrants. The government of Zaire took no action against the armed elements in the refugee camps, and subsequent actions taken by Zairian local authorities were interpreted by the governments of both Rwanda and Burundi as clear confirmation of official Zairian support to insurgencies directed against their countries.

The already desperate refugee situation in Zaire became supercharged on 7 October 1996, when the deputy governor for the Southern Kivu declared that the substantial (300,000) native Banyarwanda population of the Kivu would be expelled forthwith from the country, or be 'hunted down as rebels'. It was this mindless act which, within less than a year, led to the overthrow of Zaire's central government.

The government of Rwanda sent military trainers and equipment to its beleaguered cousins in the Kivu. Building on ever-present anti-Kinshasa sentiments in the Kivu, within just a few days there appeared an active armed Banyamulenge resistance movement, which swept through the southern Kivu, scattering Zairian army (FAZ) personnel and civilian administrators before it.[16]

One of the many unusual aspects of the events in eastern Zaire in the Fall of 1996 was the sudden appearance of Laurent Kabila, a former Lumumbist who had puttered around the fringes of Zairian politics for many years secure in his small Marxist-Leninist enclave in the hills above Fizi along the frontier between South Kivu and Katanga.[17] He was reportedly selected to serve in mid-1996 as a figurehead leader for the Banyamulenge in Southern Kivu by Ugandan leader Museveni, based on their past associations and Kabila's geographical availability. With his family roots in north Katanga, Kabila provided a useful Zairian face to the opposition. The AFDL (Alliance des Forces Démocratiques pour la Libération du Congo-Zaire), which he was selected to lead, was originally composed of an amalgamation of four anti-Mobutu groups. These groups were composed of Tutsi brought together by actions taken by the Zairian government, which had disenfranchised the native Banyarwanda in 1981, and the exactions of the former FAR and *Interhamwe* taken against the Tutsi populations of North Kivu since 1994.[18] Although hatred of Mobutu generated popular acclaim for Kabila as his Rwandan-led forces marched across Zaire between October 1996 and April 1997, he has amply demonstrated his limitations since taking power, and he has reverted to practices strikingly similar to those of his predecessor. It is an interesting question whether the interests of Africa and the West have been served by unconditionally accepting the replacement of one execrable leader by one impaired by poor judgment and seen by most Zairians as the instrument of outside forces.

Quickly capturing the key towns of Uvira, a port town on Lake Tanganyika, just across the valley from the Burundi capital of Bujumbura, and Bukavu, a key city on the southern shores of Lake Kivu, the Banyamulenge established their military credentials. International diplomatic efforts increased in early November, as the fighting appeared to spread to the Goma region. Repeated calls for a ceasefire fell on deaf ears, as both the rebel and government forces rejected a cessation of hostilities.[19] As the Banyamulenge marched north, they caused several refugee camps to dissolve as Hutu refugees, spurred by fear and/or their Hutu protectors, fled from the path of the Banyamulenge. The major refugee camp at Mugunga, some 12 miles west of Goma, quadrupled in population during October–November 1996 to over one million.[20] On 2 November, international aid workers were forced to abandon their charges in the face of fighting in the immediate area of the Mugunga refugee camp.[21] On 7 November, the UN Security Council passed Resolution 1078 calling upon the Secretary-General 'to draw up the framework for a humanitarian task force'.[22]

After the fall of Goma on 1 November, Mugunga camp was cut off from its usual food and medicine supply channels, and it appeared to the world that the camp population would provide yet another horrendous toll to the list of non-combatant deaths in central Africa.[23] Adding to the world's concern were charges, threats and imperative statements by the Zairian government designed to emphasize central government control and sovereignty. In response, United Nations Children's Fund (UNICEF) and the International Committee of the Red Cross (ICRC) announced that they would set up supply bases in Kisangani, 300 miles west of Mugunga, and to attempt to stage food and supplies from there.

On 13 November, the rebel force began to shell the Mugunga camp. The fighting was intense for three days. Quite to the astonishment of the outside world, on 15 November, the FAR and *Interhamwe* custodians of the Mugunga camp bolted toward the west, and the majority of the camp population began a silent march back to the Goma crossing point into Rwanda along the path established for it by rebel forces. Dramatic photographs of the exodus were displayed around the world. Was the central African crisis over, or was it simply to change its location?

How many Rwandan refugees remained in Zaire after the November 1996 reverse floodtide back home remains a highly controversial issue. According to René Lemarchand, an American professor who has made central Africa the object of lifelong scholarship, 'pro-Rwandan analysts tend to greatly inflate the number of returnees (up to 700,000) and scale down those who stayed in Zaire'. After analyzing often conflicting figures, Lemarchand concludes that 400,000 refugees are 'unaccounted for'.[24] This is an awesome figure, especially in the knowledge that wars between ethnic groups in Rwanda and eastern Zaire are characterized by unwillingness to take prisoners, whether they be fighters or non-combatants.

In the wake of Kabila's victorious march to Kinshasa came repeated reports of serious human rights violations. Amnesty International reported in March 1997 that 'there is mounting evidence that the AFDL has carried out a deliberate campaign of arbitrary killings and attacks of refugees who have refused or been too afraid to go back to Rwanda... particularly males of fighting age'.[25] In a preliminary survey of human rights violations in rebel-held areas of eastern Zaire undertaken in March 1997, a Special Rapporteur appointed by the UN High Commissioner for Human Rights concluded that Kabila's ADFL was responsible for 'serious violations of the right to life' and called for punishment against those responsible.[26] This led to the Special Rapporteur being barred from returning to Zaire/Congo and a six month period in which Kabila played cat and mouse with the United Nations to prevent further independent investigation of the generalized killing of both Rwandan and Burundi Hutu refugees. For many observers, the many testimonies and stories emerging from Zaire/Congo are indicative that many, if not most, of the 'missing' refugees have been slaughtered.

Waiting Out the 'Big One'

Wars in the post-Cold War period are mostly domestic in origin and their initial causes often are traced back to group myths and barely-recorded histories. Given the relatively recent creation of modern geographic states in Africa, many age-old social conflicts suppressed during the periods of colonial rule are now at the center of conflicts on that continent. Unwise leadership and consequent economic and financial decline caused political control and common services in many African states to erode during the years of independence. The scope of leadership in these states gradually shrunk to dictators' bunkers and state authorities no longer controlled much beyond those bunkers. The erosion of infrastructure and institutions in Zaire in 1996 presented perhaps the worst case of state collapse in Africa since the Somalia crisis of 1991–92.[27]

All Zaire watchers in 1996 were aware that timing was important. Many believed that the genocide which took place in Rwanda in 1994 might have been avoided if the UNAMIR force had been augmented rather than considerably diminished after the initial violence that followed the downing of the President's aircraft. In a study done at the Georgetown School of Foreign Service, the UN force commander in Rwanda in 1994 asserted that he could have nipped the mass killings in the bud if he had commanded a mechanized military force of 5,000 members. A panel of military and civilian experts generally agreed. During the two week period, 7–21 April 1994, a credible UN military force could have 'squelched the violence [and] prevented its spread from the capital to the countryside ...'[28]

In November 1996, the US government appeared more concerned with eliminating the UN Secretary-General than responding to the crisis in central Africa. For Secretary-General Boutros Boutros-Ghali, the central Africa crisis hung like an Albatross around his neck as he sought to focus international concern on the rising crisis while fighting to retain his position in the face of a sharply-focused US campaign to unseat him. The policy dilemma created by the Secretary-General election campaign obscured the international response to Boutros-Ghali's calls for action in eastern Zaire as evidenced in his careful diplomatic reply to the initial question posed at a press conference in Rome on 12 November:

> Question: What is the soonest we could expect members of the multinational force on the ground in Zaire, and how do you assess the United States hesitation to take part in it?

> The Secretary-General: I cannot give you a date for the arrival of the multinational force; we are still working on this subject; we are still having contacts; we are still planning how it will have to operate. And I don't believe that there is any reticence on the part of any member state ...[29]

The government of France, noting that 'time is pressing', called for the establishment of 4,000–5,000 man force to be stationed in eastern Zaire under UN aegis.[30] Shortly thereafter, the French government rejected a proposal from former French Minister of Cooperation, Bernard Debré, to establish 'Hutulands' to provide protected asylum for the Rwandan Hutu communities in Zaire.[31] To further complicate the situation, rebel leader Kabila announced that he might accept an intervention force 'on the condition that France did not take part'.[32]

In the meantime, to break the loggerhead over intervention in eastern Zaire, the French turned to Canada to lead the force. Canadian Lt-General Maurice Baril accepted a request to lead the UN operation. He estimated that the force would need 10,000 troops for about two months before turning the operation back to the United Nations. Gordon Smith, Canada's deputy foreign minister, stressed that the multinational troops would not use force to separate militias or disarm fighters found among the victims. Somewhat equivocally, the deputy minister stated that anyone who got in the way of the force 'would be dealt with accordingly'.[33] The first Canadian soldiers embarked for Zaire on 14 November.

Among nations responding favorably to the multinational force project were France, Spain, Italy, South Africa, Ethiopia and Mali. Like the US, the British government remained on the fence, undecided about participation.[34] In Addis Ababa, Organization of African Unity President, Salim Ahmed Salim, announced on 13 November that Eritrea, Cameroon, Congo (Brazzaville), and Senegal were ready to join the Canadian-led multinational humanitarian force.[35] South Africa demurred on an earlier-expressed desire to join the force. South African reserve was apparent on 14 November, when Deputy President Thabo Mbeki announced that his country 'was not prepared to send troops to Zaire to fight a war'.[36]

During early November 1996, humanitarian agencies continued to argue forcefully for a military response to the emergency.[37] Many agencies, including Refugees International, a prominent NGO called specifically for a major US role in the humanitarian effort.[38] The question of US involvement was hotly debated in Washington and elsewhere. Secretary of State Christopher reportedly was strongly opposed to any force commitment to the central African disaster.[39] With the recent memory of his unsuccessful trip to Africa in October, and fighting to retain his position in the new Clinton administration, the Secretary wished to undertake no new initiatives which would expose him to criticism.

The first indication of an official US response to the crisis appeared on 4 November, when the State Department announced that a USAID Disaster Assistance Response Team (DART) had been sent to the region.[40] On the following day, US officials told Reuters news service that the US 'is leaning toward backing a proposed protection force for refugees in Zaire but will not itself contribute ground forces'.[41] The bureaucracy continued to grind away in Washington, and on 7 November, the State Department stated that it was still examining the possibility of joining the multinational force led by Canada. A Department of Defense spokesman reported on 7 November that the European Command was undergoing 'prudent planning' for possible use in contingency operations in eastern Zaire. He corroborated the rumor that no US ground forces would be deployed in eastern Zaire.[42] A US military advance team arrived in East Africa on 13 November, still without any Washington commitment to joining the international force.[43]

While the world looked for a US response to what appeared to be another monumental catastrophe in central Africa, Washington continued to employ dilatory tactics. A White House spokesman noted on 12 November that the administration was 'urgently reviewing what practical steps can be taken to address the growing humanitarian crisis'.[44] The Chairman of the Joint Chiefs of Staff, General John Shalikashvili, indicated his reluctance when he stated: 'Obviously, before you commit troops you have to understand very clearly what their tasks should be, whether they are really the right solution'.[45]

Those problems appeared to have been on the way to solution when, on 13 November, the Pentagon announced that it would 'in principle' and 'under certain conditions' participate in the international force being prepared by Canada for the United Nations.[46] Michael McCurry, the White House press spokesman, indicated that the approximate size of the US force would be 5,000, with 1,000 of these actually deployed into Zaire. The several conditions laid down by the White House reflected general misgivings about the project [subject headings taken from the White House press release]:

1. *Assumptions.* There was need first to validate core assumptions about the threat: the nature of the threat, the environment in which a multinational force would insert itself into the region, the availability of other properly trained and equipped forces and the consent of concerned countries in the region.

2. *Mission statement.* The mission of the force would have to be very clearly defined: to facilitate the delivery of humanitarian aid by civilian relief organizations and to facilitate the voluntary repatriation of refugees by the UN High Commissioner for Refugees. Specifically excluded from the mission would be disarmament of militants, execution of any kind of forced entry or to provide police operations in the refugee camps set up in the border regions.

3. *UN mandate.* The mission of the multinational force would include robust rules of engagement authorized under Chapter VII of the UN Charter. The White House statement added somewhat ambiguously that the mission would not constitute what 'we would typically think of as a blue-helmet cooperation'.

4. *Funding.* Each state participating in the operation would pay its share of the operation. Special arrangements would have to be made for participating African states.

5. *Duration.* The operation would be of limited duration. A follow-on presence to ensure that the conditions which brought on the present crisis would not be repeated was being discussed with other participants.

6. *Specific US roles.* McCurry noted certain 'unique capacities' which the US force could bring to the operation. The US contribution would consist of maintaining security at the Goma airport and the three-mile corridor from Goma to the Rwandan border and help in airlifting and deploying forces to the region.[47]

Reflecting what have become standard US command and control arrangements, US forces would be under the command of a US general, who would serve as deputy to the Canadian commander. The governments of Zaire and Rwanda would be obliged to avoid hostile actions against the multinational force. The multinational force would have 'robust rules of engagement (ROE)', although it was clear that no actions would be taken which might cause the ROE to be used.[48] US Defense Secretary William Perry insisted that there would have to be 'clarity of mission' before Washington would give its final approval to the deployment of the force.[49]

With the US somewhat timidly on board, Security Council action was quick to come. On 15 November 1996, the Security Council adopted Resolution 1080, which recognized that 'the current situation in eastern Zaire demands an urgent response by the international community'. Acting under Chapter VII (Action with Respect to Threats to the Peace, Breaches of the Peace, and Acts of Aggression) of the UN Charter, the Security Council condemned the violence, called for an end to all hostilities in the region and authorized the creation:

> for humanitarian purposes of a temporary multinational force to facilitate the immediate return of humanitarian organizations and the effective delivery by civilian relief organizations of humanitarian aid to alleviate the immediate suffering of displaced persons, refugees and civilians at risk in eastern Zaire, and to facilitate the voluntary, orderly repatriation of refugees by the United Nations Commissioner for Refugees as well as the voluntary return of displaced persons ...[50]

In her explanation of the US vote in favor of Resolution 1080, US Permanent Representative to the UN, Madeleine Albright, echoed previous US civilian and military reticence about the Zaire disaster rescue operation when she referred to the 'complexities of the situation in eastern Zaire, with multiple armed groups and a fragile political environment [that] require prudent preparation'. She noted US support to Canadian leadership in the operation which would 'allow the delivery of humanitarian assistance' and 'voluntary repatriation of refugees to their home countries'. The long-term solution is 'voluntary repatriation of the refugees'.[51] By defining the immediate and long-term concerns in the same words, the US continued to define its mission in the most cautious and temporizing terms.

In the meantime, the first US elements of the military operation which was identified as Operation 'Guardian Assistance' arrived in Kigali, Rwanda, on 14 November to meet with Rwandan government officials and to look into the situation. Operating under orders from USEUCOM's Standing Joint Task Force (SETAF) based in Vicenza, Italy, the operation already had very narrow objectives:

> When directed, USEUCOM will conduct military operations in E. Zaire, Rwanda and Burundi in support of UN-directed humanitarian assistance and disaster relief operations. USEUCOM will provide only unique military capabilities to alleviate acute humanitarian crises. If required, establish CMOC to transition all support to UN agencies and NGOs/PVOs.[52]

Various humanitarian agencies immediately criticized the rules devised for the multinational operation. Without a clear mandate to disarm the warring groups, the operation would only have short-term effects. Médecins sans Frontières (MSF), one of the most active non-governmental organizations (NGOs) working in the Great Lakes region of central Africa stated:

> Disarming the militias is indispensable. It is not just a problem of security for humanitarian organizations, but a question of protection of the refugees. We know about the existence of Rwandan Hutu extremists who have been taking the refugees for hostages. If these extremists are not separated from the refugees, we will find ourselves exactly in the same situation as that which led this current conflict in Zaire[53]

A noted political scientist, Catherine Newbury, professor at the University of North Carolina (Chapel Hill), and author of several works on Zaire, reflected the general dissatisfaction of the US academic community at the slow pace of administration efforts to relieve the central African crisis, when she wrote:

> In 1994, the United States decided not to support a United Nations proposal to intervene in strife-torn Rwanda. This inaction meant that state-sponsored genocide was allowed to run its course: In less than

three months more than 500,000 people were killed. Today, though the political dynamics in war-torn eastern Zaire are different, the consequences of inaction will be similar: hundreds of thousands are at risk. The United States has exhibited a remarkable lack of urgency in this crisis ...[54]

Collapse of the World Resolve

In the meantime, dissident military strategy was working in eastern Zaire. The tactic of gradually herding the refugees towards the Rwandan border where they would be freed of control by former Rwandan Hutu forces was demonstrated by artillery attacks on the Kibumba camp north of Goma on 26 October which caused its 195,000 refugees to move south to Mugunga camp, increasing its population to 420,000 people.[55] The combined Rwandan/Zairian rebel campaign in the Kivu continued to propel the refugees back in the direction of Rwanda, with the hope of eventually separating them from their FAR and *Interhamwe* controllers.[56] On 2 November, rebel forces captured the key frontier town of Goma. Fearing the worst, all representatives of humanitarian organizations, including those mobilizing supplies for the Mugunga operation, left the area. World public opinion subsequently became electrified when the rebel decision to prevent the return of the international humanitarian workers to Goma became known.

Humanitarian workers were permitted to return to Zaire on 11–12 November. However, they were surprised to find themselves restricted to Goma's Unity Stadium. They were forbidden to distribute food or to make independent assessments of the situation. It was particularly galling for the humanitarian community to be isolated from the humanitarian battle zone during 2–11 November, especially while the flock of international journalists reporting on the crisis suffered no such restrictions.[57]

The reasons for holding back the international humanitarian community became clear on 13 November, when rebel batteries began to fire on Mugunga camp. On the following day, Kabila's ADFL forces from Goma directly engaged FAR troops and *Interhamwe* militia in the camp.[58] Reportedly, fighting was ferocious. Unobstructed by the presence of the humanitarian community, the combined forces of the AFDL and the Rwandan army, supported by Ugandan units blocking retreat to the north, set up a narrow escape passage for defending forces to the west, while readying the eastern route for the refugees to be flushed towards home. On 15 November, after three days of shelling, the 1.2 million inhabitants of Mugunga camp abandoned the facility. Their ruthless Rwandan Defense Force and *Interhamwe* 'protectors' fled westward, using perhaps as many

250,000 civilian non-combatants from the camp as shields for their movement. The vast majority of camp inmates, however, headed back towards Rwanda. Beginning on 16 November, in a virtually reverse copy of the 1994 flood of refugees into Zaire, up to 10,000 refugees an hour crossed back into Rwanda.[59] In less than two days, the Mugunga camp emptied itself, leaving, according to journalists, vast piles of rubbish and a few twisted bodies representing both warriors and the uprooted.

It must be recalled that almost simultaneously with the dramatic events in Zaire, the UN Security Council adopted Resolution 1080. By 17 November, it was estimated that 250,000 refugees had crossed the Rwandan frontier at Goma. The world's resolve to provide protective services to the hundreds of thousands of refugees in Zaire appeared to evaporate within hours of the first reports of substantial numbers of refugees arriving at Goma. On 17 November, US Secretary of Defense Perry said that there might still be a need for the multinational force, but that the 'quality of that need' had changed as the result of the refugee outflow. At Stuttgart, the 20 nations which had signed up for the UN operation agreed on the need to reassess the need for intervention. By 18 November, only France and Canada were considering active participation in the operation. The US announced on 19 November that its contingent would be reduced from 4,000–5,000 troops to 400, the size of the SETAF advance team then in East Africa. Although meetings continued to be held in various capitals, the fragile resolution of the world community to address the tragedy in eastern Zaire disappeared. In mid-December, the Canadian advance team returned home.

In several very revealing interviews in mid-1997, various participants discussed the strategy behind the events which the world somewhat uncomfortably observed in November 1996. The primary foreign actor was the Republic of Rwanda. It is a state governed by a besieged minority which had come to power two years earlier following one of the most concentrated state-sponsored genocidal campaigns since World War II. With the assistance of France and the passivity of the world, most of the Rwandan governmental and military leadership which had sponsored the genocide disappeared into UN- and NGO-run refugee camps in eastern Zaire. Many mistakes were made by the international humanitarian community in the establishment of the refugee camps in north Kivu. The camps were located too close to the Rwandan border. International standards set by the UNHCR require that refugee camps be located beyond one day's walk of a political frontier in order to diminish their effectiveness as rearguard bases for military activities directed against other states. The Zairian government asserted little control over the camps, and the humanitarian community was unable to stop the open flow of arms and munitions into the camps. It was known to all that the refugee camps in Zaire represented a critical threat to the security of the victorious Tutsi-dominated Rwandan administration. To ensure state security, the Rwandan administration decided that the camps must be broken up, and the Zairian dictator Mobutu had to go.[60]

Rwandan Defense Minister and Vice President, Paul Kagame, perhaps the key player in the 1996 central African crisis, freely acknowledged the role which his country played in the eastern Zaire campaign. It first emptied the refugee camps that provided sanctuary to his government's sworn enemies and eventually led to the overthrow of the country's enfeebled dictator. Under his command, Rwandan officers and men were present in all of the campaigns, including the final push that led to the fall of Kinshasa in May 1997. The final decision to take direct action against the camps and the neighboring dictator were taken after Kagame visited New York and Washington in August 1996.[61] In Washington, he confronted the White House and State Department with the problems which the continued existence of the refugee camps posed to his government. Kagame reported that he asked them for a solution to his country's security crisis. He told a reporter that 'They didn't come up with any answers, not even suggestions.' He returned to Rwanda and preparations for war.[62] It was essential for success of Rwandan strategy that there be no UN-mandated international military intervention in Zaire. The threat that Kagame claims he feared most was 'talk of a US-backed international intervention force for eastern Congo'. The attack on Mugunga camp on 15 November was partially developed to scuttle that effort.

Kagame had been a Ugandan exchange student at the US Army Command and Staff College in Leavenworth, Kansas, when he was summoned back home in 1990 to take charge of the campaign to overthrow the Kigali regime. He is much admired within the US military for his skills both as innovative tactician and decisive strategist.[63]

According to Kagame, the Rwandan perception that an international intervention in eastern Zaire in November 1996 would not be in its interests was based on the concern that it would have led to an effort to mediate the Zairian civil war, with the threat that this might have given new life to the Mobutu regime.[64] The reality was probably something more. Any form of effective international mediation in eastern Zaire would eventually have called for free and open elections in that country. While this would have had great value in Zaire, it would have placed the minority Tutsi government in Rwanda in an acutely embarrassing position. Again, had there been a coherent planning environment available for use in central Africa at the time of the November 1996 crisis, these matters could have been decided within a broader context. In the author's view, the total collapse of Hutu political credibility in Rwanda as the result of the 1994 genocide campaign (which, as one recalls, also liquidated moderate Hutu leaders at the same that it attempted a final solution to the Tutsi problem) provides several years of breathing space for the current Tutsi-dominated Rwandan government to work out the necessary power-sharing arrangements that appear to be the only path to long-term stability in that country.

Comprehensive Campaign Planning

The certainty of widespread suffering, suspicions of severe human rights violations including the possibilities of indiscriminate slaughter, and conflicting global and regional geo-strategic interests in far-off places provide the thorny context for many modern diplomatic crises. Whether these events occur in central Europe, central Asia or central Africa, there should be a clear and coherent planning process available to develop appropriate international responses to such uncomfortable matters. For militaries, as well as their civilian masters, the post-Cold War threat environment is increasingly defined by the 'Complex Humanitarian Emergency' (CHE), of which the central African crisis provides a prime example. A CHE is an acute man-made disaster, sometimes complicated by natural disaster(s), affecting large numbers of people, which requires some form of external political-military response. When a CHE response includes a foreign military force, it is usually called a peacekeeping, or peacemaking, operation.

Taking part in these kinds of disasters are International Organizations such as the ICRC, the specialized humanitarian agencies of the United Nations and a vast number of NGOs which have arisen to channel private humanitarian initiative.

Although it has only been significantly engaged in peacekeeping and overseas humanitarian interventions since the end of the Cold War, the US military remains at the leading edge of US government research and thinking to determine how to better perform such activities. Some of this innovative thinking led to the development of a process called the 'Comprehensive Campaign Plan' (CCP), which has been largely developed in the course of military exercises in the US Southern Command (SOUTHCOM); some parts of the CCP have been reflected in exercises in both the US European Command (EUCOM) and the US Pacific Command (PACOM).[65]

The essential nucleus of the CCP is the five-paragraph military field operations order, which has been adopted by most militaries for its simplicity and focus (see Annex A). The five paragraphs lay out the critical themes for any proposed military operation: (1) an assessment of the threat; (2) a clear statement of the mission; (3) a review of the means to carry out the mission; (4) the support requirements; and (5) the organization of the force. The ultimate goal of the CCP in the international humanitarian-political-military environment is to develop common agreement on the ends, ways and means of resolving a given crisis. Once the main approach has been agreed upon, the details of each participant's contributions to resolution of the main themes are spelled out in annexes to the agreed-upon policy document. The CCP provides a useful framework to focus discussion and debate, and its discipline ensures that policy-makers do not take artificial shortcuts to avoid deciding the hard issues.

The first attachment to the CCP ('Annex A') addresses the critical political framework of the operation. The international and domestic political context is detailed, and the options permitted under the mission authorization (mandate) are discussed. Most importantly, the first annex also lays out achievable goals (milestones) and the desired end result of the international intervention.

Had there been a CCP available to the international community in the 1996 crisis in eastern Zaire (see Annex A) , the shape of the CCP would have adhered to the following lines:

1. The *threat analysis* would have included a discussion of the various health and security issues affecting the vast numbers of refugees and persons displaced by the ongoing crisis. The initial 'enemies' on the humanitarian battlefield are impure water, disease and the lack of shelter. People can live for a few days without food, but they will not survive without water, or, depending on the climate, shelter. The CCP places these considerations up front. The other threats, including the presence of armed elements, both legitimate and illegitimate, would also be noted.

2. The *mission* would have been analyzed, taking into account the normal phases of a peace operation. Nearly all peacekeeping endeavors begin as CHEs, then enter an institutional rehabilitation stage before ending as political problems. In central Africa, there would be a range of mission goals, beginning with the plight of the refugees and displaced persons, while creating conditions for the restoration of civil society in Zaire/Congo and for power-sharing in Burundi and (eventually) in Rwanda. Arranging a peaceful handover of power in Kinshasa would be in the interest of all parties. Given the general international approbation he received at the outset of recent insurgency, Laurent Kabila would probably have received an international mandate to handle the transition to democratic rule. In so doing, he would have been accorded both legitimacy and a built-in advantage for leadership of the successor regime. The art of creating a meaningful mission statement requires both

coherence and appreciation of the long-term consequences of the intervention.

It is not difficult to develop a mission statement for the humanitarian side of the operation. The military can establish quickly the basic security requirements for the humanitarian phase of the operation. However, security means more than just the security of the intervening forces; it must include reasonable security for non-combatants. If this means that police or gendarmes are necessary to develop or restore local justice, then it should be included in the CCP planning process.

3. The *concept of operations* would provide a discussion of the diverse resources, capabilities and goals which each of the participating CCP partners brings to the crisis area. These would be matched to the threats and other requirements outlined in the threat statement. At this point the contributions of the host nation would have to be assessed and collated with the sum total of external resources. The vain effort of the Mobutu regime to impose dysfunctional restrictions on the emergency effort in October 1996 would be rejected in the face of the combined indignation of the international community. Inclusion of the government of Rwanda in this phase of the CCP process could have been justified. Contrary to the reasoning of Major General Kagame, the government of Rwanda would have had far more to gain by cooperation with the international community than by conniving to hobble its activities.

4. The specific *support tasks* of the military component are of great interest to all participants in the operation. These would be discussed in detail; the creation of a security umbrella is the fundamental reason for the presence of the military in most CHEs and peace operations. In the November 1996 eastern Zaire crisis, the US decision to extend that umbrella only to protection of the Goma airport and the refugee corridor was a minimalist solution which ignored the fact that the arrival of a substantial military force in the region would have increased the security risks to the humanitarian community. The disarmament issue is also a chronic issue in most peace operations. Unfortunately, the US military tends to look at this matter strictly in force protection terms. In fact, forcible disarmament is not a practical solution. What is needed is a comprehensive program to create political and security conditions in which the local population perceives its interests to be better served by participation in a political process rather than war. At the outset, this means the restoration of civil order. If there is to be participation of international police and legal personnel to facilitate the resurrection of a legal system, then the military component must extend its security umbrella to protect that process.

5. The process of *coordination and cooperation* (command and control) must also be well understood by all participants. The late UN Secretary-General Dag Hammerskjöld once said that peacekeeping is not a job for a soldier, but only a soldier can do it. That observation is no longer fully accurate and may, in fact, be partially responsible for some of the misunderstandings which prevail in developing political-humanitarian-military relations within modern peacekeeping operations. Contrary to the practice in some of the early Cold War peace operations (the 1960–64 UNOC activity in the Congo, for example), the military commander is not now in charge of running the peace operation mission. The UN Secretary-General usually appoints a Special Representative to act as his agent on the ground. The presence of a senior civilian representative can be a difficult pill for some military personnel to swallow, although it recognizes the basic fact that the predominant political and humanitarian imperatives in peace operations should be managed by those who ultimately bear the responsibility for its success.

It should not be forgotten that peace operations are not missions for which professional military forces traditionally are trained. The military, especially the US military, does not train its personnel to perform civilian police functions. The US military is uncomfortable about being used as the instruments of diplomats or politicians. War fighting and peacemaking are not necessarily compatible concepts for professional military officers. Humanitarian crises in the modern world are compelling human events which are usually wrapped around seemingly intractable social and political issues for which no amount of familiarity with military doctrine is necessarily useful. The manner in which professional military personnel can be employed in peacekeeping operations remains a matter of sharp debate at the highest levels of government. The various dilemmas involved in that debate were clearly exhibited in the central African crisis.

The United Nations has a natural leadership role in both peace and humanitarian operations. Under the CCP, the central support apparatus in eastern Zaire would have been led by the Special Representative of the Secretary-General (SRSG). Production of the CCP should logically be produced within a committee that would include representatives of the Department of Peace-Keeping Operations (DPKO), the Department of Humanitarian Affairs (DHA) and the Department of Political Affairs (DPA) and the prospective partners. The capabilities of these headquarters staff offices have substantially increased in recent years. Should the CCP lead to the development of a coordinating mechanism for peace operations, there should also be created a corresponding field unit, under the SRSG. This unit would have responsibility for coordinating the field mechanism which includes representatives of cooperating agencies but also to monitor the CCP to ensure that it reflects current concerns.

6. The *political annex* provides the overall focus for the operation. It is manifestly ironic that only when the military component recognizes that it is deployed *in support* of broader objectives is it possible for the operational partners to develop the milestones and end-state for which the military so desperately searches in the mission planning process. Because this approach seems to imply direct involvement in the political, social and legal realities of failed and failing societies, current US military practice in peace operations is to seek to separate the interrelated political, humanitarian and military aspects of the operation. The ongoing international operation in Bosnia has demonstrated the inefficiencies and inadequacies of creating artificial separations for the three primary elements of peace operations. Any time a foreign military force is deployed to a failed or failing state, it will have an impact on the relationships of the contending parties.

More difficult is the development of the short-term political parameters of the operation. In central Africa, the first requirement would be a ceasefire by all sides. With an active insurgency taking place in all three countries, this will be difficult, but with sufficient diplomatic pressure backed up by military force, it should be feasible on a short-term basis. In any case, the agenda of the Bamyamulenge forces, as allies of the Rwandan government, was to remove the refugee pockets providing cover to Hutu insurgents in the Kivu, and to send them home. The political incentives necessary to secure the cooperation of the belligerent parties must focus on the longer-term requirements of developing greater openness and participation in the respective countries. This could entail a very long-term process, and may be unrealizable, but it is important that all parties understand that there are rewards for cooperation. It will be very difficult for the minority governments in Rwanda and Burundi to accept the possibility of reducing their monopoly on power, but the world community must be resolute in imposing conditions on continued aid.

Had the Dayton Accords been developed within the parameters of a comprehensive campaign plan, the eventual plan would have been more transparent to the participants and would have avoided the problems of defining tasks and goals that persisted throughout the IFOR period. The integration of security issues into the political and humanitarian tracks would have made it clear to the feuding Balkan communities that the international intervention was coherent and decisive and, in the doing, might have alleviated some of the force protection issues. As an aside, it would be interesting to examine at what point *force protection*, which has always been an inherent responsibility of military command, was promoted to becoming the *primary mission* of US forces in peace operations. This has the effect of reinforcing the artificial separation of military functions from ground realities and totally obscures the development of meaningful end-states in the planning process. When *force protection* becomes *the mission*, no other mission can compete for the military commander's attention.

As indicated in Jack Prendergast's comment in the introduction, the key to integration of the various essential factors of a peace operation, whether it be under Chapters VI, VII or VIII of the United Nations Charter, is to be found in recognition of the fundamental political issues which created the crisis. Most peacekeeping operations begin as humanitarian problems; they nearly always terminate as political problems or challenges.[66] The comprehensive planning process described herein provides the necessary parameters to focus on both the immediate and longer-term political issues.

The genocide which took place in Rwanda in 1994, combined with the ongoing crises in Burundi and Zaire, changed the political dynamic of central Africa. The most important components of the new dynamic were, and remain:

- The existence of a minority government in Rwanda. It remains unable to cope with the juridical aftermath of the 1994 genocide, and tens of thousands of putative killers are housed in primitive and squalid prisons.

- An unstable government situation in Burundi following the mysterious deaths of the two central African presidents in 1994. The civilian government in Burundi was unable to develop the confidence of the Tutsi-led military, and it was replaced in 1996 by a military government.

- The inability of the Kivu province to sustain a massive refugee population and the eventual 1996 collapse of Kinshasa's feeble administration in that province.

- President Mobutu's physical health and political influence appeared to be in parallel terminal decline.

Where there is no law, or the enforcement of laws is ambiguous, there must be international agreement to defend the international conventions on the rights of non-combatants, war prisoners, human rights, and the like. The most pernicious phenomenon of post-Cold War politics is the local warlord who makes mockery of the most fundamental rules of human interaction and is willing to plunge his country into disorder for personal profit and advantage. They must never be accorded special status because of their stolen legitimacy.

If the political goals are clearly stated in overall planning document, which, of course, is an international public document, the local participants cannot be confused about the overall intentions of the international force. If a viable political dynamic is stimulated by the presence of the force, then the local warlords and thugs have a clear choice to decide to participate in the ongoing process, to lay down their arms or become outlaws.

7. The *supporting annexes* are equally critical to the comprehensive planning process. While many of the requirements for successful peace operations include resources and disciplines which can be brought to bear much more quickly by militaries, especially in the critical opening phase, modern peace operations include a substantial community of other participants. These include international humanitarian agencies, most notably the specialized agencies of the United Nations (World Health Organization [WHO], UN High Commission for Refugees [UNHCR], UNICEF, the UN High Commissioner for Human Rights [UNHCHR], and others), non-UN international agencies (International Committee of the Red Cross [ICRC] and the International Office of Migration [IOM]. Operating independently, or in contractual arrangements with international agencies and governments, are vast numbers of non-governmental organizations [NGOs]. In addition, the three central United Nations headquarters departments (Peace-Keeping Operations [DPKO], Humanitarian Affairs [DHA], and Political Affairs [DPA]) can play vital roles in marshaling international efforts in response to Security Council mandates. Each of the above organizations, as well as most NGOs, has carved out a range of specialties which are well-known and available for deployment to crisis areas. Over the years, the various international and private organizations involved in humanitarian emergencies have developed specialities. Some specialize in mobilizing and transporting large quantities of food (WFP); others work in transport and act as wholesalers to the smaller local agencies (CARE); Oxfam performs wonders in mass vaccination campaigns.

The utility of broader planning is becoming more widely recognized in the international community. In a recent study of the 1994 Rwandan crisis sponsored by the UN Department of Peace-Keeping Operations' Lessons Learned Unit, it was found that

> A comprehensive humanitarian plan, developed along with the military and security plan for the mission, would have allowed for a better meshing of objectives ... It would have sensitized the humanitarian and military actors to the mandate, procedures and culture of the other, allowing them to work better together ...[67]

There are many reasons for establishing a plan which can accommodate the many specialities, perspectives and concerns of a major multinational intervention. If such planning is developed within a regular framework, information can be developed and stored between crises and brought immediately to bear when a crisis does erupt. With a regular framework, all participants responding to a disaster can have a clear picture what the other participants plan to do; redundancies can be avoided, and gaps can be filled. With a regular multinational planning design, the resources of local governments, such as they may be, can also be integrated into the humanitarian response. A comprehensive campaign plan would provide an imperative focus on the initial needs of victims, and it should include plans for the rehabilitation and development phases of the problem. As noted above, the CCP puts the local authorities, again such as they may be, on notice that must cooperate in establishing a just society for all of their citizens. The plan plainly establishes that humanitarian operations are not military expeditions; they are multinational efforts which include defined humanitarian and political goals, and it is the responsibility of the military component to provide adequate security and support the longer-term therapy that may be necessary to lessen the likelihood of a repeat of the disaster.

Having agreed as a multinational force on political spine of the operation, with specific milestones to mark the evolution of the intervention through the humanitarian, rehabilitation and development phases, the military can plan its departure at the appropriate moment and a handover of their responsibilities to either the host government or another international force.

In order to achieve these goals, there must be a significant change in the attitudes of African governments towards foreign intervention. In the author's view, the establishment of a straightforward international framework for constructive intervention may inspire confidence among certain African leaders who realize that the continent will forever lag so long as impunity by warlords and sanctioned leaders is permitted to blot the image of Africa around the world.

No international operation can achieve anything by scaling its activities to the fickle wills of individual militia chiefs or groups of warlords. We know from the Somali case that, in doing so, we simply added to their pretensions and gave them undeserved credibility. Yet we do not want the UN to be in the situation of recruiting forces which would then have to fight their way into a country which has failed or is in advanced death throes. Again, we need to fall back on the need for internationally-accepted political criteria. On such occasions, the UN may need an overwhelming force, with the highest technical fighting skills, something which reassembles UNITAF, although with experience, it may need far less. Warlords would know, with confidence, that certain things happen when the world decides to deploy such a force.

One might reasonably ask just how practical it is to draw up a list of exceedingly difficult peacekeeping operational goals for which universal acceptance will be difficult to achieve. At present, there are few world capitals, especially Washington, which are particularly hospitable to notions of strengthening the political, legal and military activities of the United Nations Organization. However, that does not mean that reasonable people should not examine such matters. The world must be prepared to act in a decisive manner to face tragedies affecting its neighbors. The existence of coherent doctrine would simplify coalition force building and encourage greater unity of purpose. Properly presented, the proposed doctrine might make peacekeeping efforts more comprehensible to Western publics who would be largely responsible for paying the bills and providing manpower. The doctrine would facilitate the development of an understandable end-state, so that participants would know when to go home. Most importantly, the establishment of just intervention doctrine would protect the rights of victims and the oppressed.

There will be more Somalias in the future. The resources available in the world to participate in such operations are limited, and it is unlikely that the world will again commit its resources to an exercise of the scale of Somalia unless the tools and authorizations are available to provide a reasonable chance of success. It is reasonable to expect communities which will benefit from the extraordinary expenditures required to carry out such operations to cede certain sovereign functions of normal society to the agencies which are involved in the restoration of those functions. There is the likelihood of far greater support to both the United Nations and to peace operations in general if there are clearer notions of the desired results of such campaigns and that their sons and daughters will be provided the tools to achieve success. The existence of a code of doctrine for intervention in the name of humanity might provide a deterrent effect on prospective warlords who would otherwise be willing to plunge their countries into chaos in order to advance their political agendas. Without some kind of internationally-accepted ground rules for effective political intervention in failed or failing states, the world must continue to suffer the consequences of growing chaos and many more unspeakable atrocities.

ANNEX A
THE COMPREHENSIVE CAMPAIGN PLAN FRAMEWORK

SITUATION
Description of the crisis. This can easily be developed within the existing international crisis response system. A useful model is the current Consolidated Inter-Agency Flash Appeal process. See *United Nations Consolidated Inter-Agency Flash Appeal for the*

Great Lakes Region Response to the Crisis in Eastern Zaire, 1 November 1996-31 January 1997 (NY and Geneva, UN Department of Humanitarian Affairs, 18 November 1996) p.25.

MISSION

All prospective participants are invited to develop a joint description of the short, medium, and long-term (humanitarian, political, and security) mission requirements. The results should be compatible with the United Nations Security Council Resolution (the 'mandate') authorizing the operation.

EXECUTION

What is the concept of the operation? At this point, the participants should be able to agree on their roles in the steps of the disaster response process. What are the milestones to mark the steps of the operation?

SERVICE SUPPORT

Who will do what? What are the resources which will be brought to the zone of crisis? These will be spelled out in the detailed annexes attached to the CCP.

ORGANIZATION PLAN

What is the command and control structure of the operation? What is the most useful interface between the civilian and military components of the operation?

Humanitarian	Political Annex	Military
Agency Annexes	Details the background, current	Annexes
	situation and desired end-state	

NOTES

1. The author recently retired after 36 years in the US Foreign Service, having served mostly in Sub-Saharan Africa, and the opinions expressed herein do not necessarily reflect the views of either the State Department or the US Army.
2. John Prendergast, *Crisis Response: Humanitarian Band-Aids in Sudan and Somalia* (London, Chicago: Pluto Press, with Center of Concern, Washington DC 1997) p.3. Prendergast recently joined the National Security Council Staff in the White House.
3. Zaire became the Democratic Republic of Congo on 17 May 1997. For events prior to that date, we will refer to the country by the name current at the time.
4. The 1994 Rwandan crisis sparked a great deal of soul-searching and creative thinking among both soldiers and scholars. For a collection of articles outlining many of the incorrect conclusions from the 1992–95 Somalia experience, see Walter Clarke and Jeffrey Herbst (eds.) *Learning from Somalia: Lessons of Armed Humanitarian Intervention* (Boulder, CO: Westview Press 1997).
5. Robert Kaplan, 'Idealism Won't Stop Mass Murder', *Wall Street Journal Europe*, 17 Nov. 1997, p.12. Prof. Kaplan's love-hate relationship with Africa is well-illustrated in an article 'The Coming Anarchy' in the *Atlantic Monthly* (Feb. 1994) in which he decries the seeming impenetrability of the Third World, while ending his essay with the admonition that 'we ignore this dying region at our own risk'.
6. One is tempted to coin a new phrase 'counter-genocide' to describe the ongoing events in the Democratic Republic of Congo. As we will describe in greater length below, the Tutsi-dominated government of Rwanda seemingly acted quite rationally in breaking up the refugee camps which harbored officials and military units of the former government which systematically slaughtered hundreds of thousands of Tutsis and moderate Hutus in 1994.

Where it has faltered, of course, is in preventing Rwandan forces from killing thousands of non-combatants during and after the combats in eastern Zaire. See Scott Campbell, *Democratic Republic of the Congo: What Kabila is Hiding: Civilian Killings and Impunity in Congo* (NY: Human Rights Watch/Africa, Oct. 1997) 40pp.

7. The discussion of the intervention campaign plan owes a great deal to the collaborative efforts of Arthur 'Gene' Dewey, Director of the Congressional Office on Hunger, an NGO which carries on the efforts of the former Congressional Sub-Committee on Hunger (the last Congress eliminated all sub-committees), and the exercise staff of the US Army South (USARSO), which has continued its development throughout its 1996 *Fuerzas Aliadas* (which included contingents from Belize, El Salvador, Guatemala, and Honduras), and *Fuerzas Unidas* (including Argentina, Brazil, Paraguay and Uruguay) peacekeeping exercise cycles.

8. 'Tutsi' and 'Hutu', in reality, are the noun roots to which are applied linguistic prefixes to modify the meanings of the words, i.e, 'ki' for language: Kirundi is the language of Burundi; Kinyaruanda is the language of Rwanda. The singular 'mu' is used to describer a citizen of Rwanda, as in Munyaruanda (Murundi) and 'ba' for the plural: Banyarwanda (Burundi). This is not an essay on anthropology, and henceforth we will use the same ethnic shorthand used in most sources.

9. The significance of the Tutsi and Hutu ethnic divisions has been the subject of hot academic debate for some time, especially since the 1994 slaughter in Rwanda. Most scholars agree that the labels are used rather superficially in most commentary. In both Rwanda and Burundi, there has always been a good deal of mobility between the groups, with people of wealth, as measured in cattle and other possessions, moving upward to join the Tutsi caste, with the population having usually less or no land or animal stock being considered Hutu. See Gérard Prunier, *The Rwanda Crisis: History of a Genocide* (NY: Columbia UP 1995) 389pp.

10. The author's first overseas diplomatic assignment was to the Belgian Trusteeship of Ruanda-Urundi in 1960; the period leading to independence of the two territories on 2 July 1962 was somewhat overshadowed by the events in the neighboring Congo, but was nonetheless tumultuous, particularly in Burundi, as many colonial officials acted to spite the UN which was hated for its role in the process of thwarting Katanga independence.

11. Until the final months of its presence in Rwanda and Burundi, the Belgian Trusteeship of Ruanda-Urundi was governed by a single administration. Distrust of the Belgian Government, following the debacle of Congolese (Zairian) independence probably delayed the coming of independence to Rwanda and Burundi, and UN visiting missions usually received the very minimum of cooperation from Belgian Trusteeship authorities.

12. Prunier (note 9) p.212.

13. The organization and implementation of the Hutu genocide against the Tutsis (and moderate Hutu elements) in Rwanda in 1994 is also described in grim detail by Feilip Reyntjens in 'Rwanda: Genocide and Beyond', *Journal of Refugee Studies* 9/3 (Sept. 1996) pp.240–51.

14. See *After Action Review: Operation Support Hope 1994* (Carlisle, PA: The US Army Peacekeeping Institute for HQ US European Command, 1997) est. 200pp.

15. As reproduced in Carole J.L. Collins, 'Refugee crisis around the Great Lakes', *Africa Recovery* 10/1 (May 1996) p.19.

16. The Banyamulenge are a relatively small (30,000) Tutsi-related group native to Southern Kivu. They provided the nucleus of the 1996 armed Tutsi rebellion, and soon all Tutsi rebels were known as Banyamulenge.

17. Michael G. Schatzberg, 'Beyond Mobutu: Kabila and the Congo', *Journal of Democracy* 8/4 (Oct. 1997) pp.70–84.

18. See Thomas Turner, 'Kabila Returns in a Cloud of Uncertainty', in *African Studies Quarterly* 1/3 (Sept. 1997), Special Issue: 'Crisis in the Great Lakes'. [http://www.clas.ufl.edu/africa/] and Hussein Solomon, 'From Zaire to the Democratic Republic of the Congo: Towards post-Mobutuism', *Africa Insight* 27/2 (1997) pp.9, 91–7.

19. Adeline Iziren, 'Zairians snub OAU please for ceasefire. Doubts arise over organization's ability to resolve civil war', *The Voice*, 11 Nov. 1996)

20. See 'World's Biggest Refugee Camp Born in Eastern Zaire', *Los Angeles Sentinel*, 11 July

1996, and Christian Jennings, 'Disaster faces Zaire refugees as aid workers flee', Reuters, 11 Feb. 1996.

21. See Dele Olojede, 'Goma is Stormed/Aid workers flee, leaving 700,000 behind', *Newsday*, 11 March 1996 and Debbie Howlett, '1.2M Rwandan refugees trapped, 11 Aug. 1996, p.12A.

22. 'Security Council Welcomes Multinational Force Proposal for Eastern Zaire', *UN Press Release* SC/6287, 11 Sept. 1996.

23. 'Zaire: UN Seeks Cease-fire as Forces Battle in Goma', Inter Press Service English News Wire, 11 Feb. 1996.

24. René Lemarchand, 'Patterns of State Collapse and Reconstruction in Central Africa: Reflections on the Crisis in the Great Lakes', in *African Studies Quarterly* (note18).

25. Amnesty International, 'Country Report' (March 1997) [http://www.amnesty.org/ailib/aipub/1997/AFR/16201197.htm.

26. Robert Garreton, 'Report on the mission carried out at the request of the High Commissioner for Human Rights between 25 and 29 March to the area occupied by rebels in eastern Zaire', (Geneva: ReliefWeb: http://www.reliefweb.int/emergenc/greatlak/source/-un_srhrz/ reports/ 020497.html) 12pp.

27. Jeffrey Herbst, 'Responding to State Failure in Africa', *International Security* 21/3 (Winter 1996/97) p.124.

28. Col. Scott R. Feil, 'Could 5,000 Peacekeepers Have Saved 500,000 Rwandans? Early Intervention Reconsidered', *ISD Reports* 3/2 (Washington DC: Edmund A. Walsh School of Foreign Service, Georgetown Univ.) 5pp.

29. 'Transcript of the Press Conference given by Secretary-General Boutros Boutros-Ghali in Rome on 12 November, 1996', UN ReliefWeb <http://www.reliefweb.int> (Geneva) 4 p.at http://www.reliefweb.int/emergenc/greatlak/source/un_sec_g/pressrel/121196.html.

30. See 'France specifies participation in UN Operation in Zaire', Itar-Tass, 10 Nov. 1996 and Gail Russell Chaddock and Judith Matloff, 'West Split on Sending Troops to Zaire', *The Christian Science Monitor*, 12 Nov. 1996.

31. 'Zairian Tutsis Accuse Rivals of Using Refugees as Human Shield', Xinhua News Agency, 10 Nov. 1996.

32. Chaddock and Matloff (note 30).

33. See Todd Nissen, 'Canadian general's headquarters to be in Goma', Reuters, 11 Nov. 1996, and Judy Aita, 'Canada Outlines Plans for Multinational Zaire Force', *USIA* report from its UN correspondent, 14 Nov. 1996.

34. 'Confusion mounts over possible Zaire force', Reuters, 13 Nov. 1996.

35. Ghion Hagos, 'Africa-Force: Seven African Countries Offer Troops for Zaire', (Addis Ababa: PANA, reposted by Africa News Service, 13 Nov. 1996). For further details on the expected contributions to the operation from individual states, see Philip Pullella, 'Breakdown of major nations' offers of Zaire help', Reuters, 14 Nov. 1996.

36. Liu Yegang, 'S. Africa Refuses to Send Fighting Troops', Xinhua News Agency (From Johannesburg, 15 Nov. 1996).

37. See 'The Only Hope for Refugees in Zaire – A Military Rescue Force', *Refugees International* (Washington DC) 8 Nov. 1996, and 'Oxfam and Medecins Sans Frontieres joint statement on Anglo-French summit: Military intervention now to save lives and secure long term peace and justice', Oxfam Statement, 8 Nov. 1996.

38. Lionel Rosenblatt, 'Unless US Galvanizes International Action, Central Africa Will Explode' *Refugees International* (Washington DC, 11 Nov. 1996).

39. Michael Clough, 'The Africa Question: Should the US Get Involved?' *Los Angeles Times*, 11 March 1996, p.M-2.

40. 'US Disaster Response Team Sent to Zaire', United States Information Agency (USIA), 5 Nov. 1996.

41. 'US Said Leaning Toward Backing Zaire Force', Reuters, 6 Nov. 1996.

42. Jacquelyn Porth, 'US Military Considers Options for Eastern Zaire', USIA, 7 Nov 1996.

43. 'Confusion Mounts Over Possible Zaire Force', Reuters, 13 Nov. 1996.

44. Julia Malone and Bob Deans, 'Decision on US role in Zaire crisis relief could come today', *The Atlanta Constitution*, 12 Nov. 1996, p.A05.

45. Ibid.

46. 'Transcript of the Pentagon Background Briefing on Zaire' (Washington DC: USIA) 13 Nov. 1996.
47. See Michael McCurry (White House Press Spokesman), 'White House Outlines Conditions for Sending Troops to Zaire', (Washington, DC: White House Statement, 13 November 1996) and 'Q&A from White House Briefing on Zaire', *Africa News Service*, 11 Nov. 1996.
48. 'US troops to help in Zaire', *USA Today*, 14 Nov. 1996.
49. Nicholas Doughty, 'Force for Zaire: saviour or dangerous gamble', Reuters (London bureau) 14 Nov. 1996.
50. UN Security Council Resolution 1080 (1996) Unofficial transcript reproduced on the UNDHA ReliefWeb site <http://www.reliefweb.int>.
51. Rehana Roussouw, 'Albright tells Council US backs Canadian Initiative', *Africa News Service*, 15 Nov. 1996.
52. See *After Action Review: Operation Guardian Assistance* (Vicenza, Italy (?): Headquarters United States Army Southern Task Force, 1997) draft, 25 pp. For those unfamiliar with US military acronyms, USEUCOM = US European Command; CMOC = Civil-Military Operations Center. On the obvious redundancy of 'NGO/PVO', it should be noted that the US military uses NGO for non-US voluntary agencies and PVO for US non-governmental agencies. In this text, 'NGO' is used for all such agencies.
53. Martine Lochin, MSF operations director for Zaire, quoted in: 'Zaire: Limited Intervention Where Major Action is Needed', Inter Press Service English News Wire, 14 Nov. 1996.
54. Catherine Newbury, 'US Must Head Africans' Needs', *Newsday*, 15 Nov. 1996.
55. 'Zaire – Complex Emergency – Fact Sheet No. 1, FY 1997' (Washington DC: USAID, 8 Nov. 1996).
56. Buchizya Mseteka, 'Zairian rebels agree to humanitarian corridor', Reuters, 10 Nov. 1996.
57. Ed O'Loughlin, 'Political Agenda of Zaire Rebels Stalls Food Flow to Refugees', *Christian Science Monitor*, 13 Nov. 1996.
58. Rehana Roussouw, 'US Situation Report for Eastern Zaire', *Africa News Service*, 15 Nov. 1996). This report reproduces material from USAID Office of Foreign Disaster Assistance, *Eastern Zaire: Complex Emergency Fact Sheet no 2 FY 1997*.
59. Segun Adeyemi, 'UN Bent on Sending Multilateral Force to Zaire', PANA (reporting from New York, 16 Nov. 1996).
60. John Pomfret, 'In Congo, Revenge Became Rebellion: Tutsi-led Campaign Against Hutus Turned Sights on Mobutu', *Washington Post*, 6 July 1997, p.1.
61. For a more details discussion of Rwandan strategy, see Philip Gourevitch, 'Continental Shift: Laurent Kabila's rise to power isn't just a Congolese affair—it may signal that Africa is coming together to rid itself of old political evils and to seize control of its destiny', *The New Yorker*, 4 Aug. 1997, pp.42–55.
62. John Pomfret, 'Rwandans Led Revolt in Congo: Defense Minister Says Arms, Troops Supplied For Anti-Mobutu Drive', *Washington Post*, 9 July 1997, p.1.
63. Ibid.
64. Ibid.
65. I am indebted to my indefatigable friend and colleague, Gene Dewey, decorated veteran, experienced senior government official, and committed humanitarian who introduced me to the initial concepts and design of the Comprehensive Campaign Plan. See Arthur E. Dewey and Walter S. Clarke, *The Comprehensive Campaign Plan: A Humanitarian/Political/ Military Partnership in 'Total Asset' Planning for Complex Humanitarian Emergencies* (Washington DC: Congressional Hunger Center, 1 May 1997) 27 pp.+ annexes.
66. Failure to recognize the continuity of peace operations is implicit in the fact that the US Pentagon has separate offices for peacekeeping and humanitarian operations.
67. See UN Lessons Learned Unit, 'Comprehensive Report on Lessons Learned from United Nations Assistance Mission for Rwanda (UNAMIR) October 1993–April 1996' (http://www.un.org/Depts/dpko/rwandisc.htm) p.7 of 29.

The Normative Implications of
"The Savage Wars of Peace"

JOHN T. FISHEL

The Intent of *"The Savage Wars of Peace"*

When I developed the concept for the book, *"The Savage Wars of Peace":
Toward a New Paradigm of Peace Operations*,[1] I had two things in mind.
First, I sought to test the theoretical approach known as the Manwaring
Paradigm[2] with respect to its applicability in peace operations and its
validity with respect to the doctrine that it already informed. While I would
have preferred to have fully replicated the original study that produced the
paradigm, funding and time constraints dictated a different method. As a
result, I chose to use a series of comparative case studies written by a group
of authors who had either firsthand experience with the case or had devoted
considerable scholarly effort to it, or both. The result is a study of peace
operations of some depth that is organized in a way that it is both explicitly
comparative from case to case and provides a good test of the model as
theory and as the source of much current military doctrine.

Although the theory is well developed in the book, it is useful to review
it here. In essence, the Manwaring Paradigm argues that the outcome of any
conflict is the result of the peculiar combination of seven dimensions which
are, in turn, made up of 72 variables. The dimensions are Unity of Effort,
Legitimacy, Support to Belligerents, Support Actions of Peace Forces,
Military Actions of Peace Forces, Military Actions of Belligerents and
Peace Forces, and Actions Targeted on Ending Conflict. This particular
formulation of the dimensions is designed specifically to address peace
operations; nevertheless, the same seven dimensions (with minor variation
in their titles) have been used in various other studies of a variety of types
of conflict reported elsewhere.[3] While the theory does not specify the
particular combination or weight that is to be given to each dimension, it
does argue that failure to address each one adequately increases the
likelihood of failure for the side that ignores one or more dimension.

In the first and quantitative formulation of the theory, the two strongest
individual dimensions (both of which were statistically significant)[4] were
Support Actions of the Peace Forces (originally called Support Actions of

the Intervening Power) and Legitimacy. One of the individual dimensions which was not statistically significant was Unity of Effort although the entire model was statistically significant to a far greater extent than any of the dimensions alone.[5]

Armed with this theory which had greatly influenced the development of military doctrine for low intensity conflict, our effort was to test both the theory and the doctrine on types of conflict for which it had not been specifically designed. Even though doctrine for low intensity conflict included peacekeeping as one of four operational categories,[6] the theory had never been tested with respect to peace operations of any kind. Thus our research was designed to see if the theory really applied to peace operations as we hypothesized and as the US military was stating in its doctrine.

What *"The Savage Wars of Peace"* Accomplished

The nine cases which tested the theory of the Manwaring Paradigm with respect to peace operations demonstrated very clearly that the theory could not be rejected.[7] The seven dimensions of the model *were* essential in explaining the degree of success or failure in each one of the cases. Nevertheless, the study of peace operations did introduce some modification to the theory. As in the original study and all subsequent ones, the strength of the Legitimacy dimension was such that the other dimensions clearly revolved around its impact. In the earlier studies, however, the other dimension that provided a center of gravity was Support Actions of the Peace Forces (Intervening Power). In this study, by contrast, the second center of gravity is the dimension, Unity of Effort. Case after case demonstrated that success or failure, as well as the degree of each, depended on Unity of Effort. Even more important was the insight that Unity of Effort and Legitimacy had intersecting orbits.[8] Thus, Legitimacy reinforced Unity of Effort and vice versa, while a lessening of one resulted in a lessening of the other.

A second modification to the theory is in making explicit the distinction between and interrelationship of *de jure* (juridical) and *de facto* Legitimacy.[9] While *de jure* Legitimacy is necessary to the success of any peace operation it is not in itself sufficient for that success. Rather, Legitimacy must be supported by the perceptions of all the relevant audiences. In other words, there must be *de facto* Legitimacy for an operation to succeed.

Like the previous studies, this one demonstrated that all seven dimensions were interrelated. In contrast to the previous studies, the degree of intertwining of the dimensions was even more obvious. Thus, it becomes exceptionally clear that the independent variables represented by the seven dimensions are not independent of each other. They are, instead, strongly intercorrelated. This is by no means a negative conclusion; it merely indicates that war and peace represent aspects of a very complex system of human interaction.

When theory is translated into military doctrine it becomes, at the very least, guidance as to how a military force will conduct operations; that is, it becomes prescriptive in a more or less rigid sense. At the same time, competent doctrine writers (and users) all recognize that doctrine is not dogma and must be interpreted in terms of the specific conditions that a commander finds on the ground. Given this, *"The Savage Wars of Peace"* identifies in its case studies a variety of situations in which current doctrine demands modification. The logic for modification is brilliantly addressed by David Last in his concluding chapter.[10] He argues that doctrine must guide what peace forces do, how they conduct their relations with the belligerents, and the degree of force to be used as well as when it is to be used. He further argues that rather than employing a force exit strategy we must develop strategies of transition from military to civilian organizations. When military forces must be used campaign plans need to address both coordination with civilian agencies and the eventual transfer of functions from the military to those civilian organizations. 'Doctrine should acknowledge that the spectrum of forces is continuous, although the organizations may be discreet ...'[11] which is to say that the organizations which carry out the functions are as likely to be civilian as military and may operate concurrently as well as sequentially. Extant doctrine does not reflect this reality.

A second point which Last makes, and derives from the cases and their analysis according to the paradigm, is that peace enforcement operations differ from war because they make an effort to control and de-escalate violent conflict. Indeed, this is what distinguishes all peace operations from other kinds of military operations. Thus he argues that consent is as important to peace enforcement as it is to any other peace operation. Only in this way can *de facto* Legitimacy be built.

Last then addresses the ways in which peace forces need to conduct their operations. In a passage that harkens back to the late UN Secretary-General Dag Hammarskjöld's statement that peacekeeping is not a soldier's task but only a soldier can do it, Last asserts that war fighting (or combat) skills are essential to successful peace operations. He also places the British maxim for 'wider peacekeeping' of maximum strength/minimum force in the context of both the paradigm and current doctrine showing that sufficient strength, massed properly, can give peace forces a decisive advantage in the defensive phase of an operation. More important, however, is his argument that for a peace operation to be successful it must go over to the offensive. In peace operations, the offensive requires the imaginative and sustained use of contact skills (at times instead of) in addition to combat skills. Current military doctrine generally does not address these skills. Finally, Last finds that neither military doctrine nor civilian agencies' 'doctrinal' publications adequately address either the integration of military and civilian organizations for the conduct of peace operations or the training and education in the necessary contact skills to conduct offensive peace operations effectively.

"The Savage Wars of Peace" integrates empirical theory and military doctrine by means of its case studies and analysis to produce a series of instrumental prescriptions. In other words, the book focuses on the concept that if you would achieve objective X then you must carry out courses of action Y, A, and Q (but not Z). It does not, however, nor does it intend to make any normative prescriptions. Yet, the normative is clearly implicit in the dimensions of the Manwaring Paradigm and it is to that which this study must turn. To get there we must first examine the context in which the 'savage wars of peace' take place.

The Context is Policy

Peace operations take place in a political context. We can easily and correctly paraphrase Clausewitz by saying that peace operations are an extension of policy by other means. In other words, as in every other international interaction the ultimate objective of a peace operation is political. That political objective most often is articulated in the mandate which in a UN authorized or executed operation is the resolution of the Security Council (UNSCR). Since the Security Council is a highly political organization its resolutions mostly represent compromises that are significantly less than the maximum political objectives of some of its members and significantly more than what other members consider to be ideal. As a result, there is often ambiguity in the terms of the UNSCR which will be clarified by the terms of reference that the Secretary-General (or his representative) negotiates with the force contributors. Many times, however, even the terms of reference do not eliminate the ambiguity, a fact which is complicated by the general condition that the UN is less than the sum of its members.

This was most clearly demonstrated in *"The Savage Wars of Peace"* in its chapter on UNOSOM II (Somalia).[12] There the authors address the differing objectives of the force contributors and how their discord caused the breakdown of Legitimacy internal to the operation which resulted in its failure. We may conclude, therefore, that peace operations will reflect the objectives of policy of the member states of the sponsoring organization and the force contributing states. As a result and depending on the coincidence of policy interest among those states, the operation will be more, less, or equal to the sum of the national will and resource commitments of the states involved.

In the case of the United States, the policy goals with respect to peace operations are articulated in the *National Security Strategy* (NSS), usually published annually by the President. From the first publication of the document in 1987, the NSS has stressed that US policy supports democratization around the world.[13] The ideological rationale for this is found in the notion of 'the democratic peace'. As President Bill Clinton puts it, 'This commitment to see freedom and respect for human rights take hold is not only just, but pragmatic, for strengthened democratic institutions benefit the US and the world.'[14] The President goes on to link democratization with ongoing peace operations in Bosnia[15] and Haiti.[16] As stated by the President peace operations are instrumentalities to attain a normative end – the success of democracy around the world.

Peace Operations as an Instrument of Policy

Despite some backing away from the aggressive multilateralism of its early days (largely as a result of the UNOSOM II operation in Somalia) the Clinton administration has chosen to rely heavily on peace operations as one instrument of its foreign/national security policy. Indeed, peace operations are addressed in the national security strategy under both shaping the environment and crisis response.[17] Clearly, peace operations have become an essential way (in the ends, ways, and means strategic equation) of applying the instruments of power – particularly the military instrument – to achieve the desired end state of greater numbers of nations that practice democracy as well as increased institutionalization of democracy. The principal problem with this formulation lies in the fact that democracy remains largely undefined or is confused with only one of its components, free and fair elections. This problem is compounded by the direct linkage of democracy with free market economies, often in a rigidly *laissez-faire* capitalist formulation.[18]

The link between democracy and market economies, while generally empirically valid, has a wide range of variance in democratic practice from economies with a very significant governmental social spending component to ones in which the government plays a relatively small regulatory role. The findings of *"The Savage Wars of Peace"* have little bearing on this aspect of the peace building process. They do suggest, however, that economic development goes along with political development if a peace is to be truly secured. In turn, this does imply that market economics will be the mechanism of economic development while at the same time in no way specifying the role of government in that economic system. The battle over the economic role of government is something for both another day and other articles. Suffice it here to say that ideology will certainly drive the way the various governments and international organizations will seek to attain their policy goals with respect to the objects of their peace operations. In this regard, a constraint reminiscent of the political constraints of Cold War peacekeeping emerges in modern peace operations, albeit in a not nearly so obstructionist form.

Nevertheless, success in peace operations implies the need for development, defined broadly, or in the modern language of UN peace operations, peace building. A usefully broad definition of development crafted by Ambassador Edwin G. Corr more than a quarter century ago reads:

> Development is society's change of sets of opportunities and problems for other sets of opportunities and problems(probably more complex) in which more and more people in the society are able to participate in the decisions that affect their lives, to benefit increasingly in their society's growing material, civic and cultural wealth, and to fulfill better their God-given potential and rights as human beings.[19]

The utility of this definition of development both in general and for its application to peace operations is that it focuses on change in opportunities *and* problems; that is, it does not pretend to solve all problems and suggests that new problems will arise out of some of the solutions to the old.[20] The definition has a second virtue which applies particularly to peace operations in that it suggests that the direction of change is and should be toward the peaceful resolution of conflict (as is indicated by the words 'benefit in . . . material, civic and cultural wealth ...').

The clear implication of such a definition of development (read 'peace building') for peace operations is that they will be increasingly open ended. No peace operation can be perceived to have ended successfully merely when the fighting stops. Rather, successful peace operations will of necessity build the peace through a series of carefully planned and executed civil military actions and operations. These actions will entail the full participation of civilian agencies, governmental, intergovernmental, and non-governmental, in both planning and execution. Failure to achieve such Unity of Effort will result in a peace operation that, at best, resembles Cyprus whose sole measure of success is that Greeks and Turks are not now shooting at each other. If, however, the international community seeks long term peace – a peace that addresses the root causes of the conflict – then the community will have to plan for the long haul and include all the relevant players in the planning. As David Last points out, these include the belligerents themselves who he identifies as necessary allies.[21]

It is here that Corr's definition of development again comes into play. The end state that the international community sponsoring the peace operation must seek is one in which the opportunities and problems are those desired by the belligerents which all of the former belligerents can share together. Moreover, such development will clearly entail the greater participation of the citizenry who make up the belligerent parties. In turn, this should create a series of useful cross-cutting affiliations which the peace builders can use to strengthen the *de facto* legitimacy of the peace.

Unfortunately, neither building peace nor developing a nation can be done on the cheap. The development process is expensive in any case, even more so if it comes on the heels of a destructive war, whether internal or interstate. It should be particularly clear that the belligerents who are subject to a peace operation are unlikely to be in any state to provide all the resources necessary for their own peace process, although they can and must contribute to it. Peace operations, then, will certainly be resource intensive, especially so for the force contributors along with the rest of the international community. Unwillingness to commit the required resources should raise serious questions about whether the peace operation is even worth conducting.

Given that the conduct of peace operations clearly crosses over into the work of development with the peace forces acting the role of change agents, then some of the lessons learned the hard way over the years about the development process clearly apply. Controlled experimentation with human beings definitely is unethical since some of the human guinea pigs are almost certain to be hurt. Equally important is the fact that so many variables are involved that it is probably not possible to actually conduct such an experiment. Nevertheless, doing nothing is equally unacceptable since to do that does nothing to resolve the conflict thereby rendering the peace operation irrelevant.

One way to address similar situations devised in the decade and a half from 1953 to 1968 that the Vicos Project in Peru operated under the auspices of Cornell University was what Harold Lasswell called 'prototyping'.[22] Prototyping consists of setting up a quasi experimental situation in which the subjects are willing participants and all parties are prepared to alter the conditions if and when negative consequences result either as the outcome of low probability predictions or as unanticipated consequences of actions taken. This approach appears to have the virtue of providing for rigorous observation and recording of data during an intervention while minimizing the risk of doing harm and maximizing the likelihood of achieving positive results. Thus this approach, if applied to peace operations (analogous to the 'Vicos experiment' in developmental theory) will place particular weight on flexibility and the combination of combat and contact skills of the peace forces engaged.

This discussion leads directly back to the conclusion that the strategic objective, defined as an end state, is an absolutely necessary condition for the success of a peace operation. Nevertheless, it is in no way a sufficient condition. The very first requirement for an appropriate strategic objective for a peace operation is that it be agreed to by both the mandating authority and the force contributing nations. The problem with such agreements is that they tend to be arrived at the lowest common denominator resulting in an end state that can be described in ambiguous terms, at best. At worst, agreement on the strategic objective is not agreement at all but merely fine sounding words signifying nothing.

The second requirement is that the end state be defined in political terms so that the political leader and force commander of the peace operation can identify objectives that if attained will result in the desired end state. This requirement, if met in conjunction with the former, is indeed, both necessary and sufficient for a successful peace operation. It is, however, more easily stated than accomplished. In practice, the desired end state involves the *de jure* Legitimacy of formal resolution of the conflict as well as the *de facto* Legitimacy of the perception that the conflict has been sufficiently resolved such that the belligerents will not again resort to arms. In an interstate conflict, such as Ecuador/Peru, this means that the parties must find a political solution to their territorial dispute. What the Military Observer Mission Ecuador/Peru (MOMEP) case shows us is that even with belligerent parties having as few disagreements as those two countries the international community must devote an inordinate amount of attention and effort to resolve the conflict. To date, the international community has failed despite the best efforts of the militaries of both the peacekeepers (Guarantors) and the belligerents.

Internal wars are even harder to resolve as shown by the vast majority of the cases. Those which have been successful have resulted from enlisting the belligerents as allies in the fight against conflict itself. At least as important has been the definition of the end state in those cases as legitimate democratic governance that goes beyond the mere holding of elections. In point of fact, the successful cases have achieved peace because a viable electoral mechanism was chosen which allowed for real participation of the people in choosing who was to govern them but also provided the elected government the tools with which to govern.

Identified problems in building peace in those cases we have deemed to be successes focus on the tools of effective government. In many instances these problem areas are found in the judiciary being largely unreformed, the police having little support and their budget being the bill payer for other more apparently pressing needs, as well as not having sufficient training to carry out their mission. Other problem areas include electoral systems which stress representation at the expense of governing and a lack of attention to local democratic government with the authority to govern. The indicated problem areas are by no means all encompassing; they merely illustrate the complexity of the problem of effective peace operations.

Conclusion

Peace operations, like the policy they represent, express the norms accepted by the states which make up the international community. Where states agree on values there is a strong probability that policy (perhaps even the policy reflected in peace operations) will be effective. Where states fail to agree on values the same policies of the institutions of the international community likely will fail. The international community and its institutions, however, is usually less than the sum of its parts. This may create an opportunity for a player with skill and resources to exercise more influence on the game than might otherwise be the case. Many times, the United States finds itself in just such a situation. Nevertheless, the US must use its influence with skill and caution since it is not all powerful. It must also remember that the institutions of the international community most often can only be nudged in the direction that a player wishes them to go and that these institutions are like huge ships moving with a terrible inertia.

Given these constraints on success in peace operations it would appear to be difficult to make any useful generalizations. In spite of appearances, several do come readily to mind. First, in the words of Hippocrates, 'Do no harm.' This rule should be obvious yet it is the one that is most often ignored. Political leaders tend to ignore it as a result of not thinking through their actions to the point of an attainable end state. This often results in an intervention or peace operation whose reach exceeds its grasp such as Somalia with UNOSOM II or Haiti which appears to be slowly sinking into the morass of the predator state from which it was rescued by Operation 'Uphold Democracy'. In each of these instances the attempt to 'do good' ended by doing harm to the very people it was designed to help. These cases along with that of UNPROFOR in former Yugoslavia should provide caution to the force contributors of IFOR/SFOR in Bosnia as well as future interventions.

Once the 'do no harm' criterion is met, the mandate giving international organization must determine what end state is acceptable. It could be as limited as that in Cyprus; however, it must be remembered that the consequences of that peacekeeping operation have been an end state of indefinite intervention. What makes that end state acceptable in Cyprus is that all parties, belligerents and the UN and its force contributors have concluded that the status quo of *de facto* partition without armed conflict between Greece and Turkey is a legitimate outcome. Nevertheless, the continuing threat to the peace lies in the likelihood that one or the other of the communities and/or their international sponsors decides that the status quo is no longer legitimate.

What this all means – and it is confirmed over and over again by all the case studies – is that the political outcome (or end state) of the peace operation must be perceived as legitimate both in the near and long term for success to be achieved. As a result the sponsor of the peace operation must seek to find a solution that meets the terms of political legitimacy. While this will differ depending on whether the conflict is primarily internal or external, certain general conditions can be articulated. First, the solution must have *de jure* Legitimacy; that is it must be sanctioned by treaty or other appropriate international mechanism and approved by the proper international organization or organizations. In addition, it must meet the formal approval of the belligerents. Second, the peace accord must achieve *de facto* Legitimacy. To do this, it must be perceived by all the belligerents as giving them some degree of victory. In the international cases MOMEP comes closest to meeting this criterion; nevertheless, its peace could still come apart if a political solution to the boundary dispute is not agreed upon. El Salvador presents an especially good example of success in an internal case. Here the key was that the belligerents concluded that they had both won. This was only possible because the FMLN changed its objective from overthrowing the government to becoming a participant in the political system.

The Salvadoran case also suggests the third value to be stressed in any peace operation, democracy. While democracy is primarily an internal question, and therefore central to the end state in internal wars, it also has bearing on the outcome of international conflicts, especially over the long term. In the international arena, the phenomenon of 'democratic peace' has been noted far too often. While it is by no means the absolute that many of its less sophisticated advocates assert, the narrower formulation that democratic states are significantly less likely to fight each other than are states with either asymmetrical governmental forms or states with authoritarian regimes appears to be empirically valid. There is another aspect to this hypothesis that suggests that even if democratic states do war against each other, peace between them will be easier to achieve because of the habitual compromise built into their politics. Although the jury remains out on this, some of the evidence from MOMEP gives the position limited support.

With respect to internal peace, this same argument is much stronger. The processes of democracy provide the mechanisms for the authoritative peaceful settlement of disputes among individuals, between individuals and the state, as well as between organizations and the state. These mechanisms are both political and judicial and the political is the most important. The political mechanism of free and fair elections allows for the change of leadership when the public no longer has confidence in the previous leadership. This, then, institutionalizes change itself in a way that preserves order. It must be noted, however, that for elections to be free they must be competitive and to be competitive, there must be freedom to organize, speak, write, and have one's message heard. Thus, elections are a necessary but insufficient condition for democracy. The other necessary conditions would appear to be freedom (as defined above) and an independent and impartial judiciary. Finally, for a democracy to attain *de facto* Legitimacy, it must be able to govern effectively. Therefore, freedom cannot equal license and a balance must be struck between liberty and order. That balance can be achieved by many means as the established democracies of the modern world have shown, nevertheless, they all have in common the attributes of democracy noted here.

To summarize, then, the normative implications of *"The Savage Wars of Peace"* can be stated in three pragmatic rules. First, do no harm; this requires planning through a peace operation to an end state and gaining real agreement on that end state. Anything less and it is better to let the warring parties fight it out. Second, seek to achieve political legitimacy both for the end state and for the peace operation. This requires that the belligerents become allies of the peace forces. Third, seek to promote democracy among all the governments involved for it is both less likely that democratic states will fight each other and more likely that democracies will be able to settle their internal political problems peacefully.

NOTES

1. John T. Fishel (ed.) *"The Savage Wars of Peace": A New Paradigm for Peace Operations* (Boulder, CO: Westview Press, 1997).
2. Ibid.
3. See Max G. Manwaring and John T. Fishel, 'Insurgency and Counterinsurgency: Toward a New Analytical Approach', *Small Wars & Insurgencies* 3/3 (Winter 1992) pp.272–310.
4. Ibid.
5. Ibid.
6. HQDA, FM 100-20, *Military Operations in Low Intensity Conflict*, Washington DC 1990.
7. For detail see Max G. Manwaring and Kimbra L. Fishel, 'Lessons That Should Have Been Learned: Toward a Theory of Engagement for "The Savage Wars of Peace"', in Fishel (note 1).
8. Kimbra L. Fishel and Edwin G. Corr, 'UN Peace Operations in El Salvador: The Manwaring

Paradigm in a Traditional Setting' in Fishel (note 1).

9. Manwaring and Fishel, and Thomas J. Daze and John T. Fishel, 'Peace Enforcement in Somalia: UNOSOM II' in Fishel (note 1).
10. David Last, 'Winning the Savage Wars of Peace: What the Manwaring Paradigm Tells Us' in Fishel (note 1).
11. Ibid.
12. Daze and Fishel (note 9).
13. See National Security Strategy of the United States since 1987, The White House, Washington DC.
14. William J. Clinton, *A National Security Strategy for a New Century* (The White House, Washington DC, May 1997) p.19.
15. Ibid. p.21.
16. Ibid. p.26.
17. Ibid. pp.8–9.
18. Ibid. pp.2, 19, *passim*. Although the national security strategy does *not* follow the rigid *laisse- faire* line, many other influential writings and policy applications do.
19. Edwin G. Corr, 'Including the Excluded in El Salvador: Prospects for Democracy and Development', in Peter L. Berger (ed.) *Institutions of Democracy & Development* (San Francisco: Sequoia Institute 1993) p.139.
20. For further discussion see Kimbra L. Fishel, 'From Revolutionary Warfare to Criminalization: The Transformation of Violence in El Salvador', in *Low Intensity Conflict & Law Enforcement* 6/3 (Winter 1997) pp.48–63.
21. Last (note 10).
22. See Harold D. Lasswell *et al.* (eds.) *Peasants, Power, and Applied Social Change: Vicos as a Model* (Beverly Hills, CA: Sage Publications 1971).

Beyond the Logjam: A Doctrine for Complex Emergencies

JOHN MACKINLAY

The Internet reveals that there are now more than one thousand papers and reports concerning the problems of complex emergencies. Collectively it is hard to discern any single trend in this tide of academic and professional opinion, except that taken together they make a statement, so obvious to be frequently ignored, that we are swiftly moving into an era that is already challenging the assumptions which underwrote our security during the Cold War. Although North Atlantic nations profess to be feeling more secure than ever before, we are now facing changes that may overturn our comfortable rationalisation of the gap between rich and poor nations, our response to ethnic cleansing and all the problems of overpopulation, population displacement and the need to provide stability in these areas of crisis. These issues have already begun to impinge on our arrangements for global security.

This contribution takes the deeply pessimistic view that we have, through overpopulation, over use of resources and globalisation, created security risks that require collective responses which need to be so multifaceted in composition that they are inherently unmanageable and incapable of succeeding. This complexity and its unmanageable nature is manifested at both the strategic and operational level. In both cases there is a head-on collision between the conservatism of government and military institutions, still fixed under the influence of Cold War truths and the urgent need to adopt a more lateral approach to problems that do not respond to these truths. What is the nature of this collision and the need for a radical approach to change?

It is argued here that in the complex emergencies which increasingly threaten security in Eastern Europe, Central Asia and Africa, international response mechanisms have failed from the outset to take a realistic approach that reflected the needs of the crisis. These failures have been due to vested interest, conservatism and a lack of vision beyond the narrow limitations of national and professional interest. Unfortunately vested interests and conservatism are deeply rooted characteristics of human behaviour they operate as an important survival mechanisms to counterbalance attempts at irresponsible change. But in this case they may completely suffocate the optimism and inspiration that will be needed to develop an effective international response to complex emergencies.

New Era of Security Risks

The most fundamental reason for the failure of officials and senior military officers to understand the needs of complex humanitarian emergencies is that they maintain a statist approach to what is, at its heart, a sub-state problem. At the grassroots level complex emergencies have important and idiosyncratic characteristics which cannot be ignored in the determination of their solutions. In the post-Cold War era continuing conflict and humanitarian disasters were less often caused by territorial aggression than by the long term effects of:

- Population increases that imposed a growing demand for space and resources.

- Poverty increases of 40 per cent since 1980 that left 1.4 billion people on the margins of survival, vulnerable to conflict and natural disaster.

- Economic imbalance which faced poor countries with increasing debt and a lack of access to world markets while rich nations continued to maintain and exploit their dominance.

- Environmental damage.

- Competition for raw materials, vital resources including water.

- Collapsing states, particularly artificially created multi-ethnic states held together by superpower interests during the Cold War which became vulnerable to demands for recognition of their culturally distinct elements.

- Intercommunal violence fueled by ethnic and cultural self-determination.

- Population migration and the displacement of civil communities.[1]

Planners often assumed they were dealing with a system of sovereign states where for better or worse a recognised leader and government structure effectively controlled the machinery of state. However, the basis for that assumption was eroding. Complex emergencies often involved states that either had no governments or had contending sources of authority. Even in the best case scenario of IFOR in the context of the Dayton agreement, intervention forces frequently had to steer between competing factions or ignore national authorities altogether if their peacekeeping and humanitarian missions were to be accomplished. The concept of sovereignty was undergoing fundamental reassessment. The assumption, that a state's sovereign rights could not be infringed without its consent, ran increasingly against a more universal application of human rights and a more universal standard of responsibility.

In the environment of a collapsed state, a host government was likely to have lost control of a considerable part of its territories so that beyond the immediate influence of the capital city the warring factions would supplant their authority. The reins of power had fallen from the hands of the state to the warlords who operate at street and village level. Their factions would proliferate into sub-groups each with its own agenda for revenge and survival. The presence of large displaced elements of the population completely altered the operational environment and even challenged conventional wisdom on the use of force. Intervening military forces used in a conventional anner had become increasingly less useful where the disintegrating societal structures unleashed civil violence. In some cases a massive element of the population migrated to the urban areas. This could alter the social structures of the population, increasing their sense of vulnerability and fostering lawlessness and unrest. In civil conflict substate forces acted more frequently against the civil population rather than against an opposing faction, the vast majority of the casualties were now civilians. The military objectives had become the civil population; its control, division, relocation and extermination could be a faction's war aims.

In interstate conflicts of the Cold War period, especially in the desert warzones of the Arab–Israeli battles, the crisis took place in a clearly defined area. For international negotiators and the intervening forces of the UN it was a military problem which involved few players. In the post-Cold War era none of these factors could be assumed. Yet international civil servants and political leaders continued to use the same statist approach as before. Both at the strategic and operational level, national planners saw complex emergencies as narrowly military problems and applied military solutions.

National Response Assets

In established democratic states, defence expenditure is periodically reviewed to reflect defence needs. The difficulty of predicting long-term defence needs has meant that in many states there has been a gap between planned defence capabilities and the way defence assets are used in real life. In the case of most Northern Atlantic nations, planned defence capabilities refer to the defence forces that are established for homeland defence and for regional defence treaty obligations. These needs are expressed in warships, combat aircraft and army battalions which have, for the past 50 years, been designed to fight a conventional/nuclear battle in specified areas of the northern hemisphere. However in real life these same ships, aircraft and field units have very rarely been used actively in their planned role. In real life they are used in a reactive, incremental fashion to answer the needs of smaller, unexpected contingencies. In most cases the conventional war fighting characteristics of these weapon systems and the men who operate them have to be adapted to the needs of low level, out-of-area contingencies. The 'gap' is therefore the continuing difference between the design and organisation of armed forces for their perceived role, and the manner in which these assets are used in real life.

The conflict statistics of the last 50 years seem to indicate the trend continues to move away from the kind of interstate conflict, for which our defence organisations are mainly designed, towards intra-state conflict.[2] Despite the general reduction of conventional forces at the collapse of the Soviet Union, this gap in defence planning is not reflected in any general reorganisation in the armed forces of Northern Atlantic states except in the case of Denmark.[3] In most cases the priority is to maintain conventional warfighting capabilities rather than the needs of real-life, out-of-area contingencies. For several reasons defence officials are reluctant to adapt national defence capabilities to meet the statistics of the growing incidence of intrastate conflict. They argue that in the main these crises do not threaten their homelands, that their first priority continues to be to meet the perceived worst-case-scenario which is the conventional/nuclear attack on the homeland or state interest. A lapse in maintaining this capability would lead to its irretrievable loss.[4] The sophistication and expense of current and future weapon systems, and their countermeasures, has locked our defence forces into a spiral of increasing costs and commitment that they seem unable to abandon. On the one hand there is this spiral and the influence it exercises on the shape of defence forces, and on the other the continuing statistic of real-life defence needs.

The tension between the diverging trends that define the 'defence gap' is increasing. US defence experts argue that involvement in the civil emergencies of intra state violence has a seriously debilitating effect on US war-fighting capability. US forces, they say, should keep their powder dry for greater things such as the reemergence of another Saddam Hussein.[5] Unfortunately this argument effectively debars US forces from participating at operational level in the mainstream of ongoing security issues. It seems to advocate that, particularly in the case of the US, complex emergencies should only be resolved by the application of military technology and the overwhelming use of military forces. Both these attitudes are increasingly wrong and dangerous.

Planning Problems at the Strategic Level

In most complex humanitarian crises in the 1990s there has been intense intercommunal violence and many of the factors relating to collapse of power, proliferation of warlords, massive population displacement, cited above, have been manifested. In every case there have emerged deep divisions in what was once regarded as a single state. The history of Cyprus, Northern Ireland and Lebanon, to give only three examples from a much longer list, has shown that these deep wounds in a society do not heal quickly. With each new complex emergency involving intercommunal violence the international community is facing problems which will take decades to stabilise and ultimately heal. But the politician, urged on to 'do something' by a vociferous electorate, cannot opt for a response that genuinely addresses the problem. In democratic countries national leaders are generally elected for four to five years. In most cases they seek election or re-election from political constituencies which are either profoundly unconcerned about events which take place beyond their immediate region or uninformed about their real nature. But public apathy can be suddenly reversed and manipulated into a state of concern by media attention and live coverage of a humanitarian crisis overseas. Under these circumstances when political leaders are pressed to 'do something' they find themselves in a no-win situation. The media are fickle, their attention will in due course turn to other events and with it will go public concern. The politician may wish to opt for a genuinely effective response to the crisis but cannot afford to become hostage to long term commitment. For this reason in almost all cases political responsibility has been limited to a short term approach to what is fundamentally a long term problem.

In many cases governments seek to offset their lack of commitment by the use of a proxy response through the civilian relief agencies. Increasingly governments are funding relief to complex humanitarian emergencies where intercommunal conflict has torn societies apart and this use of a proxy actor avoids the need to commit themselves to the military or political involvement. However the truth remains that a strong political commitment at the strategic level is a basic essential for success. Using the relief agencies allows them to rebuff the charge of not having 'done something'. However by using this proxy conduit for their response they invite problems at a very early stage of the international intervention. Without political and military support, relief agencies are not in a strong position to respond effectively to complex emergencies. They are vulnerable to the whim of each warring faction. Even to achieve basic operating needs on a day to day basis, access to ports and airfields for example, they find themselves becoming entangled in the interests of political figures in the crisis area who may manipulate them.

At the strategic level political negotiators also introduced a self-destructive factor into the peace process. In complex emergency negotiations their main problem has been to address and contain the proliferation of interests. This could only be achieved when the regional consensus was high and warring parties put under pressure. As a result the opportunity for action would be short and impetus important. Negotiators could not afford to be wrangling over details, their approach was characterised by optimism and an energetic circumnavigation of problems. Their enthusiasm was infectious, carrying the process headlong towards signing sessions and historic embraces. The seeds of destruction became evident later when agreements translated into action; without the same pressure of international consensus, the unresolved obstacles, circumnavigated in an artificially induced aura of bonhomie, would later become the problem of the military and civil relief elements at the coal face.

National and international responses also suffer because each component of the response is planned in isolation. During 1993–94 mandates for conflict resolution were repeatedly negotiated in the UN Security Council without a carefully developed resourcing plan. Similar mistakes were made by coalition forces in 1995 and 1996. During the first hundred days of the Dayton peace process, thousands of young men were demobilised for example at military centres such as Prijedor and Banja Luka but no civil employment programme was organised to reciprocate this effort and bring them off the streets into gainful employment.[6] Similarly after the Abouja peace accords took effect in Liberia, hundreds of Charles Taylor's fighters demobilised in Gbarnga without any reciprocal civilian effort to employ them.[7] In both cases the military and civilian components of the peace process had planned in isolation and the civilian element whose funding arrangements took longer to set up were left behind in time by a military component which failed to see that they were part of a larger holistic pattern of events.

There has also been a failure to involve at an early stage, international corporations which have interests in the crisis area. In the example of Liberia several international companies were unavoidably committed to its economic recovery because they held capital investments in rubber plantations and ore mines. The resuscitation of these concerns would have had a very stabilising effect, allowing families to return to their villages and fighters to relinquish the need for weapons. Unfortunately none of these corporations and companies were brought into the planning stages of the peace process so that they could have thrown their weight behind getting the economy restarted at the same time as the demobilised fighters began to search for jobs.

Problems at Operational Level

In most complex humanitarian emergencies in the 1990s the international community has intervened in a very prescriptive manner. At an early stage of the intervention, usually through the authority of the UN's special representative at the crisis area, it draws up a programme for action. This invariably begins with a truce or ceasefire and moves on in a mechanical fashion to 'disarmament', 'demobilization' and finally to the 'elections'.[8] This programme of events has been ritually applied in Cambodia, Namibia, Mozambique, Bosnia and several times in Angola and Liberia. In none of the above crises has this calendar gone according to plan. In Namibia the UN forces arrived late, after the proposed start of the peace programme. An estimated 200–300[9] SWAPO fighters were killed during the violence that erupted and the peace process was only restored after the intervention of the South African Defence Forces (SADF). In Angola, Cambodia and Liberia one or more of the warring factions failed to support the peace process which greatly reduced the chances of a successful outcome. In Bosnia the programme to return the displaced and ethnically cleansed elements of the population has stalled. Each of the above cases is well documented by the periodic reports of the UN Secretary General, the UN Lessons Learned reports[10] and by a greater number of independently conducted research projects. Taken together their importance is that they show in every case that the overall planning of the international response has been unsuccessful: at the strategic level due to the short term, statist approaches explained earlier, and at an operational level due to the complexity of the problems of the crisis area and the unmanageable nature of the elements of the response.

In the operational area the immediate problems facing the intervention forces and agencies seem to divide under three main headings: restoring the monopoly of power to state level, reconciliation and rebuilding the infrastructure. In each case it was found that the aims and preconceptions of the intervening forces and agencies were, in important ways, out of tune with the needs of the crisis.

Restoring a Monopoly of Power

Once the level of conflict has been reduced by a truce or by the military presence of an intervening force, the problem facing the international intervention forces is to stabilise the area in a more permanent way. The overall problem is that in the crisis area power has become decentralised and the state's monopoly for violence eroded. The option to use force had passed into the hands of local warlords. In the calendar of events that is routinely arranged by the intervention forces, stabilisation is achieved by organising disarmament, demobilisation and the transportation of fighters to their homelands. The unstated purpose of these procedures is to wrest power and the ability to offer violence from the hands of local gang leaders, militias and warlords and recentralise it at a much higher level. Designed in this way the process hinges on the degree to which the factions could be effectively disarmed. However here lies a major problem. Generally speaking in a long-standing war zone every householder possesses weapons. For a warring faction, disarmament is not an absolute procedure. Fighters might hand in old weapons to satisfy the rituals of a disarmament process, but in real terms nothing has changed, power and the capability to do violence still lies in the hands of local leaders. But in past experience many of the intervening forces wrongly saw disarmament as an absolute relinquishment of power. Because they saw it in this way, they also imagined that the faction leaders, whose representatives might have agreed to it at some distant peace process in Geneva, also saw it in the same terms locally. Usually they did not. In the 1990s experiences,[11] disarmament in a complex emergency was seldom absolutely successful unless it was part of a holistic approach in which there was also a general return to normal life, employment and a degree of personal security offered by the presence of a more powerful international force.

Because disarmament is rarely successful, there is little option but to involve the warlords as active players because they are still potent forces in the crisis area. However the international community tends to place too much faith on disarmament, and fortified by this illusion exerts pressures to remove the warlords too early from the peace process. In Cambodia, Angola, Liberia and Bosnia the rituals of disarmament had not changed the distribution of power. Therefore elections were also largely ritualistic events Under these circumstances they were only significant when won by a war leader who could bring with him the power that he already possessed. Even after an election faction leaders held onto their power base for as long as possible. The concept of parliamentary opposition was undeveloped. Elections were either meaningless because none of the principal actors had relinquished their power or they were won absolutely by the most powerful faction. Whatever the formalities of the parliamentary assembly, in reality there were no prizes for a loser, only the possibility of retribution.

In recent experience these realities collided in several ways with the ethics and conservatism of international and national politicians and officials. Because most faction leaders were also war criminals the international community tended to marginalise them from the peacebuilding plans. In strictly ethical terms this approach was laudable, however in practical terms it could not work. As a rule faction leaders even after the rituals of a disarmament process continued to be the most powerful figures in the crisis area. They had to be part of the solution though not many international organisations were able to accept that.

The reorganisation of the factions into a state defence force was an essential part of a successful peace process. The absence of an effective plan to achieve this was usually the sure sign that the peace process was destined to fail. A successful reorganisation to achieve a state defence force also meant that power and the monopoly for violence would be successfully recentralised at state level. The most successful example of this so far has been the establishment of the Zimbabwean armed forces from the ZIPRA and ZANLA factions. An essential feature of this success was the overseeing presence of the Rhodesian security forces which, despite the political failure of the Smith regime, were a tactically unbeaten force. It was essential to have a larger, unassailably powerful military force to supervise and police the procedure. The significance of this overwhelming military presence was underrated by the international community. In the case of Namibia and Mozambique the continuing presence of the SADF was more fortuitous than planned. In Liberia the continuing presence of ECOMOG and in Bosnia of SFOR have been essential features of the reconstruction of both states. However the long term, overseas deployment of these intervention forces during the post emergency phase of a national recovery has been running against the political instincts of international leaders who hope for a short commitment and a quick exit strategy.

In addition to the presence of an overwhelmingly powerful force that supports the peace process, stabilisation required some form of interim government. Because stabilisation tended to be an open-ended process, an interim government might have to remain in office for a long time. The interim government's term of office ended, in ideal circumstances, with a successful election. There were few cases of genuinely successful elections, but even where there was partial success, there was usually a strong linkage between the continuing presence of a military force supporting the peace process, a successful reorganisation of the state defence forces and an effective interim government. If one of these conditions was missing the success of the process would be in doubt. In particular the success of an interim government might depend very much on the presence of a powerful supporting military force. As a result of the experiences of the 1990s it is possible to explain the initial stabilisation of a crisis as a holistic process that relied on several factors working together in an interactive fashion and not on a series of isolated events in a calendar for action.

Reconciliation

After stabilisation, reconciliation must become the priority of a peace process. In any century intercommunal violence has demonstrated a shocking degree of passion, hatred and destructiveness. As a result the societal damage is far greater than after a conventional interstate war where large numbers of civilians are not involved. The enormous bomb damage of World War II was cleared away within two decades, but after 30 years the societal damage in Ulster and Cyprus shows no sign of healing. In prolonged intercommunal violence where territory has changed hands with great brutality, violence takes on a personal quality which is absent when the uniformed soldiers of a state kill each other impersonally on the battlefield. Political leaders in the international community, who seek to 'do something' to alleviate humanitarian crisis, have so far not shown much awareness for societal problems in the aftermath of intercommunal conflict. In some cases by organising early exit strategies, they have made decisions about traumatised populations which satisfy the domestic pressures of home politics rather that the real life needs of the crisis area.

Reconciliation refers to the eventual return to a relatively more normal life of the casualties of complex emergencies, the displaced element of the population, the fighters, the war criminals, families and the children. A distinction needs to be made between people who are displaced because they flee their homes to escape the approaching violence of an ongoing conflict and people who are forced to leave their homes because of their ethnic minority status and the consequences of mounting physical threat from a hostile surrounding majority. In the case of the former category the problem was not so much a failure to understand the political ramifications of their restoration process as the sheer size of the logistic challenge. In each crisis, displaced population figures are measured in 100,000s. Their return to their farms and villages requires a high degree of coordination. The physical problem of transporting them back to their proper homes would already involve several elements of the international response including possibly a military element to ensure their security. In addition to this a simultaneous activity is required at the proposed destination to clear areas of mines and munitions, ensure houses are not occupied already and that the basis of a supporting infrastructure is available in terms of schools, hospitals and so forth. As well as the physical problems, their return has to be reconciled with a more general timetable of events. If the displaced population is to participate in a state election are they to be registered before or after their move home? And how does their registration alter the election laws for their proportional representation? In what season of the agricultural cycle will they return? If they are farmers what facilities will they need immediately to anticipate the next season?

Displaced populations in this category have been returned successfully in many complex emergencies. The comparative success of these operations relied on a high degree of cooperation between funders, relief agencies, international military forces, electoral staff, peace process planners and above all on the affected people themselves, the power brokers who may continue to control the areas chosen for resettlement and the displaced. Despite success in some areas, globally the figures for the displaced show far more people remain displaced and homeless than have been successfully returned.

For people who have been forced to leave home as a consequence of being an ethnic minority, the numbers in some crisis areas are less than those of the war-affected. The physical problems of their return are broadly speaking the same but added to this there is another dimension. In response to the urge to 'do something" international political leaders may insist on the return of displaced ethnic minorities as part of a wider programme of reconciliation, as they have in Bosnia. In this case the urge to return them has not been matched with an equal determination to ensure their physical safety. 'Ethnically cleansed' areas of Bosnia have been largely destroyed on a house by house basis or occupied by in-coming 'ethnically cleansed' families from an opposed sector across the inter-ethnic boundary line. Foreign governments, notably the US, have urged a reconstitution of the status quo ante without providing for its success, a familiar syndrome in the recent history of peacekeeping. The reconstitution of an ethnic minority would require a substantial, street by street, security and policing effort to ensure their safety, whereas future international plans for Bosnia anticipate a further reduction from the current level of international forces.

Here the international community faces a dilemma. Doing nothing to see the return of these displaced ethnic minorities would seem to be condoning the barbaric manner in which they were evicted. However sending them back to become minorities once again would be to reconstitute the ethnic imbalances of a very recent and explosive tragedy. Policing such an option to allow a new generation to emerge that could be freed from the revenge cycle would take decades, and as explained earlier no western politician is likely to have the political comitment to take this course. It is a no-win situation. The next best option would be to adopt a Cyprus partition solution. To be sure, it seems to condone 'ethnic cleansing', however if the interests of the families and the individuals are considered as a priority it does allow a degree to normality to reassert itself. Families once again have the chance to reunite, children can go about in security and parents can begin to make what is in relative terms a home. Instead political leaders insist on returning ethnic minorities, in most cases it must be said, with the strident support of the minorities concerned, but without any of the protection that would be essential for their survival. The burden of the problem is then delegated downwards to the civil agencies and the unarmed, and in this context, largely ineffective, International Police Task Force. But nationally and internationally governments can be seen to have acted.

Criminalisation of the Factions

In the 1990s men and boys became fighters for different reasons, some had idealistic motives, many particularly in the case of children and boys, joined in order to survive and some came for revenge and their own venal gratification. However once recruited, their different motives would become less defined in the day to day struggle for survival and revenge. During intercommunal fighting, they might have to participate in mortar attacks on crowded urban areas, fighting and killing in the compounds of working schools, hospitals and places of worship, vindictively destroying cultural treasures and on a day to day basis sniping, looting and 'ethnically cleansing' civilian families.

A faction fighter became guilty of all these things, not so much by deed as by association. After prolonged violence it was irrelevant how he came to be recruited, the fact that a man carried a weapon made him guilty in several important ways. In the eyes of his own immediate community or clan he might be a hero, but further afield, especially among the element of the civil population that had not themselves joined a faction, and had been the victims of the conflict, he would be associated with atrocities and horrible violence. Personally he might also be suffering himself and be extremely disturbed by his experience. There was a danger that a large number of fighters would return to society imbued with an overwhelming ruthlessness and lawlessness that would make it impossible to absorb them in the long term. This problem was recognised by the relief and development agencies. In Liberia plans[12] were made to accommodate fighters in campsites after the conflict was over to allow for a gradual introduction back to what was an extremely fragile society. Unfortunately the international pressures, peace process timetables and the lack of time to generate sufficient funds to pay for a prolonged encampment, put an end to their plans.

War criminals were only distinguished from faction fighters by being identified as such by the national, or more usually, the international community. Although a defined number of war criminals are cited in association with the most serious crimes in the catalogue of human wickedness, it is probable that a much greater number of faction fighters could also be charged as war criminals. They are not charged because their crimes were either too commonplace or unwitnessed. In many cases war criminals are distinguished from rank and file faction fighters because they were the leaders. Their leadership status however complicates the way in which the national or international community can deal with them. A society of demobilizing fighters is often a society in which there is already a proliferation of war criminals. The leaders, whether or not they are war criminals, in many cases continue to enjoy power and support in their own community. If a relief agency then has to deal with that community it may have to seek the approval of its (war criminal) leader. A relief agency's mandate is primarily to provide relief and not to make judgements about the behaviour of officials and leaders. For this reason many agencies seem to deal with local leaders who are known war criminals.

In crisis areas where large numbers of displaced people flee their homes and travel across hostile terrain by day and night, children become unusually vulnerable. A very large number become separated from their families. In African countries this has led to the boys becoming fighters as young as ten or eleven years old and girls becoming prostitutes or working virtually as slaves. In a country like Liberia where serious violence and population displacement has continued for seven years the statistic of separated children is a serious obstacle to achieving a civil society in the long term. Child fighters are just as likely to have committed atrocities as adult fighters. Adolescent fighters have never been to school or experienced a normal family relationship for most of their life. They are deeply disturbed young people and in many cases dysfunctional. Although the need for their careful rehabilitation is self-evident, the cost is beyond the resources of the involved state and probably beyond the reasonable capacity of rich donor states.

A Doctrine for Complex Emergencies

In British military thinking the function of doctrine is 'to establish the framework of understanding of the approach to warfare in order to provide the foundation for its practical application';[13] not to set the rules but to provide direction as an aid to understanding.[14] Military doctrine is not itself prescriptive but it provides the bricks and mortar from which prescriptions are made. Military doctrine is therefore written with extreme care and has to reflect the interests of each air, land and sea element as well as the key staff departments before it can be published. In some cases military doctrine is published only after lengthy revision and discussion. In doctrinal terms responding to complex emergencies in the 1990s presents a revolutionary situation to military doctrine writers and even more seriously to the military components that make up a national response. Peace support operations are not a fundamentally military activity although the military are an essential part. In a conventional military operation the political activity and objectives underpinning the military effort are separated by a strategic level of command from the execution of its tasks; but in complex emergencies, politics impact directly at the operational level. For various reasons no genuinely comprehensive doctrine has ever been written for peace support operations. If it were, it would have to have these characteristics:

- Include as equal partners in the drafting

- Military, maritime and air assets,

- Principal UN agencies (UNHCR,UNICEF, WHO, FAO/WFP, UNDP),

- UN civil elements (Human Rights, Civil Administration, Electoral Staff and Development Staff),

- UN or International Civil Police,

- International Committee of the Red Cross/Crescent (ICRC),

- Bilateral national donors,

- Non Government Organisations (NGOs).[15]

Reflect all the policy and institutional sensibilities of the above list.

Take a holistic view of peace support operations which allowed for each agency and contingent in this internationally diverse group to participate in their own function but also as part of an overall approach. This would require them to coordinate, even integrate, their activities with other elements of the group at specified stages of the process.

It is easy to see why, even with an overwhelming degree of international and cross-institutional bonhomie and cooperation, this would be an impossible document to draft. Moreover this is why currently accepted UK and US Peace Support Operation doctrine is essentially military and furthermore, land forces oriented. In the following paragraphs the purpose is not to develop any utopian doctrine but merely to focus narrowly on the political and institutional volte-faces which would be required for a realistically revised doctrine to address itself to the realities of a modern crisis.

The Risk

A complex emergency cannot be regarded in the same genre as the operations associated with war fighting. The actual violence may be extremely local, in relative terms low key and does not in itself usually threaten international security. Violence, when it is encountered, rates low in the scales for the use of force and in terms of the combat units involved and casualties to soldiers and equipment. The threat or risk to the international community cannot therefore be explained in purely military terms. The real risk is more convoluted but is nevertheless pervasive in its impact. It can be expressed in terms of the migration of large displaced populations from the crisis area and the long term destabilising effect that might have in the region. At the heart of the problem is usually the survival and security of a community or population rather than the possession of territory. The principle characteristic therefore of almost all complex emergencies is the presence of large numbers of traumatised and displaced people.

The Response

The international community's response must be to stabilise the situation in the short term and in the long term resettle the displaced population and foster the conditions to underwrite their future security. Because the problem involves so many aspects of civil society as well as security, the response has to reflect each of these needs. The response therefore has to be multifunctional, comprising principally military forces, relief and development agencies, human rights officials, police, lawyers, electoral organisers and economists. To be genuinely successful and to achieve a long term return to stability these disparate agencies and forces must, at some crucial stages, act together, supporting each other's objectives in a holistic manner. This requires the agencies and forces to plan together prior to deployment and agree a realistic sequence of events to stabilise the crisis area. The plan that results must take account of the functions of each element of the response. To achieve a holistic approach also requires accepting an essential minimum degree of coordination by a higher authority.

Political Approach

Leaders of the international community who wish to make a response of this nature (see above) would have to be prepared to commit resources and forces for long term overseas operations that will be measured in decades. A commitment would mean becoming involved in political oversight at the operational level (rather than devolving this responsibility to locally deployed civil agencies). It would also mean providing a military security oversight in the crisis area until a national defence force or its equivalent can be reconstituted to underwrite the authority of the elected head of state.

Defence Planning

Defence forces participating in complex emergencies would have to be prepared for the tasks of stabilisation as well as the less military tasks associated with rebuilding and policing a civil society. This would require them to have a well practised capability for warfighting as well a softer approach to information gathering and local liaison. The complex nature of these operations and the ill defined separation of political and military activities calls for a highly-professional military force. It also assumes close cooperation between national defence officials and state department or foreign office officials. The complex nature of the problem demands a holistic approach to its solution. The concept of defence officials unilaterally planning defence spending may have to give way to a broader concept of 'security spending', involving foreign aid and foreign departments; a process in which the costs of contributing to and strengthening international structures take a far greater priority. The gap between perceived warfighting needs and defence forces' real-life operations must be narrowed to reflect a more practically oriented defence force.

Operational Approaches

A successful stabilisation process in the crisis area will have to recognise that unless disarmament has been absolutely successful, power will continue to rest with the leaders of the biggest factions. A peace process which does not involve them as key actors is likely to fail and the ritualistic organisation of elections will not alter this situation. In these circumstances elections will only be successful if the most powerful faction leader is elected. The concept of parliamentary opposition will not mitigate a win/lose approach to elections. War criminals will continue to hold power in the operational area until the international response group can provide a long-term security presence to operate in areas under their control. A war criminal's influence over the community can only be diminished if the intervening international forces are evidently stronger than the factions controlled by war criminals. Displaced ethnic minorities cannot be safely returned to their original homes unless the ethnic imbalance that forced their departure has altered or a powerful third-party force will guarantee their security on a street by street basis.

The Intervening Military Presence

An intervening military presence may be provided from the UN, international coalition forces, regional forces or a single nation. Any operational plan should start from the basis that local forces are unlikely to consent to intervention operations if faction leaders stand to lose power and status at the outcome of a successful peace process. Although an effective intervening force may impartially uphold its mandate, local forces will see it as acting partially against their interests if it confronts them in enforcing the details of the mandate. An intervening military force should have the capability for warfighting. In a successful peace process there is a strong relationship between the intervening force, an effective interim government and the successful reconstitution of a reliable national defence force. An intervening force should not leave the operational area until a reliable national defence force is constituted.

Conclusion

This study takes a pessimistic view of the likely success of the international community's response to complex emergencies. The last section outlines some of the major changes of policy and attitude that would be needed to make a more successful approach to complex emergencies. These changes could be regarded as the basis of a new doctrine. In the main they constitute extremely obvious and practical statements. The doctrine they imply would however require a widespread change of attitude among the principle actors. This volte face would involve politicians, senior government officials, international civil servants, relief and development institutions and the general public who in the end provide the funds and manpower of a national response. Essentially the changes concern the need to recognise the real locus of power in the operational area and the resources and forces needed to reach the successful conclusion of a peace process. The reason for pessimism is that despite being extremely obvious ideas, no general change of attitude on these lines can be anticipated. Instead there will continue to be two separate realities: what is actually happening in the operational area, and the responding nations' perception of what is happening in the operational area. Responding nations, their political leaders, officials, military staff and the general public prefer the latter version. To try to respond in terms of the former would require a much greater commitment than they may ever be prepared to give.

NOTES

1. E. Childers and B. Urquhart, *Renewing the United Nations System* (Uppsala, Sweden: Dag Hammarskjöld Foundation 1994) pp.11–22.
2. C. Bellamy, *Knights in White Armour* (London: Pimlico 1997) pp.126–44.
3. John Mackinlay, 'Squaring the Circle: Europe's Armies Train for Peacekeeping and Warfighting', (with J. Olsen) *International Defense Review* (Oct. 1995).
4. J. Hillen, 'Military Might', *National Review*, 30 June 1997, pp.38–40.
5. J. Clarke, 'To Follow' *Proceedings*, Feb. 1995, p.47; J.F. Hillen, 'Peacekeeping is Hell', *Policy Review* 66 (Autumn 1993) pp.36–9.
6. In May 1996 the military timetable of the Dayton peace process had outstripped the civil arrangements for rehabilitation. Consequently towns like Prijedor were thronged with demobilised young men who had nowhere to look for further employment. Author's unpublished research report from a visit to Banja Luka and Prijedor May 1996.
7. J. Mackinlay and A. Alao, 'Liberia 1994: ECOMOG and UNOMIL. Response to a Complex Emergency' (NY: UN Univ., Occasional Paper No.1, 1995) p.22.
8. Stiftung Wissenschaft und Politik, 'Winning the Peace; Concept and Lessons Learned of Post-Conflict Peacebuilding' (SWP Ebenhausen, Germany, 1996) pp.54–63.
9. United Nations, *Blue Helmets* (NY: UN Dept of Information, Aug. 1990) p.364.
10. 'Multidisciplinary Peacekeeping. Lessons from Recent Experience' (UN Lessons Learned Unit, Dept of Peacekeeping Operations, Dec. 1996).
11. World Bank Discussion Paper, 'Demobilisation and Reintegration of Military Personnel in Africa', Africa Regional Series Report No IDP-130, Oct. 1993, pp.11–35.

12. UN Lessons Learned Unit (note 10) p.44; and Mackinlay and Alao (note 7) pp.31–5.
13. Joint Warfare Publication (JWP) 6-01, 'British Defence Doctrine,' (London: Ministry of Defence 1996) p.1.2.
14. Chief of Air Staff, *Royal Air Force Air Power Doctrine* (HMSO 1993) p.7.
15. John Mackinlay, *A Guide to Peace Support Operations* (Providence, RI: Thomas J. Watson Jr Inst. for Int. Studies, 1996) p.21.
16. JWP (note 13) p.1.8.

Policing the New World Disorder: Addressing Gaps in Public Security during Peace Operations

MICHAEL J. DZIEDZIC

The searing image of a US soldier being dragged through the streets of Mogadishu has defined for the American public, perhaps as much as any single event, the troubling character of the contemporary era. 'What in the World are we Doing?' the cover of *Time* magazine demanded to know on behalf of an outraged nation.[1] Less than a year later, US troops were again spearheading a multilateral coalition in the midst of chaos. The venue: Port au Prince. This time the defining image was an American soldier, pistol drawn, holding a seething Haitian mob at bay. Sprawled on the ground behind him, the intended recipient of popular justice. The photo caption reads, 'As Haitian police fade from view, US troops are being drawn into conflict.'[2] Two years later, thousands of American peacekeeping troops had been deployed to Bosnia as part of a NATO-led peace operation. Among their duties, to provide area security in the strategic, Bosnian Serb-controlled town of Brcko. In August 1997, that location became the flashpoint of an internal power struggle aimed at removing indicted war criminal, Radovan Karadzic. In retaliation for SFOR actions that aided his rival, Karadzic supporters incited street violence against US troops positioned there. Two soldiers were injured, and UN Civilian Police (CIVPOL) were forced to evacuate to nearby SFOR bases. These jarring images form a mosaic of the post-Cold War era and our reluctant role in it. In tandem with various coalition partners, we are confronting the uncertainties and peculiar challenges associated with policing a new sort of disorder in the world.

Like it or not, contemporary usage of the US military instrument in peace operations has often born little resemblance to the high-intensity, high-tech battlefields that American soldiers, sailors, and airmen have been well prepared to dominate. Indeed, the most frequent demands have come from the opposite end of the conflict spectrum, where the skills of the mediator are often more relevant, and the essence of the mission is to rehabilitate, not annihilate.

The conceptual framework sketched out below seeks to portray the

FIGURE 1
PEACE OPERATIONS CONCEPTUAL FRAMEWORK

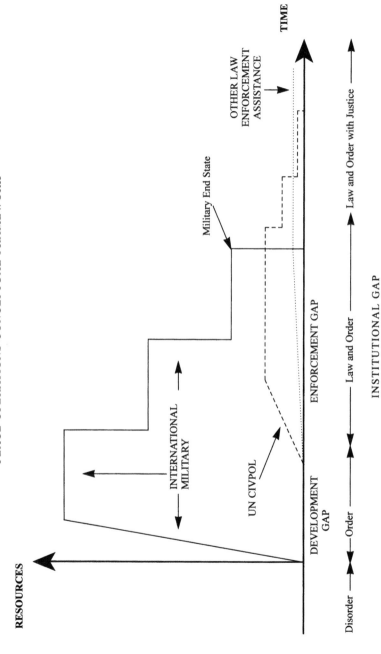

relationship of these various elements over time.

One of the more potent therapies for this new world disorder, whether administered prior to state collapse or during an international intervention, is to have local institutions of public security – policemen, judges, and jailers – function properly. Most military officers have been in uncharted territory when dealing with these matters, particularly when thrown into this complex task with a host of other international actors with whom they are largely unfamiliar (e.g., relief workers, human rights monitors, election supervisors, police trainers, etc.). Much of the learning has been on the job.

Since the dynamics producing the 'new world disorder' are unlikely to diminish any time soon, it behooves the US and the entire community of nations to refine our collective capacity to mount effective multilateral responses. This analysis seeks to address the issue by identifying gaps in public security typically confronted during peace operations and recommending measures intended to increase international proficiency at coping with them.

Peace Operations and the New World Disorder

Historically, conflict *between* states has been a predominant source of concern for soldiers and statesmen. During the post-Cold War period, however, it has been anarchic conditions *within* the sovereign state that have repeatedly posed the most acute and intractable challenges to international order. Some notable internal conflicts that have attracted international attention since 1989 had been exacerbated by the superpower rivalry (e.g., Nicaragua, El Salvador, Namibia, Angola, Mozambique, Cambodia). More recently, however, the international community has been called upon to act purely in response to dysfunctional or disintegrating states (e.g., Somalia, Yugoslavia, Liberia, Haiti, Rwanda, Zaire, Albania). Throughout the present decade (1990–97), the vast majority of battlefields have been internal to individual states; very few conflicts have resulted from inter-state warfare, the traditional concern of statecraft.

Domestic disorder, of course, is not new. The essence of this problem in many Third World states is the fragility and decay of governmental institutions, especially those devoted to responding to citizen demands, preserving law and order, and resolving internal disputes. Domestic pressures, brought on by ethnic cleavages, overpopulation, poverty, maldistribution of wealth, environmental degradation, and rapid social mobilization often outpace and even overwhelm governmental ability to respond. When internal unrest either causes a governmental meltdown or provokes draconian spasms of repression, the consequences can spill over international boundaries. Transnational forces such as massive refugee

TABLE 1

MAJOR CONFLICTS FROM 1990–1997
INVOLVING AT LEAST 1,000 BATTLE DEATHS

Continent	Civil War/International Conflicts	Interstate Conflicts
AFRICA	14 Algeria, Angola, Chad, Ethopia, Liberia, Mozambique, Rwanda, Sierra Leone, Somalia, South Africa, Sudan, Uganda, Western Sahara, Zaire	2 Chad/Libya Rwanda/Uganda
ASIA	10 Afghanistan, Bangladesh, Kampuchea, India, Indonesia, Laos, Myanmar, Philippines, Sri Lanka, Tajikistan	1 India/Pakistan
EUROPE	5 Azerbaijan, Chechnya, Georgia, Northern Ireland, *Yugoslavia	1 Armenia/Azerbaijan *Yugoslavia
MIDDLE EAST	6 Iran, Iraq, Israel, Lebanon, Turkey, Yemen	2 Iraq/Kuwait/US-led Coalition Israel/ Lebanon/Syria
LATIN AMERICA	5 Colombia, El Salvador, Guatemala, Nicaragua, Peru	0 Note: Battle deaths in the conflict between Ecuador and Peru were less than 100
TOTALS	40	7

Sources: Major armed conflict chapters, *SIPRI Yearbooks 1991–1996* (Oxford: OUP 1991–97), and 'Status of Armed Conflicts': 1994–97 map insert, *The Military Balance, 1997/98* (London: IISS, 1 Aug. 1997).

* The conflicts involving Bosnia, Croatia, and Serbia are derivatives of the disintegration of Yugoslavia.

migrations, guerrilla movements, and international criminal syndicates have increasingly been unleashed or exacerbated, threatening surrounding states. The humanitarian implications have also become more compelling. The specter of genocide or starvation, televised graphically to global audiences, has the demonstrated capacity to stir world opinion. International politics has, thus, been turned on its head: instability today often tends to emanate from the weakest of states (i.e., the 'failed state') rather than the most powerful. This anomaly has been labeled the *new world disorder.*

The consequences of this disorder for regional and international stability and the compelling humanitarian implications have eroded traditional inhibitions against intervention in the internal affairs of states. Unilateral action, however, is not considered legitimate because this could degenerate into the classic pattern of suspicion and regional/great power rivalry. The international community has preferred to act in concert, under UN or other auspices, devoting an unprecedented amount of attention and scarce resources over the past decade to ameliorating this intra-state source of international instability. The challenge for contemporary statesmen has been to organize their 'anarchic' global community for the purpose of collectively restoring order in states that are often only marginally viable.[3]

The multinational peace mission has been the preferred response. Owing to the need to separate armed domestic rivals while simultaneously restoring law and order, post-Cold War peace operations have increasingly required the contributions of both military personnel and civilian police.[4] Normally, an internationally sanctioned mandate directs the peace mission to establish a secure and stable internal environment. To fulfill this mandate, particular attention must be given to coaxing indigenous institutions of law and order into functioning in rough accordance with internationally acceptable standards. International Civilian Police (CIVPOL) members have been called upon to perform an array of tasks, therefore, including monitoring the conduct of local police cadres, training and mentoring police recruits, mediating local disputes, and even maintaining public order themselves. Owing to the complex nature of the public security challenges

TABLE 2
SIZE OF CIV-POL CONTINGENTS IN RECENT PEACE OPERATIONS

Country (Mission)	Maximum Personnel	Countries Contributing
Cambodia (UNTAC)	3,600	32
Bosnia (IPTF)	2,015	38
Haiti (IPM)	821	20
Haiti (UNMIH)	870	12
Mozambique (ONUMOZ)	1,086	29
El Salvador (ONUSAL)	341	8

involved, peace operations since the end of the Cold War have typically required sizable CIVPOL contingents. (See Table 2.)

Disorder is the phenomenon certain to be present at the inception of this genre of peace operation. It is disorder in the form of an appalling incapacity of the state to perform its most basic function – protecting its citizens. Indeed, the 'public security' apparatus itself has often been the instrument of massive public insecurity, almost to the point of genocide. Restoring *order* becomes an urgent priority.

The Deployment Gap

The initial phase of a typical, post-Cold War peace operation entails separating local armed groups (normally pursuant to a peace accord), restricting them to cantonments or assembly areas, impounding their weapons, and demobilizing many of them. In some instances, one or more of these armed forces may be totally disbanded. Owing to the uncertainty of this process and the firepower available to the disputants, a military peacekeeping force is required to inspire confidence in and verify compliance with the peace process.

Since local law-enforcement agencies have normally ceased to function or have become oppressive and even murderous forces, the international peace mission will likely confront an immediate need to perform certain police functions. Mobilizing a CIVPOL contingent is inherently time consuming, however, because most police forces do not have a significant surge capability, international mobility, or experience in operating beyond national boundaries.[5] In the early days of an intervention, therefore, the military is often the only source of order, since military forces have a capacity to deploy rapidly in unit strength, and police organizations typically do not. The military is a blunt instrument when used alone for this purpose. It is capable of imposing a basic, rigid form of order, limiting loss of life and destruction of property, but that is about all. Until the CIVPOL contingent has been deployed, therefore, the peace mission is invariably forced to deal with a deployment gap. It is one of several public security gaps that military peacekeepers are apt to confront. In this case, the gap is temporal in nature.

During this early phase, the peace mission is apt to be tested, and one vulnerable area will likely be the void in public security. If a single soldier errs by using excessive force, the entire mission can be placed in jeopardy because local consent may be squandered. Inaction, on the other hand, risks the loss of credibility and can give the impression the mission is failing. In either case, the peace operation may confront a 'defining moment' before it is well postured to respond. The media spotlight will be unavoidable, since the actions (or inaction) of a deploying peace mission invariably produce dramatic TV news footage. The consequences of failing to cope adequately with such challenges on public opinion and the credibility of the peace mission can be enduring.

US policy makers received early warning of the pitfalls associated with a deployment gap by virtue of their experiences with the 1989 Panama operation. Although the US intervention to remove General Manuel Noriega was a purely unilateral action, it demonstrated a fundamental point for future peace operations: any intervention force – unilateral or multilateral – that removes or replaces local authority will find itself responsible for maintaining public security. In Panama, a breakdown between planning levels resulted in an initial failure to provide public security.

The intervention in Panama was coincident with the end of the Cold War, and the UN was soon being called upon to mop up the vestiges of superpower rivalry in places like Cambodia, El Salvador, Mozambique, and Angola. The United Nations Transitional Authority in Cambodia (UNTAC) was established shortly after the four factions vying for power there agreed to the Paris Accords in October 1991. Although deployment of UNTAC's military contingent required about five months, the CIVPOL unit was not fully fielded until November 1992, when the planned 18-month mission was half way to completion. This deployment gap, among other factors, contributed to the loss of vital credibility from which the mission never satisfactorily recovered.

The magnitude of the deployment gap was reduced but not eliminated in subsequent operations in Haiti and Bosnia. Although provisions had been made by the US to field International Police Monitors (IPMs) in Haiti, soldiers of the US-led Multi-National Force (MNF) were still left on their own with the task of maintaining order during the first chaotic weeks of the intervention. When Haitian police began openly brutalizing their own people, the military force was compelled to reassess its Rules of Engagement (ROEs) and assume a law enforcement role. In Bosnia, the first crucial test of compliance with the Dayton Accords involved the transfer of Sarajevo suburbs to Muslim control. Even though the transfer was postponed for 45 days, the International Police Task Force (IPTF) had scarcely begun to be fielded when that 'defining moment' arrived. The civil disorders that accompanied this process and the mass exodus of Serbs, despite the presence of the IPTF and IFOR, were not reassuring occurrences for those aspiring to a multi-ethnic Bosnia.

Recommendations for Addressing the Deployment Gap

There are two basic remedies. To minimize the gap, *the capacity of the international community to mobilize CIVPOL personnel should be strengthened*, both within contributing states and at the United Nations. Since this gap probably cannot be closed entirely in most cases, *the military also needs to be prepared to discharge this function, on an interim basis*, until the security environment has been sufficiently stabilized and the CIVPOL contingent has become operational. The recommendations put forth in the following section are intended to address these two requirements.

Develop a Stand-by Force of Trained CIVPOL Personnel

The Stand-by Force concept for assembling military troop contributions to peace operations should be adapted for use in CIVPOL mobilization.[6] The most significant difference would be that individuals, rather than entire units, would need to be designated as notionally available. Member states would have to assume responsibility for ensuring their volunteers had received advanced training, either in-country or in certain third countries specializing in international police training (e.g., Norway, Spain, Canada, etc.). The CIVPOL office within the UN Department of Peacekeeping Operations (DPKO) would require additional staffing so it could establish training standards and procedures, identify the spectrum of specialized skills required, establish a team to oversee this function, and maintain a database of stand-by personnel and organizations (See CIVPOL Resources, below). A CIVPOL Stand-by Force would also require rapid access to necessary equipment and supplies. The United Nations should also seek to identify a cadre of judicial experts for standby status and rapid deployment alongside police specialists.

At present, recruitment of US personnel for UN CIVPOL missions or 'coalitions of the willing' is essentially *ad hoc*. It badly needs improvement. A first step would be to establish a cooperative arrangement between the Department of Justice's International Criminal Investigative Training Assistance Program (ICITAP) and major city police chiefs allowing them to identify their best candidates for CIVPOL duties. Additional measures to recruit qualified local and state police personnel should also be developed. Similar action needs to be taken to recruit qualified personnel with backgrounds in penal and judicial reform, working with organizations such as the Bureau of Prisons, state prison systems, and the American Bar Association. Another, parallel measure could be the consolidation and standardization of databases within DOD which indicate US Reserve and National Guard personnel with civilian police experience or with military experience as MPs or Special Forces. This database would be a step toward establishing a national CIVPOL stand-by force. (The latter would require a program of identifying, recruiting and training standby personnel for UN or US bilateral civilian police programs.) The next step would be to incorporate volunteers from state and local police forces into this database. (Key Actors: United Nations and Member States)

Include CIVPOL in UN Assessment Teams and the Deployable Headquarters

Experienced CIVPOL personnel should be incorporated into the UN's Rapidly Deployable Mission Headquarters (RDMHQ) and all UN pre-mission assessment teams. To support the RDMHQ, a cadre of prospective supervisory personnel with experience in international policing and in administering police and judicial organizations would need to be identified and maintained in a reserve status by the UN CIVPOL office (perhaps as a special category of the Stand-By Force recommended above). The assessment team should include civilian law enforcement specialists to examine all aspects of the impending CIVPOL mission, the resources required, the viability of the current public security apparatus (police, judiciary/legal code, prisons), and the extent of consent among elites and the local population to accept the peace mission. It would also be beneficial to include specialists in the legal tradition and culture of the nation-state involved so that mission-specific planning can be tailored to local circumstances. The assessment should strive to do more than describe the structures of public security and their present capabilities; it should also seek to understand the popular legitimacy of each, the prevailing 'legal culture', and the dynamics that determine their actual functioning. (Key Actor: United Nations)

Recruit a Full Spectrum of Skills for the CIVPOL Contingent

Until recently, the typical pattern of recruitment by the UN had been to solicit volunteers from member states using a very basic set of criteria, such as a given number of years experience in policing, fluency in the mission language (normally English), and driving ability. For the most recent cadre of police monitors in Bosnia, however, the UN has also asked contributing nations to provide volunteers who have the specific skills and ranks needed for that operation. This is a major advance, and recruitment of future CIVPOL contingents should continue to be done on the basis of specific personnel needs (e.g., administration of justice and of police academies, penal system reform, internal affairs/inspector general, criminal investigations, organized crime, and field training). Future recruitment should also specify the seniority or years of service desired for each position to avoid inundating CIVPOL headquarters with an excess of superannuated officers interested primarily in sinecures and perquisites. An effort should also be made to recruit personnel proficient in the indigenous language of the country where the mission is taking place.

Continuing emphasis should be placed on obtaining credible performance evaluations on CIVPOL personnel during each mission. The purpose would be to identify both incompetent personnel, so they can be removed expeditiously, and the most qualified, so they can be groomed for potential supervisory positions in future missions.

(Key Actors: United Nations and Member States)

Improve CIVPOL Training

Over the past several years there has been progress in developing handbooks and field guides on international human rights standards for CIVPOL and screening/testing of prospective CIVPOL personnel prior to deployment. The performance of CIVPOL personnel could be further enhanced through a standardized program of advanced training. This would cover such universally applicable subjects as the international standards that apply across the full range of public security functions; the general differences among legal systems based on the Napoleonic Code, English Common Law, and the Sharia; and techniques for effective monitoring and mentoring. This would be in addition to country-specific pre-mission training dealing with local cultural traits, contemporary political realities, and security threats in the mission area. English language training should also be made liberally available to CIVPOL stand-by volunteers. Such programs would need to be conducted by the member states (perhaps using regional training centers) according to standards developed by the UNCIVPOL office.

In addition to basic CIVPOL training programs, there is a need for multilateral training and exercises. This would emulate the considerable number of multilateral military peacekeeping exercises, such as those conducted by NATO and PFP militaries and by US and Latin American militaries. This would substantially improve collective civilian capabilities for police operations, as it has for military forces. In addition, military planners should incorporate CIVPOL elements in their exercise scenarios.

(Key Actors: United Nations and member states)

Expand CIVPOL Resources

The UN CIVPOL office is authorized one full-time official who is presently supplemented by five specialists seconded from member states at no cost to the UN. This is woefully insufficient given that there are some 3,000 CIVPOL personnel in the field under the nominal supervision of this office.

Present requirements for mobilizing, training, equipping, and sustaining CIVPOL field operations greatly outstrip current capabilities. Yet, there is pressure from the Non-Aligned Movement to end the practice of secondment, which would deprive the CIVPOL office of its five *pro bono* specialists. This would be highly counterproductive and tantamount to abandonment of concern for this function. Implementation of the recommendations made here, moreover, such as a CIVPOL Stand-by Force, would require additional staffing, computerization, and financial resources.

The UN and member states need to assign a higher priority to supporting CIVPOL activities. The CIVPOL office has been commendably flexible in welcoming various forms of assistance for CIVPOL activities via bilateral government programs and NGOs. To a limited degree, CIVPOL's personnel shortcomings might be ameliorated by greater integration with and support from other elements of DPKO (for equipment, logistics, etc.). However, DPKO also faces severe personnel and budgetary pressures. Thus, an increase in funding for CIVPOL is essential but, given present UN budgetary stringencies, highly unlikely until the US has paid the bulk of its arrears.

(Key Actors: United Nations and Member States)

Develop a Generic Public Security Plan

An effective CIVPOL operation plan will be much easier to prepare if there is a generic plan to use as a template. Each mission will confront anew various fundamental choices: whether CIVPOL should be armed and have 'executive authority' to enforce local law; whether the military and CIVPOL should have common communications and logistics systems and engage in joint patrolling; and how civil disturbances and other types of unrest are to be handled. The generic plan should discuss the pros and cons of the basic courses of actions available. To ensure that vital lessons gleaned from previous peace operations are reliably acted upon by future CIVPOL commissioners, UN DPKO should oversee this process. A Public Security Plan should also be an integral component of the US interagency political-military planning process.

This plan would identify the functions to be performed by members of the international community (e.g., UN CIVPOL, bilateral governments, and NGOs), address all elements of public security (i.e., judiciary/legal code, police, and corrections system), specify the resources and personnel normally required for each function and the likely sources for each; and provide general guidance regarding the relationships that should be developed with local authorities, the military contingent, and other entities contributing to the mission. Other functional issues to be considered would be how former combatants are to be demobilized, disarmed, and reintegrated into civil society; the potential for vigilante activity by police if the judiciary does not function; whether the international community should provide funding for judicial and police salaries until the government can do so adequately; the sanctions and inducements available to encourage compliance with reform of the public security apparatus; possible placement of experienced international advisors within ministries involved in public security; how the safety of CIVPOL personnel will be preserved; and if necessary, how evacuation will be accomplished.

While a generic plan can serve as a rough and ready guide, it must be tailored to the circumstances of each contingency. The generic plan would, thus, be the starting point for mission-specific planning for each new operation. The plan will need to be reviewed and revised as the mission unfolds, as conditions change, and as more is learned from exposure to reality on the ground. Rigidity is to be avoided. In addition, there should be a dynamic mechanism for capturing lessons learned after each peace operation and for revising the generic plan as warranted.

(Key Actors: United Nations and Member States contributing to CIVPOL)

Include Constabulary Forces and Civil Affairs Police Specialists in Initial Military Contingent

While steps can and should be taken to accelerate CIVPOL mobilization and overall capacity, there will continue to be a high probability that in most cases there will be a considerable lag between the deployment of the military and CIVPOL contingents. Additionally, a high threat of violence during the initial period of international intervention may militate against effective CIVPOL operations until the military contingent has been able to stabilize the situation (e.g., until the process of cantonment of former combatants has begun). Military peacekeepers will need to be prepared to perform constabulary functions on an interim basis, therefore, during the earliest stages of such peace missions. Military planners should ensure that adequate military police or gendarme units are incorporated in the initial deployment.

Careful attention must be given to specification of the mission, tasks, and Rules of Engagement (ROEs) for these units. ROEs must be crafted with prudence and precision indicating circumstances under which military forces are to act to preserve law and order. Issues to be addressed include responses to violence within the local population, authority to arrest and detain local citizens and their subsequent disposition, and the extent of training assistance that troops are permitted to provide indigenous police and judicial authorities. Other issues are the nature of the relationship with local police forces, the process by which CIVPOL will ultimately assume its responsibilities from the military, and the nature of the subsequent CIVPOL/military relationship.

In addition, US Army Civil Affairs personnel with backgrounds in planning, logistics, and police operations should be assigned to work with the CIVPOL commissioner, as soon as one has been designated, to facilitate CIVPOL deployment and military support to it. Intelligence and public information assets, along with communications and logistics capabilities of the military contingent should also be closely coordinated with CIVPOL since they can make vital contributions to restoration of public order.

(Key Actors: Military and CIVPOL Planners at the United Nations and Member States)

Increase Constabulary Capabilities

Some military establishments already possess a very significant constabulary capability, that is, units capable of maintaining public order by performing both law enforcement and light infantry operations (e.g., US Military Police and Special Forces, French Gendarmerie, Spanish Guardia Civil, Chilean Carabineros, Argentine Gendarmes, and Italian *Carabiniere*). Such units should be explicitly solicited from donor nations when there is a serious prospect that an impending peace operation will have to cope with significant public disorder. In circumstances where the potential for violence is not high, constabulary forces could be considered as a substitute for regular combat forces in peace operations.

Overuse of this remedy could overtax the finite number of member states currently possessing such a 'constabulary' capability. Additional training, manpower, and other resources would undoubtedly be required if there were to be significant and recurring missions for such units. Thus, there are inherent limitations in this approach, unless member states would be amenable to expanding their constabulary forces and/or assisting other countries to develop an enhanced capability in response to this need. Owing to sensitivities about the possible impact on civil-military relations, assistance to member states for the purpose of developing new 'constabulary' forces would need to be considered on a case-by-case basis.

(Key Actors: UN; Member States)

The Enforcement Gap

Whereas the deployment gap was about timing, the gap in enforcement is about function. When serious lawlessness breaks out or when one of the disputants acts to thwart the peace process, the peace mission can be acutely challenged since the capabilities of the military and police contingents to deal with these situations normally do not overlap. After sufficient CIVPOL members have been deployed, they monitor the indigenous public security apparatus (assuming the latter remains in existence) or assist with the creation of an entirely new police force and judiciary, if that is necessary. The 'inner shell' of public security for individual crimes and small-scale disturbances, therefore, will usually be provided by some hybrid of the indigenous police and CIVPOL. The military component normally shifts to a 'rapid reaction' mode, thus providing the 'outer shell' or area security. An *enforcement gap* is likely to arise when the peace mission is confronted with the need to perform functions that fall between these inner and outer layers. Typically, these actions relate either to *serious challenges to law and order* or *noncompliance with the peace agreement*.

In the first case, international CIVPOL are incapable of dealing with organized crime, heavily armed gangs, and violent domestic disorder, all of which may flourish in post-conflict situations. This applies whether or not CIVPOL are armed and have arrest authority added to their mandate. The local government is typically characterized by an extremely weak or dysfunctional domestic law-enforcement apparatus while society is awash with automatic weapons and unemployed ex-combatants whose job prospects are extremely limited. The latter may be tempted to join the criminal underworld, and international criminal syndicates may seek to exploit any void in law enforcement by insinuating themselves into the fabric of government and society. While the military intervention force may have great firepower, only specialized units such as military police, gendarmes, or Special Forces have the training and resources to engage effectively in law enforcement activities. Such units have not always been included in peace forces. Even when they have been available and the mandate has permitted military involvement in law enforcement, there has sometimes been considerable reluctance by military commanders to use them for this purpose, out of concern this could make it difficult to disengage or incite popular opposition.

The second variant of this gap deals with enforcement of the peace agreement, as opposed to local laws. When one or more of the former disputants is unwilling to abide by or implement aspects of their peace accord, the military contingent may be prevailed upon to compel compliance. To the extent this is done, the peace mission runs the risk of losing consent from at least one of the parties, potentially leading to civil disturbances and more violent forms of opposition to their continued presence. In many cases, moreover, the international community will also be attempting to promote the transformation of the police force from an instrument of state repression into a servant of the people. Policing is inherently political, and such a role reversal for the forces of public security can profoundly affect the domestic distribution of power.[7] This is another area that could precipitate serious local resistance.

Military forces are reluctant to engage in confrontations with civilians because, with the exception of constabulary units, they are generally not trained in the measured use of force, control of riots, negotiating techniques, or de-escalation of conflict. As noted above, CIVPOL is not capable of handling violent challenges, either.

The Cambodian experience reinforced the need to be attentive to political consent, especially when implementation of the peace accord has the potential to alter the internal balance of power. The incapacity of the UN Transitional Authority in Cambodia (UNTAC) to enforce the cantonment process as specified in the Paris Accord caused a fundamental reorientation at the mid-point of the mission. Military and CIVPOL resources were reconfigured so they could operate jointly, and their mission was reduced to manageable proportions (i.e., providing security for the electoral process).

The Haitian case demonstrates several promising approaches to this issue. Among them is the benefit of unity of purpose for military and police components, pre-mission training, and a comprehensive political-military plan for US government agencies involved. The experiences of the Multi-National Force (MNF) and UN Mission In Haiti (UNMIH) might serve as a model for achieving smooth transitions and overall unity of effort. There was a single individual in charge of the operation, to whom both the police and military contingent commanders were subordinated (for this to function well, these individuals must be capable of working together as a team). At the operational level, police and military command posts were co-located, and both forces used the same communication network, information/intelligence structures, and logistics support system. At the tactical level, military policemen were temporarily assigned to duty in local police stations to accompany CIVPOL and local police on patrols. In Bosnia, the enforcement challenge was even more demanding and unity of effort was much more difficult to achieve owing, in large part, to the division of international responsibilities among a welter of divergent actors. Although the final word on Bosnia is far from written, IFOR/SFOR and the IPTF (International Police Task Force) have traveled an arduous path in their struggle to narrow the enforcement gap for implementation of the civilian aspects of the Dayton Accords.

Somalia provides both positive and negative examples of the enforcement gap. The UNITAF phase provided a remarkable example of the value of a reasonably professional indigenous police force, supported by military peacekeeping forces in dealing with the enforcement gap (in this case without CIVPOL involvement). The Somali Auxiliary Security Force (ASF) was actually capable of functioning in the absence of other governmental structures. The subsequent demise of the UNOSOM II mission is a classic case of the enforcement gap, as the military intervention force sought to apprehend Muhammed Farah Aideed, becoming a protagonist in the internal violent dispute without the means or the will to do so.

Recommendations for Addressing the Enforcement Gap

To address the void in local law enforcement, the most workable option is generally *an interim police force* assembled, after careful screening, from local government security forces and monitored closely by CIVPOL.

When the enforcement gap involves a need to promote compliance with provisions of a peace agreement, the most promising approach is to bring all resources of the peace operation to bear in a coordinated fashion. In particular, this entails *integrated and mutually reinforcing operations by the military and CIVPOL contingents.* Absent such unity of effort, this gap in public security can become acute and threaten the success of the entire mission.

Create an Interim Police Force from Vetted Local Personnel

In most cases, the local police force will not be held in very high public esteem. Thus, in seeking to fill the law enforcement gap, the challenge will be to convert what may have been a predatory and illegitimate force into at least a visible facade of law enforcement (as in Haiti with the Interim Public Security Force). This allows local law to be applied and minimizes confrontations between the peace force and the local population. This will entail vetting of notoriously corrupt or sadistic personnel, a retraining program to make those retained on duty aware of their new performance standards, adequate matériel support, supervision by CIVPOL monitors, and, perhaps, joint patrolling with military police, as well. A mechanism for funding salaries and operational expenses of this interim police force must be anticipated, since revenue collection is apt to have broken down along with other government functions.

One of the inherent dangers that must be guarded against is the inclination for interim policemen to exploit what they may regard as their final opportunity in a police uniform to enrich themselves through extortion or outright banditry. Stifling this requires a competent, adequately staffed, and fully engaged CIVPOL force, often with military support. It also means holding out opportunities for individuals in the interim force to become members of a permanent force if their current behavior and past records meet proper standards. Throughout this process a public information campaign should keep the general public informed about the mission's intentions and the new standards to expect from the police.
(Key Actors: Special Representative of Secretary General or Equivalent in Charge of the Peace Mission; CIVPOL; Military Contingent Commander; Local Officials)

Resolve the Demobilization Dilemma

In a post-conflict environment, the rates of violent crime, especially assault with automatic weapons, are apt to be soaring. Government security forces are typically restricted to cantonment areas or demobilized, creating a void in public order. As public alarm mounts along with the crime rate, the retention of elite police units and supervisors who have had the benefit of extensive training and years of experience becomes very appealing. The dilemma arises because these same individuals and specialized units are often guilty of grave human rights abuses and rampant corruption.

Past experience indicates it is generally preferable to disband elite units, vet the personnel, require the holdovers to be fully retrained, and permit them back only on an individual basis to prevent them from coalescing as a group and usurping control over the fledgling police force. Similarly, there will be a great temptation to retain experienced police supervisors because the remainder of the police force will be comprised of newly trained rookies. Once again, extreme care must be exercised, because whoever is allowed to assign these individuals to senior posts will be in a strong position to monopolize power over the long haul. In the long run, prospects for law enforcement that is both proficient and endowed with an ethos of public service hinges on fundamentally altering the police culture. Retaining specialized units or cadres of previous supervisory personnel (especially mid-level supervisors) could constitute an insurmountable barrier to essential change.

Another dimension of the demobilization dilemma is the concern that former security personnel may be unable to find gainful employment and will therefore turn to criminal activity to support themselves. Given their training, discipline, and knowledge of the criminal underworld, this is a realistic possibility. Demobilization or retraining programs are an obvious answer, but, as in Haiti, there may be considerable political resistance to providing special assistance to the same nefarious group that had formerly victimized their fellow citizens.

(Key Actors: Special Representative of Secretary-General or equivalent in charge of the peace mission; CIVPOL; commander of military contingent; local government officials; donor nations funding retraining programs; ICITAP and other bilateral government agencies)

Establish Unity and Continuity of Effort between CIVPOL and Military Contingents

The most effective way to deal with a gap in enforcement of the peace accord is via mutually reinforcing operations between the international military and CIVPOL contingents. Haiti provides the model, enhancing unity of effort in a variety of areas. First, information about potential threats, forthcoming operations, and other mutual concerns can be passed freely between the military and CIVPOL organizations by virtue of a common communications net, a shared command post, and intermingling of personnel in the field. Second, the presence of military forces serves as a deterrent against armed resistance to CIVPOL and their local counterparts, boosting their morale and effectiveness. Third, the use of common communication and logistics networks allows for economies of scale, interoperability, and other efficiencies. Finally, joint planning by the military and CIVPOL should make the response to contingencies much more timely and effective.

Maximizing unity of effort also requires recognition of the need for Civil Affairs personnel to work with CIVPOL, as well as for effective coordination of public information and intelligence capabilities. CIVPOL personnel also serve as a rich and timely source of raw intelligence data. Assuring a continuous and timely exchange of information should be a high priority. The efficacy of the military's public information campaign in shaping local attitudes toward CIVPOL activities was clearly demonstrated in Haiti. Such capabilities are not found in normal UN CIVPOL deployments, therefore, arrangements for military support in this area should be included in military planning. After the military peacekeeping mission has ended, a few Military Police, Civil Affairs, intelligence, and public information personnel may be required to remain with CIVPOL temporarily to ensure a smooth transition and continuity of effort. (Key Actors: UN DPKO; Special Representative of Secretary-General or equivalent in charge of the peace mission; CIVPOL and military contingent commanders; member states contributing military or police personnel)

Sanctions and Inducements

Even the most unified and well-coordinated peace mission will not, by virtue of this factor alone, be able to overcome deficient political will on the part of one or more of the parties. Assuming the international coalition is reasonably unified regarding the desired outcome (or end state), it may be possible to encourage greater compliance through a coordinated package of international sanctions and inducements. One of the dilemmas for those concerned with reforming the instruments of public security is that suspending public security reform programs as a sanction for misconduct might be counterproductive. The lack of effective measures against defiance by Bosnian Serb police and interior ministry officials was a chronic liability for IPTF Commissioners.[8] (Key Actors: UN DPKO; Special Representative of Secretary-General [SRSG] or equivalent in charge of the peace mission; CIVPOL and military contingent commanders; member states contributing military or police personnel)

The Institutional Gap

Whereas the deployment gap was *temporal* and the enforcement gap was *functional* in nature, the institutional gap is a matter of political *development*. The first two gaps pertain to the relationship between the military and civilian police components of a peace operation. The institutional gap, in contrast, refers to the incapacity of the host government to provide public order, especially when measured against international standards for policing and human rights. Law and order alone do not guarantee sustainable security, since, without justice, the likely result is oppression. That, in turn, could set the stage for another cycle of institutional decay and collapse. *Sustainable security,* therefore, requires that *law and order* be combined with an adequate measure of *justice* for all. The *institutional gap*, therefore, is the difference in development between a public security apparatus that is responsive to the entire citizenry and one that is dysfunctional (or not functioning at all).

For society to begin resuming normal activity, law and order are required. This is the domain of police, judges, and jailers. Rather than becoming a surrogate for malfunctioning institutions of law and order, the international community aspires to foster their progressive development. Domestic police forces, however, are often ill-trained, inadequately equipped, and lacking in discipline. They usually do not command the trust or respect of the citizenry and are often themselves among the more notorious criminal offenders. The judiciary and penal systems are apt to be similarly dysfunctional and overwhelmed. Thus, before local authorities can effectively assume responsibility, a reorganization of the entire public security system (i.e., police, courts/legal code, and prisons) may be necessary. The international community, including CIVPOL, will need to play an integral role in this institution-building process.

Closing the institutional public security gap normally entails removal of unsuitable local personnel from the ranks and formation of a new cadre of police and supervisors. After replacements complete basic police training, they will require mentoring (or on-the-job training) for a considerable period. Until the local police force has been reconstituted and is able to maintain public security autonomously, there will be a continuous need for international assistance. This entails use of international civilian trainers and mentors, including CIVPOL and other forms of international policing assistance. This assistance begins while the military contingent is present, but it ought to continue well after their departure (five years is often used as a rule of thumb for such major institution-building projects). Even if the local police force eventually proves to be willing and capable, the entire process will ultimately be of little benefit unless the courts, criminal code, and penal system have also undergone a similar transformation. If these potential deficiencies are not adequately addressed, the likely result will be the re-emergence of conditions that precipitated the peace operation in the first place.

This is, in essence, what transpired in Cambodia. Rehabilitation of the public security infrastructure was not one of the missions. This and other factors made UNTAC's contributions 'highly perishable' and the political regime it had ushered into existence at great expense was ultimately vulnerable to collapse. In El Salvador, in contrast, the international community undertook to replace the entire police force. The spectrum of challenges included assembling sufficient human and financial resources from the international community, eliminating incompetent or corrupt former members of the police, developing a leadership hierarchy, and training a new force. Although the Salvadoran case deserves its acclaim as the poster child of peace operations, it also serves as a cautionary tale about the damage wrought by neglecting to undertake judicial and penal reform in tandem with enhancements in policing. Similarly, Haiti shows the corrosive effects on a replacement police force, even one receiving substantial ongoing international assistance, when judicial reform lags far behind.

Recommendations for Addressing the Institutional Gap

A blueprint for achieving sustainable security ought to be considered a centerpiece of any 'Exit Strategy'. First, the structural components of indigenous public security (police, judiciary/legal code, and prisons) must achieve at least *a basic capacity to maintain law and order* by capitalizing on the international assistance available to them. This process should begin as soon as possible during the peace operation.

The second and more challenging task is to *imbue these structures of public security with an ethos of public service* and impartiality, and to bolster societal mechanisms of accountability. Achieving law and order with justice under these circumstances is a long-term process requiring international and indigenous mechanisms for generating and sustaining the requisite political will. This process brings a host of additional players to the forefront. Among the more prominent are specialists in public administration, human rights, electoral processes, and journalism.

Strive for Multilateral Cohesion

The UN CIVPOL office has been commendably flexible in blending bilateral assistance programs together with the efforts of CIVPOL operations in the field. This has ranged from US ICITAP taking responsibility for creating and operating police and judicial academies and training programs (e.g., Haiti and Bosnia), to France and Canada providing personnel for police and judicial activities in parallel with CIVPOL, to Norway and Spain offering training to prospective CIVPOL personnel from other countries. This is constructive and should be continued, especially given CIVPOL's resource limitations. However, it should be more systematic and more member states should be encouraged to become active if there is to be an enduring improvement in the law enforcement capability of states being assisted.

Multilateral cohesion requires a process of coordination embracing not merely member states but also key IGOs and NGOs involved in a peace operation, as well. There needs to be greater integration of DPKO with the Crime Prevention and Criminal Justice Division, the United Nations Development Program (UNDP) and other elements of the UN system, since public safety assistance goes well beyond policing and is a long-term developmental as well as peacekeeping function. A suitable method for achieving this would be to establish a clearinghouse within the United Nations for pre-mission coordination. While this process could never be mandatory or binding, it should at least aim to identify the external actors expected to be involved, their anticipated contributions, and how they will interact/coordinate with each other.[9] The purpose would be to facilitate the sharing of intentions and coordination of plans among the various actors associated with a pending or ongoing peace mission, (public security would not be the only aspect of peace operations that would benefit from such a mechanism). A centralized database, perhaps building upon the computerized system used for refugee integration in Bosnia by SFOR, UNHCR, and the Office of the High Representative could be developed as the centerpiece of this effort.

Once the mission has begun, the CIVPOL Commissioner and the senior international civilian and military representatives should take the initiative to establish a suitable mechanism for communication and coordination with other actors providing assistance in the realm of public security, including NGOs, IGOs, and member states conducting bilateral assistance programs. The Commissioner should also work closely with the military commander and under the unifying direction of the senior civilian authority (e.g., UN SRSG, High Representative, etc.) to coordinate with other actors in the areas of human rights, elections, refugee resettlement and related issues.

(Key Actors: UN DPKO; the SRSG; the CIVPOL contingent; the military contingent; member states; relevant IGOs and NGOs)

Strengthen Follow-on Assistance Agencies for Public Security

To redress severe deficiencies in the public security system effectively requires a prolonged commitment by the international community. Thorough reformation of the police force alone is normally at least a five-year proposition; the judiciary requires even more time, due to the extensive educational requirements and experience required for most judicial posts. Public attitudes and expectations toward the legal system must also be altered, and support for the rule of law must be engendered within civil society (including human rights organizations and a free press). These reforms should begin as soon as possible during the peacekeeping phase and continue as a foundation for peace building. Once this has begun to happen and the peace process has become irreversible, there is no further need for the presence of a military intervention force.

One of the areas requiring particular development is follow-on assistance after the departure of military forces. Resources and programs need to be marshaled to consolidate and sustain advances made during the military phase of the peace operation. In the US, the Agency for International Development (AID) and ICITAP are crucial for this purpose, yet their funding is far from robust. ICITAP is the only US government agency with an exclusive focus on assistance to public security organizations outside the US. In spite of its pivotal role ICITAP is only a temporary organization within the Department of Justice, without permanently funded staff or programs. To protect US interests from transnational criminal activity abroad, it is crucial that this be corrected. Other bilateral public security assistance programs and NGOs can also make a crucial contribution to development of institutions in civil society that will provide accountability for the police, judiciary, and prisons. (Key Actors: AID, ICITAP, and other bilateral assistance programs; human rights organizations; American Bar Association; other relevant NGOs)

Refine Standards for Public Security and Criminal Justice Activities

International standards for policing have been prepared by the UN Crime Prevention and Criminal Justice Division (UNCPCJD). However, they are general in nature. The IPTF in Bosnia developed Commissioner's Guidance, which specifies the actual conduct expected of policemen in the Federation and the Serb Republic.[10] The UNCPCJD also developed a Guideline for the Conduct of Public Justice in Cambodia (even though its utility there was rather limited). Building on these initiatives, the UN should endeavor to refine international standards for policing, as well as for the judiciary and penal system. As the IPTF Commissioner's Guidance has done, emphasis should be on providing specific, observable, and objective measures that can be used by monitors to evaluate the conduct of personnel involved in public security functions. Prior to deployment, CIVPOL monitors should receive training on these standards and a Field Training Guide should be developed reflecting them. (Key Actors: UN DPKO; UN High Commissioner on Human Rights; UN Crime Prevention and Criminal Justice Division; member states)

Include Public Security and Criminal Justice Responsibilities in the Mandate

If warranted, authority for CIVPOL and military peacekeepers to reform the police, judiciary/legal code, and penal system, in conformance with internationally accepted standards, should be explicitly articulated in the mandate. The more detailed the mandate and peace agreement are about required reforms, the more leverage CIVPOL will have to press effectively for compliance. If possible, international standards for public security institutions should be incorporated into any peace agreement that serves as a basis for the peace operation. Authority to resolve conflicts between local law and international standards should be allocated in the mandate to the Special Representative of the Secretary-General or equivalent. If warranted, the mandate should also include authority to certify the fitness of local police and cashier those deemed by the CIVPOL Commissioner to be responsible for gross human rights abuses or serious corruption. Provision should be made in both the mandate and the law enforcement plan to establish an indigenous police oversight body to ensure accountability to the public after CIVPOL departs and for civilian assistance to continue after the military phase has concluded.

Seize the Initiative

The early phase of an intervention is likely to be fraught with uncertainty about the willingness of the disputants to cooperate with the intervention force; however, this is also the moment of greatest opportunity to set in motion the dynamics necessary to complete the mission successfully. Institutional reformers should capitalize on local war weariness, the state of flux, and the positive shock effect of international intervention to obtain necessary concessions and acceptance of a robust interpretation of the mandate. The emphasis ought to be on securing broad freedom of action for the peace force, but care should be taken in actually asserting this authority until commanders gain a clearer understanding of local political realities. The military phase of the intervention should not be squandered, since this presence in significant numbers is of limited duration. The longer an external military force remains deployed on the ground, the more it is apt to

be perceived as an occupation army.
(Key Actors: UN Security Council; UN DPKO; member states; the military contingent)

Strengthen Civil Society

In the long run, the objective of sustainable security will only be assured when impunity is no longer the norm, and justice is perceived to be available to all, even if not on a totally equal footing. Achieving this aim entails mobilization and strengthening of civil society. This is the only way that institutions of public security will ultimately be held accountable for their conduct. Specific functions that are conducive to this outcome are a free press, open elections, availability of *pro bono* defense counsels for the indigent and minorities, domestic human rights monitoring organizations with international sponsorship, ombudsmen or similar mechanisms to promote transparency of public security institutions, and public access to police via hot line (911 equivalent). The exact form that these take must be carefully crafted so as to be compatible with local culture and tradition.

This process involves arousing a sense of efficacy in the average citizen and a conviction that public security ought to be a public good not a private privilege. The political culture must be altered, therefore, so repressive behavior by the police is not reinforced because that is what the populace expects. Public education is a crucial component of the process of altering expectations. In this regard, the public information resources of the military intervention force, as well as civilian agencies, ought to be put to maximum use. There should be planning for coordinated actions by both military and civilian elements of the peace mission to strengthen civil society as well as promote good communication with local authorities. It will also be vitally important to nurture public support when sanctions are required to promote needed reform of the police, penal system, or judiciary. At the end of the day, civil society is the constituency that stands to gain if justice and order become the norm.
(Key Actors: UNDP; UN High Commissioner on Human Rights; UN Crime Prevention and Criminal Justice Division; CIVPOL; member states, relevant NGOs)

Promote De Facto *Separation of Power Between the Executive and Judiciary*

Injustice, impunity, and exploitation of the police and legal system to repress political opponents are often major contributing factors to the governmental meltdown that causes an international intervention. If the judicial process has been co-opted by the executive branch, its primary function invariably becomes perpetuation in power of the current governing elite. To alter this fundamentally, so justice ultimately prevails and the cycle of repression and governmental decay does not repeat itself, the power of the executive over the judiciary should be checked by other forces, such as the legislative branch and civil society. This would likely include limiting or balancing executive prerogatives in such areas as judicial appointments, budgetary allocations, and physical security.

(Key Actors: Local government; SRSG; human rights organizations).

The conceptual framework sketched out above in Figure 1 (p.133) seeks to portray the relationship of these various elements over time.

Conclusion

To address all three public security gaps adequately is a challenging proposition. As a provisional guide for those assuming peace-building responsibilities in the future, the following summarize the central propositions:

Sustainable Public Security Is Not Always Possible

Not all internal conflicts are ripe for the ministrations of a peace operation. Even if all the recommendations cited above were to be heeded and all lessons faithfully applied, the outcome of any given peace operation will still remain hostage to the political will of the parties enmeshed in the internal dispute. No peace force can compel reconciliation if the powerbrokers involved are unalterably opposed to this. Nor can the best efforts of the international community ensure that local law enforcement institutions will use this opportunity for reform to begin functioning according to 'international standards' (which have yet to be universally accepted for all aspects of public security). Careful attention must be given, therefore, to the sanctions and inducements available to achieve compliance.

Prior to mounting such a mission, it is absolutely crucial to perform a rigorous assessment of the prospects for successful intervention. Apart from other pertinent considerations, reform of public security will require two developments: commitment of resources over time capable both of overcoming deficiencies in the capacity of public security structures and of generating political consensus among former disputants that these structures should function in a reasonably impartial manner. It is essential to address both if the efforts of the international community are to have lasting impact. The most daunting of these challenges invariably will be to obtain the consent of powerful political elites who calculate they will be disadvantaged by the outcome of the reform process. Doing a proper job of institution building could undercut the political interests of certain powerful actors whose consent is likely to be required for the peace mission to continue functioning or for its results to be sustained. Pressing too hard in the wrong areas may produce a backlash that places the mission in jeopardy and retards the reform process. Even in more promising circumstances, expectations must be realistic, since the clout of the international community is normally insufficient to induce all changes that might be desired in the subject nation's public security apparatus.

Public Security Reform Needs to be Comprehensive

The task of rebuilding or reforming the public security apparatus requires that the judicial process (including the associated legal code) and penal system be addressed during the earliest stages, along with reform of the police force (Collectively referred to as a public security 'triad'). Compared with policing, judicial reform not only takes longer, but it is also even more difficult because of its intimate connection with national sovereignty and the distribution of power in any regime. By waiting until the latter stages of a peace operation to come to grips with shortcomings in the judiciary, legal code, or penal system, the clout of the international community will likely have faded, and a window of opportunity will probably have been lost. This is self-defeating, since police reform is of little value when the judicial process is corrupt and abusive behavior is rampant within the penal system.

Taking a holistic approach to the criminal justice system entails, *inter alia*, conducting a detailed assessment of the local judiciary, legal codes, and penal systems, along with the police force; identifying the major deficiencies in each; and engaging in a dialogue with local authorities to determine how the resources of the international community can be applied to overcoming these shortcomings. It also means getting an early start on these programs in order to build momentum. None of this will matter, however, unless bilateral and multilateral assistance programs give judicial and penal reform adequate priority when resources are allocated and local authorities manifest a willingness to cooperate.

Public Security Reform Is Vital

One of the defining features of post-Cold War peace operations is domestic disorder. Since these are internal conflicts, a lasting resolution will require erstwhile antagonists to live together as part of a single political community. The parties must thus have with adequate assurances that future political disputes will be resolved through peaceful means rather than violence.

Merely restoring order will not be sufficient. Unless attention is also given to establishing effective safeguards against abuse, there is the very real possibility that international public security assistance will have the perverse effect of making an existing instrument of repression even more efficient. Justice must be included as an objective otherwise public security will not be sustainable. This does not require creating an ideal society. It does require functional mechanisms to deal with abuses of authority within the public security 'triad'. These mechanisms only need to function well enough initially that no significant segment of the political community feels compelled to resort to force once again to correct systemic injustice.

This process takes time, and it will almost assuredly take longer than the US and other countries are prepared to leave their military forces deployed in significant numbers in some distant land. However, the military contingent can be progressively reduced as law and order are restored and civilian assistance programs come into effect. There are clear operational advantages for the military contingent if international law enforcement assistance is effectively carried out. It can reduce the threat to military peacekeepers, enhance popular support for the ongoing mission, improve respect for human rights, accelerate the reduction and withdrawal of military peacekeepers, and increase prospects for long-term stability.

Perhaps the most daunting constraint for the US is the impatient character of the American people, especially when they do not understand why tax dollars and especially lives are being spent in some forlorn and obscure corner of the globe. On the other hand, policy makers are apt to be bombarded by vocal and well-organized special interest groups pressing for an aggressive policy to rectify past wrongs immediately and to remake an uncivil culture promptly into an incubator of democracy. If peace operations are going to result in sustainable security over the long haul, the American people must come to a much clearer understanding of what we are about, what interests are at stake, and what our expectations realistically ought to be.

NOTES

1. *Time* 142/16, 18 Oct. 1993, Cover.
2. Ibid.
3. The absence of any supranational authority is the trait that theoretically distinguishes the international system of states from politics within states. Thus, international politics is said to be 'anarchic' because of this lack of an authoritative source of order. The state, in contrast, is sovereign within its territory. When the apparatus of the state collapses, however, or dissolves into several armed factions, each claiming the right to sovereignty, then anarchy prevails within that state, as well. The first irony of the post-Cold War period is that anarchy within the state has become a more frequent source of disruption for the international system than armed conflict between states. The second is that the anarchic global community must undertake the task of creating order for the sovereign state. It is for this latter reason that international unity of effort during a peace operation is so necessary yet so difficult to attain.
4. *International Policing*, in this context, involves a flexible combination of participants. The

mainstay invariably will be a contingent of policemen recruited from member states by the UN (or some other multilateral organization or coalition). When acting under United Nations mandate, such civilian police are referred to as UN CIVPOL, and they are administered by the Civilian Police Unit within the Department of Peacekeeping Operations (DPKO). Typically collaborating with UN CIVPOL are an eclectic mix of bilateral law enforcement assistance programs (e.g., the US International Criminal Investigative Training Assistance Program-ICITAP), multilateral activities (e.g. UN Crime Prevention and Criminal Justice Division), and NGOs (e.g., the American Bar Association). Also typically involved with aspects of policing and public security on a UN mission are the military contingent, human rights and election monitors, and UN civil affairs personnel.

5. As a practical matter, moreover, CIVPOL in the absence of a credible military back-up would be of dubious value and perhaps even in considerable risk.

6. Sweden and Norway have already taken the initiative to establish a reserve of dedicated civilian police personnel for use in future UN CIVPOL or other multilateral missions. This includes the development of specialized training programs for international policing. Canada and Australia also have established procedures for identifying personnel in advance for CIVPOL missions and providing training for them.

7. Professor David Bailey made this point most persuasively at an US National Defense University (NDU) workshop on 15–16 Sept. 1996 devoted to the search for themes and recommendations for this work.

8. IPTF Deputy Commissioner Robert Wasserman was particularly compelling in his discussion of this point during our 15–16 Sept. 1997 conference at NDU.

9. The US government recently recognized the need to prepare an inter-agency plan with the adoption of Presidential Decision Directive 56. Other governments have already instituted similar planning processes.

10. *Commissioner's Guidance for Democratic Policing in the Federation of Bosnia-Herzegovina*, Part 1 (Sarajevo: UN Mission in Bosnia-Herzegovina, May 1996).

The Future of
Peace Support Operations

ROBERT H. DORFF

The end of the Cold War has certainly not meant an end to conflict in the international system. To the contrary, if measured by the number of UN-sanctioned responses that have been mounted since the fall of the Berlin Wall, the level of conflict in the system has actually increased.[1] While the overall threat to systemic stability posed by such conflicts may have decreased, the fact remains that we have witnessed an increase in conflicts and in multilateral responses to them. As the threat of global annihilation in a world war has subsided, the challenges posed by these 'lesser wars' persist.

An underlying premise of this analysis, and indeed of this entire special issue, is that these lesser conflicts, the so-called small wars and insurgencies spawned by ethnic, religious, and nationalist animosities and hatreds, will continue to be the most prevalent form of conflict in the international system well into the next millennium. Of course, the United States must continue to prepare for, and thereby hopefully deter, the outbreak of future major regional conflicts (what are now called 'major theater wars'). And the US must remain vigilant and prepared to address the possible emergence of potential peer threats in a rapidly changing world. But the new era in international relations that is still emerging seems to be especially clear in one key characteristic: The 'small uncomfortable wars' that have characterized the recent past will very likely persist as the dominant form of conflict confronting us.[2]

If this is true, then the next logical issue to address is what we can and should do about these kinds of conflicts. Answers are not as obvious as we once thought. In the early stages of the post-Cold War era there was considerable enthusiasm for a form of response that resulted not so much from any conscious decision as from a series of ad-libbed reactions. From the 'coalition of the willing' in the Gulf War to the crisis responses in Somalia and Bosnia (at least in its early phases), the answer appeared to be 'peace support operations'.[3] One need only recall the boundless enthusiasm for the concept embodied in Boutros Boutros-Ghali's 'Agenda for Peace', keeping in mind that no less a conservative and ostensible realist than George Bush was caught up in the same kind of optimism (though perhaps somewhat more tempered than Ghali's).[4] Unfortunately, the enthusiasm was soon to die (at least for Americans), first in the hard reality of the streets of Mogadishu and later in the seemingly endless vacillation and do-nothing responses to the unfolding tragedy in Bosnia.

As with so many things, the reaction to the failures and shortcomings of the responses probably swung the pendulum too far in the other direction. Just as the initial enthusiasm was too great, creating unfulfillable expectations, the pessimism that now set in helped create excessive caution. Militarily, current US policy is guided by an overly strict and narrow set of criteria represented by PDD 25 and embodied, for example, in the Dayton Accords. End states have been transformed into 'end dates' and exit strategies into 'exits'. What has been missing in all this is a sound strategy, and that absence has contributed to the wild swings of the pendulum. We did not spend the time to understand the nature of the conflicts that were arising, and a tendency emerged to assume that they were essentially all the same (or at least of the same basic genus). There was therefore little serious effort directed toward understanding the nature of the objectives that we should seek in addressing those conflicts, and then the ways with which we could address them.

The purpose here is to contribute to the elucidation of just such a strategy; not to lay out the strategy in its entirety but at least to suggest some of the component parts of it. We begin with a consideration of the nature of conflict in the post-Cold War world. Then we look at the implications of the different forms of conflict for the strategic objectives we might have in addressing them. Finally, we consider some current policy alternatives for addressing the challenges, and then discuss some of the component parts of a strategy that could contribute to a broader kind of success in dealing with them. The news will certainly not be all good. For one thing, not all problems with which we are confronted have solutions. Despite our Enlightenment-based enthusiasm for applying human skills to the successful solution of problems, there are limits on what we can do, and the limits are considerable in some of these conflicts. There are also limits on our resources, not the least of which is money. But the limits also include time, human resources, and operational opportunity costs. And finally, there are limits on our will, nationally and also internationally. In the end, however, a better understanding of the nature of the conflict will help us better identify what we can reasonably accomplish in a given situation. A better understanding of what we can accomplish will help us devise a more sound strategy for actually accomplishing it. That in turn will give us an enhanced likelihood of successfully implementing that strategy and hence dealing with the kind of conflicts that we are most likely to see in the near term.

Nature of Conflict in the Post-Cold War World

There are several characteristics of the contemporary international system that help explain why these 'small uncomfortable wars' are likely at a minimum to persist and, perhaps, to be the predominant form of post-Cold War conflict. The coexistence of forces of integration and disintegration in the international system is a theme running through all of these characteristics. On the one hand, much is made of the extent to which the globalization of the world economy and the revolution in telecommunications technologies are bringing the world closer together. It is difficult to deny this integrative influence of modern communications and international commerce. At the same time, increasing awareness of what others have tends to cast into greater relief what one does not have. We can argue about whether the disparities between the 'haves' and the 'have nots' are in fact increasing. But even if they are not, the awareness of those disparities certainly is. When that awareness is combined with resources, action to redress the disparities, or simply to express the associated frustrations, usually follows. This is the stuff of which revolutions and insurgencies are made.

The ability to communicate freely and quickly with large numbers of people has also played into the hands of those who desire to press ethnic and nationalist identity as a mobilizing force for action. Instead of simply making the world increasingly borderless, as one thrust of the argument emphasizes, the telecommunications revolution also makes it easier to exploit basic differences in religion, language, and race as a basis for organizing and mobilizing. The influence of more and easier communication need not be linear and positive; it can also be quite negative, and the process may be characterized by lateral movement and even 'backsliding' as subnational groups are whipped up into emotional frenzies by leaders willing and now increasingly able to exploit those group differences for their own personal political and financial gain.[5] Rather than guaranteeing a safer, friendlier, and more peaceful world, improved telecommunications also brings the potential for increased tension and conflict. Once again, we see forces of integration and disintegration at work.

Another factor at work in the contemporary international system that contributes to the increased likelihood of 'small uncomfortable wars' is the continuation of the democratic wave.[6] Whether viewed as an extension of the decolonization that occurred earlier in this century or as a wholly new phenomenon associated with the final conquest by market democracy over its authoritarian, command economy adversaries, the fact remains that new countries have been thrust on the world scene at a time when being a 'democracy' with a 'market economy' is the *only* choice. But democracy as a form of government is based on a complex set of tradeoffs and a balancing act among competing rights and responsibilities (individual vs. group, individual vs. individual, group vs. group, and so on). As such, the institutions for resolving conflicts in a democracy, particularly in a fledgling democracy, are often quite weak because they depend so much on the willing consent of the participants rather than on an underlying fear of coercive power. For participants unfamiliar with this kind of political conflict resolution, democracy can be a strange and not visibly effective system. Coupled with the tools offered by modern communications and weapons technologies, the exploitable weaknesses of nascent democratic institutions may offer an attractive target of opportunity for those actors whose objectives may be based more on disintegration than on integration. And much the same argument can be made about liberal economic institutions.[7] So we not only have more 'new' countries, but we also have them choosing forms of social, political, and economic organization that are often easier to exploit by their opponents than other forms of organization.

The tension of our age may reside most clearly in the two concepts of sovereignty and self-determination. On the one hand, we have the traditional notion of the nation-state as a sovereign entity. A core characteristic of the contemporary Westphalian nation-state system, sovereignty in its absolute form has increasingly come under attack today, in no small part because of the transparency of international relations brought on by the influences of global communications and commerce with which we began this part of the discussion. Should a state be allowed to use force, at times quite brutally, against its own population and subgroups within it? This was a question hardly raised only 138 years ago as the United States was moving down the path toward a civil war, when the desires of the Confederacy to secede were deemed to be so counter to the concept of the Union that Americans would fight and die to impose the will of one group on the other. Today, any group that desires to secede simply declares its 'independence', supports it with a vote by its people that demonstrates its belief in self-determination, and then calls on the international community to sustain it and its 'liberal' values. In such an environment, it is no surprise that we should expect these 'small uncomfortable wars' to continue.

A quick survey of the literature suffices to illustrate the situation. Much of the work points in varying degrees to ethnicity, religion, and nationalism as the primary sources of conflict in today's international system.[8] But these sources of potential conflict are hardly new. What is 'new' is the current international context in which these sources operate, and the influence that context has on the likelihood of conflict occurring, the form that it takes, and the kinds of responses to it that can be generated. Just as the Cold War international system influenced these aspects of conflict (likelihood, form, responses), the post-Cold War system does so as well. In the absence of the constraining and moderating influences of the Cold War system, these sources of conflict are today more likely to lead to conflict in part because many actors perceive the risks of that conflict as being less than they were in the bipolar, superpower-dominated system. And the range of possible responses seems greater today, from no response on one end of the spectrum to full-scale coalition warfare on the other. Somewhere between these two ends of the response spectrum is the set of responses which is the focus of this special issue: peace support operations.

Increasing Ungovernability and Failing States

These various sources of potential conflict exist in an international system characterized by increasing global ungovernability, and it is that contextual characteristic that we need to examine and understand more fully in order to devise an effective strategy for dealing with today's challenges. Ungovernability has been defined as 'the declining ability of governments worldwide, but particularly in the Third World, to govern, to carry out the many and various responsibilities of managing a modern state in an increasingly complex environment'.[9] Peters argues that 'Future wars and violent conflicts will be shaped by the inabilities of governments to function as effective systems of resource distribution and control, and by the failure of entire cultures to compete in the post-modern age.'[10] A related aspect of the problem is the increasing unwillingness (or inability) of some populations to be governed. Ethnicity, religion, and nationalism are not the core challenges we face, although they play important roles in generating conflict. The core challenge comes from increasing ungovernability.

Elsewhere I discussed some of the implications of ungovernability for the US strategy of democratization, and by extension for peace support operations.[11] I shall reconstruct some of that discussion here as it also bears directly on the future of peace support operations. An important point for this discussion is that there are different types and forms of ungovernability, and the appropriate response to the challenges will depend to a great extent on the nature of the problem with which we are confronted.

Perhaps the most widely discussed form of ungovernability is the failed or failing state.[12] Manwaring and Corr call it the core problem underlying a host of issues, including the 'wars of national debilitation, a steady run of uncivil wars sundering fragile but functioning nation-states and gnawing at the well-being of stable nations'.[13] One of the perplexing problems of failed states is that they do not simply go away. Experience suggests that they linger, and the longer they persist, the greater the potential challenges to neighboring states, regional stability, and international peace. In 1992 Boutros Boutros-Ghali addressed this issue in his discussion of the reduced significance of sovereignty in the post-Cold War world and the concomitant possibility that the UN would be compelled to intervene in the domestic affairs of member states. He suggested that such intervention would be appropriate in the face of a collapse of domestic governing authority, displaced populations or gross violations of human rights, or when developments within the failed state posed a threat to international peace and stability.[14] Helman and Ratner observe that failed states threaten neighboring countries because civil strife, economic collapse, and the breakdown of food and health systems 'force refugees to flee to adjacent countries'. These states may also 'be burdened with illicit arms traffic, solidarity activities by related ethnic groups, and armed bands seeking to establish a safe have'. There is also a 'tangible risk that such conflicts will spill over into other countries'.[15] The problems of failed or failing states frequently do not remain neatly contained within the state's boundaries. Brian Atwood, head of the US Agency for International Development (AID), concluded that 'disintegrating societies and failed states ... have emerged as the greatest menace to global stability,' and he considers them a 'strategic threat'.[16]

In addition to these general threats to stability and security, a failed or failing state is itself a potential target for internal or external disruption and insurgencies. A transnational or sub-state actor, operating either within the troubled country or from points nearby, may exploit the failing state to promote its own objectives. Such activities could lead to the destabilization of an entire region, thereby quickly escalating into a security threat well beyond the relatively minor interests originating from the failed or failing state. These states also provide an environment in which such actors can thrive, exploiting the lack of effective governance to consolidate their power and influence. So, for example, the inability of a state to control criminal activities such as drug or weapons smuggling, money laundering, and terrorism may eventually transform the country into a kind of 'safe haven' from which the criminal can effectively consolidate and expand operations. To the extent that such actors gain strength in these safe havens, the failed state becomes a security concern for other countries, including the US.[17]

Failed states pose an additional challenge because they frequently generate significant and highly visible violations of human rights.[18] The pain and suffering of large numbers of refugees, especially women and children, make for compelling photo-journalism (Somalia, Bosnia). Similarly, people suffering under the chaos and near-anarchy of a collapsing government, or the brutal authoritarianism of an autocratic regime desperately trying to maintain its weakened ruling position, appear to much of the world as innocent victims who deserve serious outside assistance (Haiti, Rwanda). There are at least two relevant dimensions to this humanitarian side of the problem. First, humanitarian interests are one of the three categories of national interests addressed in the US national security strategy.[19] Consequently, visible cases of human rights violations will certainly raise questions about US willingness to respond to such violations consistently and universally. When the US chooses not to respond, for whatever reasons, one can expect to hear criticism based on the selectivity with which the policy is applied.

A second dimension of the problem is the public outcry that frequently accompanies these highly visible cases of human rights violations. The outcry, often fed by the extensive media coverage that such crises engender (as well as by the efforts of involved groups to generate sympathy, support, and revenue), increases domestic and international pressures to 'do something'.[20] Such pressures can all too easily lead to responses that are less than carefully thought out in advance. The point is this: by their very nature the human rights dimensions of failed states raise critical issues for the US in terms of our national security strategy and our ability to be selective and effective in responding to them.

At the international level, trends in demographics, development and industrialization, and the global distribution of wealth, to name just a few, make it highly likely that these sources of conflict generating the need for peace operations will persist, and with them the operations themselves.[21] Furthermore, as several writers have observed, the international system is likely to remain a tiered system.[22] Following Metz's argument, that system will consist of three tiers. The first tier will be comprised of the advanced industrialized countries, and it will be characterized by stability and economic prosperity. The second tier will be more diverse, with some countries on the verge of moving into the first tier and most occupying a kind of mid-twentieth century position consisting of industrial-based economies with little of the information-age influences seen in the first tier. This tier will be characterized by less stability, as there will be the occasional 'regional' war waged between them as they struggle for relative power gains. The third tier (what Singer and Wildavsky see as the worst part of their second tier) will consist of the economic and political outcasts, the countries that will continue to be unable to move into the modern industrial age, let alone to gain entry into the post-modern information age. This tier will be 'characterized by endemic violence, ungovernability, and a range of ecological problems. Armed forces would take the form of militias, warlord armies, and terrorist gangs.'[23] The kind of conflicts likely to generate the hue and cry for peace support operations will be found almost exclusively in this tier, and the size of the tier alone suggests that there will be no dearth of such conflicts.

Our discussion of ungovernability and failing states also suggests a future as bleak as Metz's analysis does. Struggling countries with little to non-existent functioning governmental and economic institutions will find it all that much more difficult to make any real progress toward building legitimate mechanisms of governance. The problems they already face today will be exacerbated by the forces and technologies at work in the system. Proponents of disorder and chaos will have significant advantages over those who wish to establish order and rule by law. It is not a very bright or encouraging future for those who value peace and stability.

Types of Conflict

Conflict in the international system is likely to fall into three broad categories. First, we must still be wary of a major regional conflict of the traditional inter-state variety. Saddam Hussein's past and recent actions certainly reinforce the fact that we cannot lose focus on preparing for, deterring, and if necessary fighting and winning such wars. The notion of a tiered system suggests that such conflicts, if they occur, will take place in the second tier, and will most likely involve those actors that we in the US consider rogue states.

Second, in both the second and third tiers we are likely to see continued cases of intra-state conflict that closely resembles traditional inter-state war. This is the 'classic' civil war, with the wars over the dissolution of Yugoslavia, including the on-going Bosnian conflict, as contemporary examples. It resembles inter-state conflict primarily because there are clearly identifiable protagonists, with clearly identifiable leaders, and usually with some clearly identifiable territorial base with which they began the conflict.

Finally, to some extent the second, but especially the third, tier will be characterized by the kinds of conflict that grow out of increasing ungovernability and the resultant failing or failed state. In some cases we will see more of the warlordism and chaos that we witnessed in Somalia, and which we probably failed to understand in time to prevent us from making serious mistakes. A more common variety of conflict, however, may be similar to what occurred in Haiti, which was less a case of rampant criminality and warlordism than of a state and people that were simply exhausted. Each of these kinds of conflicts results from a somewhat different configuration of causes and precipitating events, and consequently, the nature of their problems and the proper approaches to addressing them will be different. For the remainder of this assessment I shall concentrate on the latter category of conflict, primarily because I think it will be the most frequent, and the one that is perhaps most perplexing to policy makers and the public today.[24]

The Nature of the Challenge: Some Dilemmas

The complexity of these conflicts in terms of origins, operations, and the search for effective ways of addressing them poses a significant challenge. Based on the preceding discussion we can recognize generally the difficulties that would be involved in designing and implementing a strategy to deal with the potential threats that grow out of them, and we will come back to some of them in the concluding section as we examine some of the implications for US policy. But first a closer examination of some underlying issues and the dilemmas they create is necessary.

Most of the conflict occurring in the system will be of the 'small uncomfortable war' variety. Moreover, most of them will take place in the second or third tiers we described. There are several important implications of these two observations. First, there will almost always be an 'interest-threat mismatch' for the US in these conflicts. In other words, the threats posed by these conflicts (to neighbors, sub-state groups, even regions, etc.) will almost never involve vital US interests, and perhaps only occasionally important ones. For the most part US interests affected by such conflicts will be peripheral. As suggested earlier, potentially there will be a host of humanitarian issues and interests involved, but it will take some highly creative redefinition of US security interests to transform them into matters of even important, let alone vital interests. Arguing that 'stability and security' on a global basis is always an important US interest, no matter where and under what circumstances the potential threat to it occurs, runs the risk of creating another 'peace is indivisible' argument. That would have the US actively engaged everywhere and with no criteria for being even somewhat selective in our decisions to engage.

Second, precisely because of these humanitarian consequences of state failures, the conflicts will be extremely difficult for the US simply to ignore. Recall the observation that even if the humanitarian consequences are not in and of themselves sufficient for generating a response, parties to the conflict will have strategies for fueling highly emotional reactions and generating external support for their causes. Such actions will feed into other factors frequently discussed in analyses of such conflicts, not the least of which is the often insatiable appetite of international media for covering such tragedies relentlessly. As the consequences for international inaction in such a crisis are brought home to millions of people worldwide, it is easy to recognize that pressures will grow on countries to act, especially those countries with a visible capacity to do so.

Yet the interest-threat mismatch now comes fully into play. Therefore, the third implication is that public support for a response, if it does result from the humanitarian dimension of the conflict, may be broad but not very deep. The consequences of this are quite important. For one thing, if a more comprehensive and focused 'engagement' strategy is needed for addressing some of the root causes of these conflicts, it will be severely limited in scope and length if the support is shallow. For another thing, in those conflicts where military force has an appropriate, indeed necessary, role to play, studies suggest that in democracies generally, and certainly in the US, public support for, or even tolerance of, the following will be quite low: (1) high levels of violence applied against the offending parties, and (2) even minimal levels of US casualties.[25] This leads to the kind of strict limitations on the use of military force and the nature of military operations that I suggested earlier exist today under PDD 25. It also leads to strict limitations on military 'rules of engagement' which can potentially increase risks to soldiers on the ground, and which can in turn limit the effectiveness of the military instrument as a tool in support of overall US strategy.

Taken together, these implications lead to a highly problematic dilemma for US, and indeed other, policy makers in confronting these 'small uncomfortable wars' and the underlying influences of ungovernability and the failing state. A democratic public is likely to turn at some point in an unfolding crisis and tragedy to the 'do something' strategy mentioned earlier. A growing sense of humanitarian compassion will translate into a general notion that 'we have to do something about the atrocities and human suffering.' Yet at the same time, that public mood (reflected of course in the Congress) will insist that we stop the atrocities, but of course we should not injure or kill other people in the process (even if they are the ones committing atrocities), and we certainly should not risk American lives. One might also add that we should perform this miraculous feat at little or no cost to the US taxpayer. Small wonder that our policy guidance for dealing with such conflicts has been so uncertain and vacillating, and our record for succeeding so spotty.

To date this dilemma has been mostly addressed by limiting the role played by the military even as we have deployed it more and more. To be sure, this is not an argument to put more soldiers at greater risk, or to unleash massive firepower against all protagonists with no regard for the consequences in human lives, additional suffering, and retributions against those same soldiers. But it does help explain why the biggest danger today to such military operations is not that they will be exposed to excessive risk, but that they have virtually no chance of succeeding in anything other than a short, transitory way. As I wrote in another place, these military operations in such ungovernable and failing or failed states will ultimately fail, either in theater where they will not be able to address the nature of the conflict effectively, or after they withdraw, when all of the violence, tragedy, and suffering will simply resume unabated. In the end, all of us, military and civilian alike, will be left to wonder why we ever deployed in the first place. Declaring victory and going home, usually after some token 'elections' have been held, may be useful salve for the wounded conscience, but in my view it is hardly worth the risk of US blood and treasure in the first place.[26]

Possible Responses: Some Current Policy Alternatives

There is no lack of suggestions as to what the US should do in the face of these conflicts and the continuing demands for peace support operations. What is lacking is a strategy for addressing the issues and guiding the formulation of appropriate responses. Before we turn to a consideration of some of the elements of a more comprehensive strategy, it is useful to look at existing policies and suggested approaches. This will shed some light on what it is we should be striving for in the way of strategy.

One of the more obvious, comprehensive suggestions is that we simply do nothing (or very little) in response to such conflicts. This suggestion grows out of the ongoing debate about the future of US grand strategy and is grounded in the isolationist option.[27] In its simplest form it resolves the interest-threat mismatch by concluding that the absence of vital or clearly important US interests means that we should not become involved at all in the conflicts or in addressing the underlying causes of them. There are at least two immediate problems with this approach, however. First, it obviously depends critically on what one defines as vital or important interests. It may be easier to draw a blanket conclusion that no such interests exist than to apply that conclusion to a specific case. And that brings us to the second problem, discussed earlier, namely the difficulty of ignoring the humanitarian consequences of such conflicts. Recent history suggests that it will be very difficult indeed to adopt an overall 'do nothing' strategy.[28] For the purposes of this argument, we conclude that such suggestions are at best unrealistic.

Another recurring suggestion is that we move to develop and implement much better early-warning mechanisms in support of a system of preventive diplomacy.[29] While I do not dispute for a moment the need for improved early-warning mechanisms, especially in the areas identified with the sources of state failure (ethnic and religious conflict, socio-economic instability, sub-state nationalistic movements, etc.), I am less sanguine about the capabilities of such mechanisms to provide much in the way of relief from the basic problem. In my view the lack of early warning and indicators of potential violence has been neither the primary nor even a central reason underlying our inability to deal effectively with such crises prior to their becoming critical. Rather, the critical factor has been the lack of political will, either by individual countries or the collective international community. We shall return to this in a moment, but the point here is simply that it is dangerous and misleading to think that we can effectively address the problems of ungovernability and state failure only by improving our ability to receive early warning. In the former Yugoslavia, as well as in most of the recent crises in Africa (e.g., Rwanda, Zaire), policy makers were well aware of the potential for violent conflict well in advance of hostilities actually breaking out. It was not the absence of early warning that caused the delay in or absence of an effective response. It is at best only a part of an effective response capability.

Yet another suggestion that focuses on a component part of a response is the notion that we need to develop more robust, full-spectrum military capabilities (either national or multilateral) for dealing with the conflicts. Here, too, the problem has been not so much with the absence of military capabilities (although some would still argue that this is precisely why the UN needs a standing military force to conduct peace operations), but with the attendant lack of consensus on whether a response is warranted and, if so, precisely what it should consist of. No amount of military capabilities, residing at either the national or international institutional level, will make up for the absence of an overall strategy and the underlying consensus on the objectives and the proper ways with which to deal with the challenges.

That leaves us with one other suggestion that does take on more of the appearance of a comprehensive, strategic approach. This is the notion that what is needed is the broadest possible engagement, by the US and all other national and international actors, in a global attempt to punish all aggression and to eradicate the root causes of conflict. While perhaps laudable for the nobility of the 'call to arms' embodied in this approach, it encounters at least two major problems discussed earlier. First, it will almost always get bogged down in the sovereignty vs. self determination tensions. Second, it will raise the 'indivisibility of peace' problems. Despite the desires of many of us to the contrary, true collective security has never been realized as a mechanism for ensuring security and stability in the international system. Rather, and to varying degrees of scope and effectiveness, it has functioned at best as a system of 'selective anti-aggression'.[30] While it may be worthwhile to continue the search for such a system, the impracticality of achieving it any time soon makes it a poor candidate for a strategic framework with which to address the potential crises, collapses, and chaos of the present. Another approach is surely and sorely needed.

Conclusions: Some Recommendations

Based on the discussion so far, we conclude that the most prevalent form of conflict in the international system will occur in the second and third tiers, will result from increasing ungovernability in failed and failing states, and will rarely involve vital or important US national interests. The crises that grow out of this conflict will nonetheless be extremely difficult for the US to ignore altogether, but they will almost certainly be beyond our means and desires to confront across the entire globe. And the means and form of our involvement will be severely constrained by, among other things, the lack of clear public support for any cohesive approach in the absence of an articulated, defensible strategy. It seems evident, then, that what is most needed is precisely such a strategy for confronting these kinds of challenges to security and stability in the post-Cold War world.

The kind of strategy needed to provide some coherence and guidance to US and indeed to international security policy generally has been suggested by Max G. Manwaring and Edwin G. Corr in an earlier work.[31] They argue that the US should pursue a strategy based on a 'legitimate governance theory of engagement'. They further define legitimate governance as 'governance that derives its just powers from the governed and generates a viable political competence that can and will manage, coordinate, and sustain security, and political, economic, and social development'.[32] Such a strategy would be more than the 'democratization' component of our previous 'National Security Strategy of Engagement and Enlargement', although there are some basic similarities.[33] The main point is that the kinds of conflicts to which we find ourselves increasingly responding in an *ad hoc* fashion today will persist as long as the lingering problems of ungovernability exist throughout the international system. So for Manwaring and Corr, the task for the US is to construct a set of organizational and policy guidelines that will focus our collective national instruments of power, and coordinate them with those of allies and other international actors (NGOs, IGOs, PVOs, etc.), toward the strategic objective of promoting legitimate governance. As they recommend, '... when US interests are threatened by events in a weak and menaced state, the main element of US policy and strategy must go beyond promoting simple "democracy" (i.e., the election of civilian leaders) to guiding supported leaders in a long-term, patient, but firm and vigilant pursuit of moral legitimacy.'[34]

What happens today, without such a strategy and the corollary understanding of the nature of the conflicts that are occurring, is a host of *ad hoc* responses by the US, frequently acting as part of a multinational operation, to situations as they arise and are pushed along by events, media coverage, and the ebb and flow of public interest. Susan Woodward has described this as 'crisis responses to locales considered unimportant'.[35] For reasons we have already presented here, such responses will continue to create problems for the US as long as we have no systematic approach for determining answers to such questions as when to go in, what to accomplish while there, and when (and how) to get out. We respond primarily militarily, and with the idea that it will be a short-term operation only. But the problem of failing states is not first and foremost a military problem, and the solution (along the lines of Manwaring and Corr's recommendation) is anything but short-term. What is required is a long-term, multifaceted engagement that will lay the groundwork and then promote the growth of institutions and patterns of legitimate governance.

This can be accomplished only if we can devise an integrated strategy, employing all components of national and international power (political, economic, and military), in a focused effort to achieve the strategic objective of promoting legitimate governance. Conducting military peace support operations fails to recognize that the nature of the conflict rests squarely in the socio-political-economic arena. Piling civilian and political requirements on already over-burdened military commanders in the field is not a strategy for integrating the full range of instruments necessary for dealing with the problem. Separating the warring parties, holding elections, declaring victory, and then heading home is certain to result in our being called upon over and over again to repeat the same operations. It is, quite simply, a formula for failure, and it will contribute to increasing frustration on the part of US military forces and policy makers, and to increasing desperation on the part of many suffering people throughout the world. The tragedies that ultimately compel us to 'do something' will continue unabated.

Therefore, if we wish to make progress out of this dilemma, we must face the critical issues head on. Because I believe that Americans will be unable or unwilling simply to ignore these tragedies, I conclude that the recommendations by Manwaring and Corr and their colleagues provide the only reasonable guidance we can adopt at this critical juncture in our search for a strategy with which to address the most likely source of conflict in the contemporary international system – the failed state and the forces that contribute to its failure. The root problem is not 'ethnic conflict' or 'religious conflict' or 'nationalism'. The root problem is the collapse of formal institutions of legitimate governance. We must develop ways of employing national and collective resources to reverse state failure and to reestablish legitimate governance. That will take careful analysis, planning, coordinating, and resourcing. We will have to build support for the objectives domestically and among our allies and partners (institutions as well as other countries). We must be able to identify and enlist the support of legitimate partners to assist in the comprehensive, long-term policy approaches that are needed. We will need the kind of unity of effort at a coordinated international level that we have become so accustomed to implementing in our military operations, especially the multinational variety. We will need the kind of managerial and organizational arrangements, particularly in our Executive Branch, that will allow all of this to take place in pursuit of clearly articulated objectives. And we will need patience, because such a strategy will not be easily and quickly implemented. And, as an important qualification, we should recognize that our policies for dealing with an imperfect situation will also be imperfect. Our goal should not be to make the entire world a better place all at once; rather we should be accepting of smaller scale progress, in carefully selected situations where the likelihood of success appears greatest, to guide us along the way toward a more effective approach to conflict management through peace support operations in the millennium that lies ahead.

Finally, we need to recognize that there are important differences in the kinds of conflicts we will be called upon to address. I have suggested here that many of them grow out of a broader problem of increasing ungovernability and the concomitant reality of failed and failing states. But I have also suggested that not all failing or failed states are the same, and this should provide a basis for answering some important questions in the face of specific crises. Let me conclude by illustrating some of the kinds of questions we need to ask and answer as part of the process of deciding how to respond. First, what is the nature of the crisis? Is this a purely humanitarian crisis (like a flood) or a larger crisis with humanitarian consequences (Somalia)? Are we in fact dealing with a failed state? If so, is it a failing state of the Bosnian variety (with identifiable protagonists, reasonably clear chains of command, and so on) or of the Somali variety (where the enemy is violence, chaos, and disorder)? Or is the failing state of the Haitian variety (a collapse of exhausted institutions and processes)?

Second, based on answers to the preceding questions, what should our objective be? If the crisis is purely humanitarian, the answer could be as simple as deciding to provide immediate relief such as food and temporary shelter. This tends to work very well when the immediate crisis is not compounded by the collateral influences of, say, state failure or civil war. The United Nations has conducted any number of successful operations of this kind. But if in fact the humanitarian crisis is a part of, or even the result of state failure, we must ask other questions about our objectives. Is our objective to provide immediate relief from the short-term humanitarian crisis, recognizing that the crisis is likely to recur given the underlying causes of it? Or is our objective a long-term eradication of the problems that ultimately caused or exacerbated the humanitarian crisis? Can the humanitarian crisis in fact be separated from the broader crisis and the symptoms treated separately? The final step is to assess, given the objectives we have decided to pursue, the best policies for pursuing them and the resources needed in order to ensure that we can maximize our chances for success.

This brief list of questions is certainly not comprehensive, but it serves to make my basic point that, in my view, we have too often failed to understand adequately the nature of the problem we are facing, the alternative objectives we might have, and thus the best approach to take in dealing with it. It should also be apparent that the option of doing nothing is not ruled out by any of this. In fact, by addressing the crises in this more strategic fashion, we should be able to recognize those situations more clearly, and to justify them more effectively, when we simply cannot and should not respond. Knowing when not to respond is one important part of a strategy for enhancing success in those cases where we choose to respond. It is my hope that this discussion may contribute something to our ability to make just such critical decisions about future peace support operations.

NOTES

1. According to the United Nations, there are 15 current authorized peace support operations and 18 completed operations begun since the fall of the Berlin Wall. That compares to a total of 12 operations begun and completed prior to the fall of the Berlin Wall. See the United Nations Peacekeeping Operations Home Page at http://www.un.org/Depts/dpko/.
2. I believe that Gen. John R. Galvin first introduced this term. For a definition and discussion of it, see his 'Uncomfortable Wars: Toward a New Paradigm', *Parameters* 16/4 (Dec. 1986) pp.2–8. Also published in Max G. Manwaring (ed.) *Uncomfortable Wars* (Boulder, CO: Westview Press 1991) pp.9–18.
3. I refer here to what is now understood to be the full range of military operations that to varying degrees fall short of full scale war. This has most recently been labeled Military Operations Other Than War or MOOTW, and includes purely humanitarian operations on one end of the spectrum to peacemaking on the other. This distinction recognizes that there can be some combat roles in the high intensity end of the MOOTW spectrum. Of course, what are called United Nations 'Chapter 6 1/2' peace-keeping operations emerged during the Cold War under the auspices of the UN, and the policies and procedures for conducting them were reasonably well developed and understood. But new criteria for operations such as peacemaking and peace enforcement have been evolving in the post-Cold War world, often on the ground as operations were on-going.
4. See Boutros Boutros-Ghali, *An Agenda for Peace 1995*, 2nd ed. (NY: UN 1995). This publication contains the original 1992 report of the Secretary-General and the Supplement to it dated 3 Jan. 1995.
5. For a discussion of the role of elites in exploiting these differences for personal gain as opposed to the notion that such conflicts arise spontaneously out of historical ethnic and religious hatreds, see Robert H. Dorff, 'Federalism in Eastern Europe: Part of the Solution or Part of the Problem?' *Publius* 24/2 (Spring 1994) pp.99–114.
6. On the notion of democratic waves see especially Samuel P. Huntington, *The Third Wave:*

Democratization in the Late Twentieth Century (Norman: U. of Oklahoma Press 1991).

7. Although this simplifies the arguments tremendously, one can see the interaction of the negative elements in places such as the former Soviet Union. New freedoms are hard to distinguish from license. Political rights become the basis for mob-like organizations to build illegal but highly effective powerbases. Market economies become the basis for criminals to create and then exploit black markets. Citizens are left to ponder, not without justification, whether these liberal systems are in fact so much better than the authoritarian systems they supplanted. Those of us raised in the late-twentieth century versions of American liberal institutions would do well to remember that at a time when our institutions were less developed and robust, only some 100 years ago, democracy and capitalism helped the 'Wild West' flourish. Most of us would not care to live in such a period today where the rule of law often depended on the six-shooter, and supply and demand were abstract theoretical terms as opposed to the realities of bootlegging, smuggling, and rampant criminal activity.

8. Among the numerous and diverse sources one can cite in this regard, consider the following. From the military perspective come: 'Threats in Transition: Marine Corps Mid-Range Threat Estimate 1995–2005' (Nov. 1994); US Army Field Manual No. 100-23 *Peace Operations* (Washington DC: US Army Headquarters, 1994); and the policy-oriented piece by Robert L. Pfaltzgraff Jr, and Richard H. Shultz J. (eds.) *Ethnic Conflict and Regional Instability: Implications for US Policy and Army Roles and Missions.* (Carlisle, PA: Strategic Studies Inst., US Army War College 1994) esp. pp.59–75. From an academic perspective: Jacquelyn K. Davis, *Forward Presence and US Security Policy* (Cambridge, MA: Inst. for Foreign Policy Analysis 1995), esp. 'Introduction: Managing Chaos in the Post-Soviet Era'; Susan L. Woodward, 'Failed States: Warlordism and 'Tribal' Warfare', Paper presented at the conference on 'The Role of Naval Forces in the 21st Century', Fletcher School of Law and Diplomacy, Cambridge, MA, 19–20 Nov. 1997; and Ralph Peters, 'The Culture of Future Conflict', *Parameters* 25/4 (Winter 1995–96) pp.18–27. A more journalistic approach is found in Peter Maass, *Love Thy Neighbor: A Story of War* (NY: Knopf 1996), and Robert D. Kaplan, *The Ends of the Earth: A Journey at the Dawn of the 21st Century* (NY: Random House 1996).

9. William J. Olson, 'The New World Disorder: Governability and Development', in Max G. Manwaring (ed.) *Gray Area Phenomena: Confronting the New World Disorder* (Boulder, CO: Westview Press 1993) p.10.

10. Ralph Peters, 'The Culture of Future Conflict' (note 8) p.18.

11. See Robert H. Dorff, 'Democratization and Failed States: The Challenge of Ungovernability', *Parameters* 26/2 (Summer 1996) pp.17–31.

12. See for example ibid. esp. pp.3–7; Gerald B. Helman and Steven R. Ratner, 'Saving Failed States', *Foreign Policy* 89 (Winter 1992–93) pp.3–20; and Leslie H. Gelb, 'Quelling the Teacup Wars', *Foreign Affairs* 73/6 (Nov.–Dec. 1994) pp.2–6.

13. This is Gelb's description in ibid. p.5. The Manwaring and Corr discussion is found in Max G. Manwaring and Edwin G. Corr, 'Confronting the New World Disorder: A Legitimate Governance Theory of Engagement', in Max G. Manwaring and Wm. J. Olson (eds.) *Managing Contemporary Conflict: Pillars of Success* (Boulder, CO: Westview Press 1996) p.34.

14. Boutros-Ghali, *An Agenda for Peace*, (UN 1992) esp. Section VI, 'Post-Conflict Peace-Building', pp.61–2.

15. Helman and Ratner, 'Saving Failed States' (note 12) p.8.

16. Quoted in Jeremy D. Rosner, 'Is Chaos America's Real Enemy?' *Washington Post*, 14 Aug. 1994, p.C-1.

17. For example, see the discussion in Manwaring and Corr, 'Confronting the New World Disorder' (note 13) esp. pp.33–6. They argue: 'Because instability in one place can cause instabilities elsewhere, related threats can ultimately become directly menacing to the United States. Again, failure to recognize and deal with a threat in its early stages is a threat in itself', p.36.

18. Rosner observes: 'For it is almost always the absence of responsible governance that causes humanitarian disasters (witness Somalia, Rwanda and Haiti), not the other way around'. Rosner, 'Is Chaos America's Real Enemy?' (note 16) p.A1. A similar argument is made by

Manwaring and Corr: 'Ultimately, the spillover effects of national and regional instabilities place demands on the international community, if not to solve the problems, at least to harbor the victims.' Manwaring and Corr, 'Confronting the New World Disorder' (note 13) p.33

19. They are listed along with vital and important interests in the National Security Strategy. See *A National Security Strategy for a New Century* (Washington DC: US GPO 1997) p.9.

20. This so-called 'do something' strategy is of course not a strategy at all. It is also dangerous for precisely the same reason it is not a strategy: It fails to consider what objectives are to be accomplished, what appropriate resources are to be used and how, and whether the application of those resources will in any way contribute to the successful resolution of the problem.

21. See for example discussions in Max Singer and Aaron Wildavsky, *The Real World Order: Zones of Peace/Zones of Turmoil*, rev. ed. (Chatham, NJ: Chatham House 1996), and Helman and Ratner, 'Saving Failed States' (note 12).

22. For different examples and arguments about the nature and implications of the tiers see: Singer and Wildavsky, *The Real World Order* (note 21); Donald M. Snow, *National Security: Defense Policy for a New International Order*, 3rd ed. (NY: St Martin's Press 1995); and Steven Metz, 'Strategic Horizons: The Military Implications of Alternative Futures' (Carlisle Barracks, PA: Strategic Studies Inst. 1997).

23. Ibid. p.vii.

24. One additional observation at this point is worth considering. The second and third categories roughly laid out here are often referred to as 'failed states'. While I have no problems with that general reference, what I am suggesting is that there are some important subcategories of the failing and failed state that have different implications for policy. For one thing, a state that has collapsed because of challenges to its formal authority from organized criminal groups and competing warlords has a very different set of problems, and poses a different set of challenges to our use of political, economic, and military instruments of power than a state that has more accurately just collapsed under the weight of its own incompetence or the people's weariness. A military operation in a country with multiple contending groups, only somewhat organized and following no clear chain of command (as we saw in Somalia) poses serious risks of a unique nature to an intervening military force. In Haiti there was virtually none of the same risks inherent in the Somali operating environment. Similarly, a state that is 'failing' because of a classic civil war being waged between contending parties (what I argue has been the situation in Bosnia virtually since the inception of that conflict) also presents different kinds of risks, but is also an environment in which there is more predictability because the parties to the conflict are essentially known and identifiable, and they more or less follow the commands of their superiors. While I do not mean to downplay the risks that exist in any of these environments, it seems clear to me that military operations in a Bosnia are much more easy to plan and execute than in a Somalia. Neither military operation may contribute ultimately to a successful strategy for resolving the conflict, but getting in and getting out may be a qualitatively different kind of challenge, and we need to do more work on addressing these subcategories of failed states, and their policy implications (for military operations, remedies for the country's ills, and our willingness to become involved in the first place).

25. I am indebted to Dr Gil Merom, Tel Aviv University, for his insights on this particular issue. See his 'Blood & Conscience: Recasting the Boundaries of National Security', Ph.D. Dissertation, Cornell University, July 1994, esp. pp.446–54.

26. Another way in which this dilemma is too often resolved is in the 'indefinite extension' approach of the military operation, as we are currently witnessing in Bosnia. If the extension were in fact tied to meaningful operations being undertaken in other areas necessary for resolving the conflict, using other instruments of national and international power, a prolonged military presence could be justified in terms of its continuing contribution to a strategic solution. But of course, all of that would still have to be justified to a skeptical or downright opposed public. The point here, and in the section that follows, is that without such a strategy in the first place, no amount of *ad hoc* justification will ever succeed in building the sustained support necessary for effectively addressing the kinds of conflicts I believe will most characterize the end of this century and the beginning of the new millennium.

27. While there are several published works that address this debate, one of the best is by Barry R. Posen and Andrew L. Ross, 'Competing Visions for US Grand Strategy', *International Security* 21/3 (Winter 1996/97) pp.5–53. See esp. the section on 'Neo-isolationism' pp.9–16. Richard N. Haass also has a similar review of grand strategic options in his book, *The Reluctant Sheriff: The United States After the Cold War* (NY: Council on Foreign Relations, 1997) esp. Chapter 2, 'A Doctrine of Regulation'. Haass discusses 'isolationism' on pp.55–60.
28. This does not necessarily mean, however, that there will never be cases in which the decision is to do nothing. Rather, the suggestion here is that an overall presumption of doing nothing in all such cases is probably very hard to sustain on a strategic level in today's world.
29. Recent examples of work in this area include Alexander L. George and Jane E. Holl, *The Warning-Response Problem and Missed Opportunities in Preventive Diplomacy* (NY: Carnegie Corporation 1997); and Ashley J. Tellis, Thomas S. Szayna, and James A. Winnefeld, *Anticipating Ethnic Conflict*, MR-853-A (Santa Monica, CA: RAND 1997).
30. For an incisive discussion of this term as well as the notion that true collective security has not and probably never will be fully realized, see Inis L. Claude J., 'Collective Security After the Cold War', in Gary L. Guertner (ed.) *Collective Security in Europe and Asia* (Carlisle Barracks, PA: Strategic Studies Inst. 1992).
31. Manwaring and Corr, 'Confronting the New World Disorder' (note 13) pp.31–47.
32. Ibid. p.32.
33. See *A National Security Strategy of Engagement and Enlargement* (Washington DC: US GPO 1996). The latest version (1997) of this document is *A National Security Strategy for a New Century*. The direct reference to 'enlarging' the community of market democracies has been eliminated from the title, but the emphasis on promoting democracies as part of US security strategy remains (see esp. pp.19–20).
34. Manwaring and Corr, 'Confronting the New World Disorder' (note 13) p.44.
35. Comments made in a presentation to a conference on 'The Role of Naval Forces in the 21st Century', Fletcher School of Law and Diplomacy, Cambridge, MA, 19–20 Nov. 1997.

Facing the Choice Among Bad Options in Complex Humanitarian Emergencies

DAYTON L. MAXWELL

By failing to examine the mid- to long-term effects of following short-term, politically acceptable solutions concerning conflict countries, better options may be discarded. The willingness on the part of the international community to spend billions of dollars over the last few years in relief and minimal security protection for relief efforts has led to the use of the term 'fig leaf'. Providing relief hides the fact that more vigorous actions and greater risks are required to bring a conflict to a close. In the case of Bosnia, this 'fig leaf' now appears to extend through the reconstruction effort, given that sectarian political leadership is unwilling to implement the multi-ethnic society provisions of the Dayton Accords.

Those who provoked the strife in the first place are still prepared to renew the strife without continued international intervention. The hostile parties in the Bosnian conflict have not agreed on how to establish a multi-ethnic state, per the Dayton Accords, causing a growing number of leaders to declare that partition is the answer. It required eight years for ECOWAS/ECOMOG to achieve an elected government in Liberia. Angola, Haiti, Guatemala, Armenia/Azerbaijan, Tajikistan, Sierra Leone, Cambodia, and Burundi are examples of other conflict countries which need continued nurture by the international community to avoid the recurrence of conflict.

Experts are increasingly concluding that all aspects of reaching a sustainable peace ('structural peace' is used in Europe) need to be considered early in the policy/strategy decision process. In a World Bank and Carter Center conference early in 1997, 'the participants advocated an *integrated strategic framework* characterized by:

- a coherent and comprehensive approach by all actors;

- partnerships and coordination between the various members of the international community and the national government;

- a broad consensus on a strategy and related set of interventions;

- careful balancing of macroeconomic and political objectives;

- the necessary financial resources.'[1]

Future historical analyses of the current, immediate post-Cold War period will likely treat the 1990s political process used to reach intervention decisions as inappropriate, antiquated vestiges of the decision-making process used during the Cold War. The challenge is to find more effective means of decision-making appropriate to the post-Cold War climate. If not, the lesson would-be warlords will learn is that their actions can be conducted with impunity and the rewards may be significant. 'Impunity is becoming very, very, very contagious', says Emma Bonino, European Economic Commission Humanitarian Affairs Commissioner.[2]

Examples of Tough Choices[3]

Somalia 1992: Converting the Joint Task Force Intervention to a UN Operation

The decision on the timing to turn over the peace enforcement operation in Somalia to UN forces was made by the US Republican administration after the election of a Democratic administration to occur prior to the Democrats taking office. This was a political decision both to minimize the duration of the US armed forces' stay and to limit the political liability of the Republicans. Very little analysis was performed on the root causes of the conflict, the political process needed to sustain progress toward a stable peace, the military tactics of the warlords and effective means of mitigation, and the host country institutional change options available in a post-Cold War Somalia. *The tough choices were not addressed.*[4]

Sarajevo, Bosnia 1994-95: UNPROFOR Enforcement of Ceasefire

The Sarajevo market massacre of February 1994 led to a vigorous NATO response, a ceasefire agreement, an agreement to permit access to Sarajevo, and the launching of a reconstruction effort. The Bosnian Serb military held the overwhelming balance of power, however, and began to test and abrogate many elements of the agreement. Sniping and occasional mortar/rocket attacks in the city resumed (albeit some of it was retaliation for Bosniac provocation), the airport was closed down, checkpoints were established and access/transport of goods limited, water/gas/electricity utilities cut off, and general non-cooperation increased. From the military standpoint, UNPROFOR seemed to have no choice but to accede to the superior military authority facing it. Yet civilian deaths due to the conditions of strife, including senior American diplomats, increased for well over a year until the Dayton Accords were finally accomplished. That did not happen until after the Srebrenica catastrophe. *The tough choices were not faced until after disasters occurred.* Evidence that disasters would come was ample.[5]

General 1992–97: Civilian Deaths Outnumber Military Casualties

The UN recently released information that the number of civilian humanitarian workers killed in the past five years is 250–300. No statistical data base exists on civilian mortality figures, but these numbers far exceed military deaths in complex humanitarian emergency countries. Political decisions which limit effective military engagement to minimize military casualties in effect place civilians at risk. *The tough choice which is not faced is that either indigenous civilians die in significant numbers, civilian humanitarian workers are killed, or soldiers are put at risk to achieve a stable peace.* Soldiers have selected a risky occupation but are protected. By implication, the decisions on actions (or non-actions) taken in conflict countries lead to the conclusion that civilians are expendable.

Rwanda 1994: Taking Preventive Action

The evidence was available to determine that a potential catastrophe was brewing in 1994. Hate radio programs were broadcast. Information was quietly passed to the international community that sinister plans were being developed. People at high levels in the international community debated about what should be done. Nothing was done, and no rapid reaction was taken even when the atrocities began to mitigate them. *An inability to face the tough choices led to the killing of well over a half a million people.*

General: Mitigating the Costs of Conflict

There are both human and economic costs to conflicts. The economic costs are both the costs to the donors for humanitarian assistance, peacekeeping, and reconstruction, and the costs to the country in conflict in terms of destruction and lost economic progress should the conflict not have occurred. 'The impact of conflict on human lives, economic development and the environment is devastating.'[6] To take just the Bosnia conflict, while actual costs are not easily available, a reasonable estimate places the cost from 1992–97 at around $17 billion. *No one calculated that by not making the tough decision to intervene assertively at the outset the costs would mount to this magnitude.*

Democratic Republic of the Congo (DRC) 1997

Today the conditions for ethnic conflict among the many groups comprising the Democratic Republic of the Congo exist. The long-term support of an authoritarian government not only delayed an evolutionary transition of the DRC into a stable democracy, but it created the conditions for a fragmentation of the country. Like Bosnia, it will be necessary to assist the leaders and the peoples of DRC determine how to create a viable multi-ethnic society after years of oppression and atrocities. *The choices which must be confronted on how to do that will be tough.*

Contribution of the Development Assistance Community

Economic assistance is a necessary but not a sufficient component of establishing a stable peace. Multilateral and bilateral donors are making progress, but still struggling, to determine their appropriate roles. The World Bank has just issued 'a conceptual and operational framework ... designed to facilitate the transition from conflict to peace',[7] and is using donor country trust funds to begin reconstruction work in Bosnia in spite of the conditions not yet being satisfied to grant loans. The UNDP has established the Office of Emergency Response to bring resources quickly to respond to needs in post-conflict countries. Bilateral donors are gradually improving their ability to provide relevant assistance in transition countries.

Equally important is determining how to use limited resources in the most effective manner.

Assistance is needed in many areas at the same time. The following is an illustrative list:

- establishing a neutral and professional security and justice system,
- re-establishing normal economic activity,
- restoring essential public services and utilities,
- determining and initiating the most appropriate economic and social policies,
- creating a governance which respects minority rights and evolves toward a viable democracy,
- planning and holding free and fair elections,
- disarmament, demobilization, and demining,
- refugee and internally-displaced persons repatriation,
- empowering civil society as a viable representative of the population,
- developing viable financial management, and
- creating a credible investment climate.

No wonder the civilian sector lags, given the extensive and intensive requirements. Priorities must be established, a strategic approach developed, and the host country leaders and population fully engaged in the phased tasks. Host country leaders are ultimately responsible for creating and implementing the solutions which lead to a stable peace. Far more work is required to help them do this. This is the most important deficit in the international community's approach to a more effective response to overcoming conflict.

Contribution of the Military Community

Peace enforcement efforts by an intervening military force is often a *necessary but not a sufficient component* toward establishing a stable peace. Of the three communities working together in conflict countries (political, military and humanitarian), the military is the most constrained in being able to perform to its maximum capacity. The intervenors conform to different ethical standards than the conflicting parties. No matter what level of atrocities are being committed by the conflicting parties, constraint on the part of the intervenors is the mandate. In addition, 'mission creep' and 'force protection' orders constrain it from contributing to a greater extent than simply establishing and maintaining security.

Yet the principal threat to peace in conflict countries is the likelihood, demonstrated in most of the conflict countries over the last few years, of warring faction commanders using their military power to achieve their objectives rather than patiently implementing peace agreements. The military leaders in the intervening nations face a dilemma. They say they will follow the orders of their political leaders, yet they actively work to influence the political decisions to minimize the risk because the military is blamed should something go wrong.

The military has generally been successful in halting fighting and establishing stability. It established a secure zone in northern Iraq to protect the return home of the Kurds – and redeployed in only two months; it halted the famine in Somalia – before the ill-fated and much-publicized loss of lives; it restored an elected government in Haiti; it established the conditions for the Bosnian peace agreement to be worked out in Dayton; it restored order in Albania; it established (finally) conditions for elections to be held in Liberia; and it placed a small peacekeeping force in Macedonia which has prevented violence from occurring there. The successes are not as easily remembered as the failures, unfortunately. In addition, successful exits are rare, and peacekeeping operations seem to last indefinitely.

Contribution of the Political/Diplomatic Community

The political efforts lead all the others. They, too, are a *necessary but not a sufficient component* toward establishing a stable peace. The general directions are set in the United Nations Security Council through resolutions. Actions to achieve diplomatic solutions are engaged by special representatives of the UN and of concerned governments. Joint efforts among governments are launched through diplomatic missions, 'contact groups', high profile personalities, and at times in combination with 'Track Two' efforts (e.g., NGOs, established religious organizations,[8] the media). By definition (or by default), sooner or later the political efforts lead to a solution. It's unfortunate that in the 1990s it is usually later rather than sooner, for various reasons.

Preventing conflict in the first place is the desired state. Successes exist, they probably happen frequently, but are seldom noted. Nor is a comprehensive process institutionalized. A 'Tool Kit' has been published for diplomats and practitioners.[9] But a 1996 US Institute of Peace study concluded:

> Though preventive diplomacy is becoming more widely used and discussed ... only limited progress has been made in translating this emerging approach into workable operating strategies and ongoing practice. ... Standard operating procedures for early warning and preventive response have yet to be widely instituted and regularly applied by the United Nations, the US government, and regional organizations, and preventive diplomacy has yet to be elevated to the status of accepted official governmental or international policy.[10]

The need for a determined political will to use 'all necessary means', the common phrase in the UNSC resolutions, is the commonly accepted weakest link today. The most detailed study of this phenomenon was written about Bosnia by James Gow under the fitting title, *Triumph of the Lack of Will*. He concludes, '... the Bosnian conflict and the Yugoslav war as a whole could have been drawn to a close two and a half years earlier at the time of the Vance-Owen Plan.'[11] Similar conclusions can probably be drawn for Liberia, Angola, and several other countries.

A Whole Greater Than the Sum of Its Parts

Orchestration of the efforts engaged in creating a sustainable peace is the responsibility of political leadership, not only international leaders but also the leaders of the conflicting factions and the civil society leaders in the country in conflict. But the Cold War created institutions and mandates which limit the flexibility to react rapidly to changing conditions, and in particular conditions of crisis. The term 'stovepipe' operations is frequently used, even within institutions. A report evaluating the performance of the

US military in Bosnia says, 'Stove-pipe, independent planning prevents integrated planning, invites "ad hoc-ery", and sows confusion.'[12] Contained in an Agency for International Development (USAID) report is, 'Within the USAID "corporate culture", disaster and development experts are philosophically, fiscally and physically divided, with separate funding sources, offices, programming systems and objectives.'[13]

Even if each organization engaged in a conflict country completely accomplishes its mandate, the goal of re-establishing stability and normal economic activity in a conflict country is not likely to be easily accomplished. Few have the expertise or the mandate to perform the comprehensive conflict resolution efforts required, complementary to economic, political and military efforts, to assure that a strategic plan is established and maintained toward achievement of a sustainable peace. The need for a greater effort toward sustainable peace is the theme of another piece by the author. This study lists current on-ground operational mandates of the civilian and military organizations, plus a second list suggesting extended mandates for each to include efforts which contribute to resolving the conflict.[14]

Thus even if a decision were reached to perform integrated strategic plans for all future interventions, it probably could not be done effectively in the near term. The term 'complex' means just that. Today's conflicts cannot be resolved by simply returning to the status quo ante. Given that pre-conflict conditions either caused the conflict or permitted it to be exacerbated, changes must be introduced as part of the resolution. Democratization, privatization, new governance systems, establishing independent and neutral police and judiciary, ethnic reconciliation, demobilization and reintegration of military, and developing a free market economy are all examples of changes *required* in the transition from pre-conflict to post-conflict conditions. Assistance to the conflicting parties to move through the transition period and resolve the conflict will require new skills and techniques which need to be developed. Thinking on how to do this has already begun. The United States Government has issued its Presidential Decision Directive 56, referred to as the Pol-Mil Plan directive.[15] General (Ret.) John R. Galvin, in the lead article to this publication as well as Lt General (Ret.) William G. Carter, III, former Chief of Staff of IFOR in Sarajevo, both indicate that the military needs to perform political analysis. While still active, General Carter spoke to the participants of the Bosnia-Herzegovina After Action Review on 16 April 1997, saying (paraphrase):

> During the Cold War period NATO was a military organization with a political annex; now, however, NATO has become a political

organization with a military annex. New and innovative thinking is very much required in these changed circumstances. For example, 'mission creep' is an unfortunate term and should be replaced by 'mission evolution.' The military must be more forthcoming in making a contribution to the achievement of a stable security in crisis countries, and even do more of the political analysis if necessary.[16]

The State Department and USAID have begun integrated strategic planning and implementation in the President's Greater Horn of Africa Initiative. The World Bank plans to work in post-conflict reconstruction by 'initiating a process of detailed assessment and planning which would ... culminate in a Transitional Support Strategy. ... The extent of the Bank's involvement and risk-management strategies would ... include entry and exit strategies.'[17] The European Union is addressing these new issues as it works toward a new, post-Maastricht treaty.

But we need to admit in all humility that we face an extended period of Applied Research efforts. All the players need to learn new skills and techniques. Negotiation skills must be combined with technical expertise to analyze, prioritize and develop implementation plans to effect *rapidly and patiently* (a clear challenge) the new policies/technologies/governance systems. Today's information technology can *surely* contribute to more effective conflict resolution.[18] The US Institute of Peace dedicated a full conference to 'Virtual Diplomacy' to examine this need.[19]

We need to accept that certain risks must be taken, either taking risks early or risking worse consequences later. Certainly good judgement on what actions are appropriate will come with experience. (Early action, while usually important to quell crises before they grow in magnitude, may not necessarily be appropriate. Timely action, however, is critical. Much more attention on what constitutes effective timing is certainly needed.) A more systematic approach to learn how all organizations can work more effectively together to achieve a whole which is greater than the sum of its parts is vitally needed.

Facing the Tough Choices

A systematic approach begins with a clear understanding of the issues that need to be researched. This process can be stimulated by asking a series of questions which summarize the tough choices to be examined. Examples:

- Given that long-term aspects of intervention are not considered in the political decisions taken in the interventions over the last six years for fear of the cost commitments, and given that the costs of NOT examining these options are resulting in far greater costs, will this lead to a *requirement* to examine the long-term effects of decisions?

- Might a study of the costs of prolonged conflicts result in the need to examine the nature of the interventions? Should we become more fearful of the resource drain and harmful humanitarian and human rights effects on prolonged, inconclusive crises than a more vigorous intervention which establishes total control an creates a new, more appropriate government, that is, the post-World War II model for Germany and Japan?

- With public resources devoted to conflict countries limited, will private resources of foundations, philanthropists, NGOs and commercial companies become increasingly important and solicited? If so, will this require a new definition of partnership between the public and private actors?

- What is the nature of the complementarity among government and UN diplomats working at upper levels, official donor reconstruction programs working at the technical levels, the military in establishing a stable security, and the NGOs working at the community levels, in formulating strategic approaches which will assure sustained progress toward peace?

- What organizational restructuring and institution-building is necessary to become more effective in achieving a stable peace by the UN, donor governments, NGOs, the military, the independent financial institutions, etc.? What new resources will need to be devoted to support this donor 'structural adjustment'?

- What is the validity in the rationale that the world is becoming more interdependent economically, and that conflicts in almost any region of the world will hurt the developed nations economically as well as the region where the conflict takes place. Can this be studied in more depth to determine the nature and magnitude of the negative effects?

- Can the citizens of intervening countries be educated to understand and accept a reasonable level of risk which must be taken to achieve peace, even in distant countries where national interests are unclear? What level can be considered reasonable? How do governments do this most effectively?

- What specialized skills and techniques must be developed among expatriate communities to work comprehensively and intensively with host country representatives that will assure a sustainable peace process?
- What tools and techniques can be passed to host country representatives

which will permit them to more effectively address and resolve their conflicts?

- How can economic incentives and sanctions be used more effectively, either separately or in conjunction with military pressures?

- Can *regional organizations* (e.g., OAU, OAS, ECOWAS) be strengthened to mount effective diplomatic/economic/military efforts to bring conflicts to an early conclusion? Would a long-term strategy to do that make intervention more palatable as a training mission, particularly if conflict is mitigated and potential substantial loss of life avoided?

- How much does the determination of an exit date for peacekeepers based only on political criteria affect the disposition of the conflicting parties to cooperate to achieve a stable peace?

- To what extent do elections *really* contribute to achieving a stable peace? Is the objective of establishing a multi-ethnic society with respect for minority rights contrary to the objective of democratization of a country?

- Will reconstruction efforts, with some inter-ethnic cooperation built in, be sufficient to assure long-term ethnic cooperation, or will activities directly addressing long-term institutionalization of inter-ethnic cooperation be necessary?

- Can military peacekeeping units be given the task of in-country training of indigenous military to facilitate reconstruction, participate in conflict resolution efforts, and in general convert to a peaceful military supporting a democratically-elected civilian government?

- Is it possible for NGOs and the military to work together in such programs? Strengthening of civil society organizations is one of the most important tasks in democratic governance. Can NGOs and the military cooperate in finding ways to work with and strengthen indigenous civil society organizations?

These are representative of many questions which need to be addressed. Others would address the need to determine priorities in uses of resources among, *inter alia,* facility reconstruction, training of police and judges, revitalizing enterprises to provide employment, ethnic reconciliation, holding elections, bringing to justice war criminals or holding truth commissions to put injustices behind, and restoring education and essential services.

The tough choices will not really be understood without a more systematic approach to research the answers to these questions.

Conclusion

Correct identification of the problem is often said to be the key to achieving a solution. With the possible exception of Haiti, that is not done in any sophisticated manner for most complex humanitarian emergency countries prior to a decision to intervene. But even Haiti remains problematic because the tough issue of establishing a viable economy with a poor resource base which holds the hope of bringing the country out of poverty was not sufficiently addressed.

Perhaps *the toughest choice is the first one*, admitting we have not developed the capability to develop rational entrance and end-state plans which address the fundamental issues causing the conflict. With respect to Bosnia, James Gow says:

> Like losing gamblers, the masters of international involvement in the Yugoslav crisis constantly hoped that they would strike lucky. Having laid one losing bet after another on half-measures, diplomacy and non-violent pressures which did not achieve their prime objective of resolving the conflict, the major powers and the principal bodies responsible for European security played double-or-quits. International diplomacy ... finally came good and Dayton was signed, but only in the ironic shadow of past failure and present surrender of principle.[20]

The term 'end-state planning' really needs to replace the term 'exit strategy'. The latter is too much associated with a political date and a strategy to withdraw based on that date, rather than determining what conditions are appropriate to establish before withdrawal, namely, end-state conditions. This is what the *Washington Post* means in a recent editorial, 'An exit strategy is the answer to the needs, even prayers, of a president caught between the tugs of politics and foreign policy. . . . Pulling out on an arbitrary date when the gains are incomplete and still reversible is a recipe for unraveling.'[21]

If the choice to perform competent and comprehensive end-state planning prior to determining departure dates is not made, we will continue to react to crises in a costly, *ad hoc* manner.

NOTES

1. The World Bank and the Carter Center, 'From Civil War to Civil Society', 19–21 Feb. 1997 conference proceedings report, July 1997.
2. B92 Open Serbia Daily News Service, 14 Nov. 1997. President Jimmy Carter and Emma Bonino both signed a declaration on 13 Nov. urging the UN to set up a permanent international court to deal with war crimes and human rights abuses. Carter said that had such

a court been in existence, some of the terrible atrocities in Rwanda could have been avoided. Bonino also said that failure to bring the indicted Bosnian Serb leaders to justice could tempt others to commit copycat crimes.

3. 'In politics, the choices are often between bad and worse' states Amos Perlmutter, American University, in a *Washington Post* article entitled, 'Saddam: It's Up to Us', 16 Nov. 1997. This article addresses the Iraq dilemma. He goes on to say, 'There is an inherent lack of resolve in the United States since the end of the Cold War and an absence of a mission that can mobilize the nation.'

4. The author was the Acting Director of the Office of Foreign Disaster Assistance (OFDA) and the senior representative of the Agency for International Development (AID) to the Interagency Task Force on Somalia during this transition period.

5. The author was the AID Representative to Bosnia during 1994, and frequently participated in UNPROFOR meetings. The UNPROFOR commander in Bosnia, Lt.-Gen. Michael Rose, was equally critical of the Serbs and the Bosniacs. He was obliged to accept the Serb power dominance, however, and for tactical reasons declined to blame them publicly for continuing their targeting of civilians. Nor did his UN civilian supervisor, Akashi. Political analysis by the military which would serve to make effective recommendations for appropriate action in these conflict situations remains very weak. This UNPROFOR weakness is a good example of the surrender of principle James Gow writes about – see his quote in the concluding section of this contribution.

6. Michael Cranna (ed.) *The True Cost of Conflict* (London: Saferworld [UK NGO], Earthscan Publications 1994) p.197. This book includes seven case studies of East Timor, Iraq, Kashmir, Mozambique, Peru, Sudan and the Former Yugoslavia, and examines the economic and human costs to both the donors and the countries in conflict. Saferworld plans to do a significant update of this study.

7. World Bank, 'A Framework for World Bank Involvement in Post-Conflict Reconstruction', 25 April 1997.

8. See, for example, Douglas Johnston and Cynthia Sampson (eds.) *Religion, The Missing Dimension of Statecraft* (Center for Strategic International Studies, OUP 1994).

9. Creative Associates International, Inc., 'Preventing and Mitigating Violent Conflicts: A Revised Guide for Practitioners', April 1997. (This was prepared for the US Department of State and AID under the Greater Horn of Africa Initiative.)

10. Michael S. Lund, *Preventing Violent Conflicts: A Strategy for Preventive Diplomacy* (US Inst. of Peace Press 1996) pp.26–7.

11. James Gow, *Triumph of The Lack of Will, International Diplomacy and the Yugoslav War* (London: Hurst 1997) p.299.

12. Max Manwaring, 'Bosnia-Herzegovina After Action Review (BHAAR II) Conference Report', US Army Peacekeeping Institute, proceedings from the 13–17 April 1997 conference.

13. AID document prepared by the Inter-Agency Team on Rapid Transitions from Relief to Development, The President's Greater Horn of Africa Initiative (GHAI), 'Linking Relief and Development in the Greater Horn of Africa', May 1996, p.7.

14. Dayton Maxwell, 'Can I Do That and My Job, Too?', presented at The Cornwallis Group conference, Analysis for and of The Resolution of Conflict, 7–11 April 1997. The conference proceedings are being published by the Canadian Peacekeeping Press of the Pearson International Peacekeeping Training Center.

15. 'White Paper – The Clinton Administration's Policy on Managing Complex Contingency Operations: Presidential Decision Directive – 56', dated May 1997. Known as PDD-56, this paper outlines the US Government organizational procedures when a crisis hits. It includes directions to develop an exit strategy. Skeptics conclude that this does not necessarily mean a change from the current practice of determining a politically acceptable date.

16. Dayton Maxwell, 'Adaptive Command & Control: Future Mission Statements in Peace Operations', a paper in the Proceedings of the Third International Command and Control Research and Technology Symposium, National Defense University, 17–20 June 1997, p.26.

17. World Bank, 'Framework' (note 7) p.v.

18. See, for example, Joseph S. Nye Jr and William A. Owens, 'America's Information Edge',
    Foreign Affairs, March/April 1996.
19. US Inst. of Peace conference on 'Virtual Diplomacy – The Global Communications
    Revolution and International Conflict Management', 1–2 April 1997.
20. Gow (note 11) p.325.
21. Exit Strategy', *Washington Post*, 28 Sept.1997, p.C6.

The 'Almost Obvious' Lessons of Peace Operations

MAX G. MANWARING and EDWIN G. CORR

The unstable 'peace' of the post-Cold War era is rife with myriad instabilities and destabilizers. They include human starvation, widespread disease, environmental devastation, increasing poverty, lack of socio-economic and political justice, criminal anarchy, refugee flows, illegal drug trafficking and organized crime, extreme nationalism, irredentism, religious fundamentalism, militant reformers, ideologues, demagogues, civil and military bureaucrats, terrorists, insurgents, warlords, ethnic cleansers, and rogue states.

The hard evidence over time and throughout the world shows that instabilities and destabilizers are the general consequences of misguided, corrupt, insensitive, and/or incompetent governance.[1] Such governments are unwilling or unable to provide basic services and to maintain basic security and functioning legal systems that protect individual rights and provide a sense of societal equity. These governments do *not* derive their just powers from the governed and do *not* generate a viable political competence that can and will manage, coordinate, and sustain internal change and conflict affecting individual and collective well-being in a morally acceptable manner. This illegitimate governance or malfeasance can be seen when disparate ethnic, religious, or other political groups in a society become insistent on establishing separate identities, and governments react to them with thuggish and brutal violence.

In this security environment, the United Nations (UN), other regional international organizations, the United States, and other interested parties have become increasingly involved in some form of direct or indirect intervention to achieve a desired level of stability and peace in pursuit of multilateral collective security interests or overriding unilateral national security or humanitarian interests. Thus, the concept of 'peacekeeping' has gone from monitoring agreements between a relatively few absolutely sovereign, consenting, and responsible parties to a considerably larger number of more difficult and ambiguous peacemaking and peace-enforcement tasks among less-than-sovereign, and sometimes nonconsenting and irresponsible parties.

The implacable challenge in pursuing nation-state stability and legitimate governance is one of accepting the responsibilities of political leadership that the international security environment imposes. The task is to mount a coordinated political-economic-psychological-humanitarian-military effort. The purpose of such an effort is to create internal conditions within failed or failing states that can lead to peace and stability with justice. Once this has been accomplished, 'only sustained, cooperative work to deal with underlying economic, social, cultural, and humanitarian problems can place an achieved peace on a durable foundation' – and avoid an eventual relapse into conflict.[2] Thus, political solutions circling back to 'preventive diplomacy' must be a part of the endgame, and all other peace operations in a given context must directly support that agenda. Otherwise, peace operations risk becoming little more than static and limited military occupations.

Related Lessons That Should Have Been Learned

The problems and questions related to the violence of the new world 'disorder' imply five highly interrelated and reinforcing lessons that should have been learned by now. The consistency of these lessons in the more than 60 cases the UN Security Council has declared as formal threats to international peace and security is impressive. That consistency warrants confidence that these strategic-level lessons take into account the major unifying dimensions of effective peace efforts and should begin the process of rethinking both problem and response in a world of dangerous uncertainty and ambiguity.

These five closely connected lessons focus on internal political requirements for successful involvement in complex humanitarian emergencies; the relationship of legitimate governance to stability; the relationship of development to security and stability; the relationship between legitimacy and political competence; and the external political requirements necessary to generate the capability to sustain a durable foundation for peace.

Internal Political Requirements for Successful Involvement

The days of delineating a successful international political end-state as simple short-term self-protection, limited adherence to human rights and the election of civilian political leaders, or material compassion for a humanitarian problem are over. The American public expects US efforts, especially if they involve the expenditure of large amounts of tax dollars and/or the expenditure of even a few American lives, to make the world – and the United States – a better place in the long term.

Thus, the main element of US foreign policy, military management, and public diplomacy in the current international security environment must go beyond the notion of democratic enlargement to that of a selective, long-term, patient but firm and vigilant pursuit of responsible and competent (i.e., legitimate) governance. This is not simple idealism. The concept of legitimate governance is a marriage of Wilsonian ideals and *realpolitik* that provides a pragmatic foundation for national and international stability and well-being.[3]

The Relationship of Legitimate Governance to Stability

Political legitimacy is based on the moral right of a government to govern – and the ability of the government to govern morally. Popular perceptions of corruption, disenfranchisement, poverty, lack of upward social mobility, and lack of personal security tend to limit the right, and the ability, of a regime to conduct the business of state. Until and unless a population feels that its government deals with these and other issues of political, economic, and social injustice and security fairly and effectively, the potential for internal or external factors to destabilize and subvert a government is considerable.

The Relationship of Development to Security and Stability

The international security dialogue is focusing on national development. That requirement equates to a holistic national capability-building effort. The generally uncoordinated, piecemeal, and *ad hoc* approach to socio-economic development must be brought to an end. Unless solutions to development problems are addressed on a coherent and long term basis, there will be no self-sustaining national development. National development provides the capability for the nation-state to develop the political and economic strength to provide internal order and progress. National development also provides the capability for the state to protect and enhance its interests in the international security arena. Thus, self-sustaining national development provides both security and stability.

The Relationship between Legitimacy and Political Competence

Another lesson that should have been learned that helps define an appropriate response to the problem of legitimate governance and positive stability is that of the relationship between legitimacy and political competence. Legitimacy is necessary to generate the capability to effectively manage, coordinate, and sustain political, economic, and social development. This capability implies the political competence to develop responsible governance and a resultant national and international purpose and will to which a people can relate and support. This capability thus implies the competence to legitimize and strengthen national political institutions. The degree to which this political objective is achieved at home will determine the level of influence that can be exerted abroad. It will also define, more than anything else, progress toward viable national security and well-being.

The External Political Requirements for Success in Generating a Durable Foundation for Peace and Stability

The principal circumstance that has plagued UN and US efforts to assist Bosnia-Herzogovina, Cambodia, the Congo, Haiti, Panama, Rwanda, Somalia, and any number of additional examples to establish credible and legitimate public security and stability is a lack of commitment to take responsibility for the consequences of intervention.

Commitment presupposes a great deal more than taking control of a contended area, stopping any escalation of violence, enforcing law and order, and imposing an acceptable level of security. It presupposes knowing where you are going, understanding and implementing the ways and means of getting there, and taking responsibility for action.

An international organization acting multilaterally or a government acting unilaterally that defers to arbitrary 'end-dates' and fails to make a commitment to a clearly defined vision of ultimate political success makes it possible to lose control of both the process and the end-state. As a consequence, a peace operation or complex humanitarian emergency frequently cycles back to the beginning of the process, and the seeds of the next problem are sown in the present one.

Two Keys to Putting It All Together

The fulfillment of an imperative for holistic responsible governance and just stability consists of two principal elements. They are both conceptual and operational. The first requires a rethinking and restructuring of the stability equation. The second is end-state planning. Together, a new stability equation and end-state planning constitute the prime lesson for failed or failing regimes and their international supporters in the coming decades.

Toward a New Stability Equation

The three dimensions of a new stability (S) equation that must be developed are: (1) the military-police capability (M) to provide an acceptable level of internal and external security; (2) the economic ability (E) to generate real security and socio-economic development; and (3) the political competence (PC) to develop a type of governance to which a people can relate and support.

The security and the socio-economic components of stability are generally well understood. Clearly, however, the key concept of political competence is not as well understood, developed, and operationalized as the other two. The United States and the international community, generally, have emphasized economic development and military security under the assumption that social and political development would automatically follow. That has not happened.

It is heuristically valuable to portray the relationships among the three components of stability in a mathematical formula: $S = (M + E) PC$. The political competence element of the equation is so critical that it means the sum of the whole can be substantially altered by the elements that constitute national political competence. The ultimate value of the economic and security elements of the equation can be reduced to nothing or nearly nothing if the leadership competence component is absent or weak. For example, $100 \times 0 = 0$.

Governments that are not responsive to the importance of political competence can find themselves in a 'crisis of governance'. They face growing social violence, criminal anarchy, terrorism, insurgency, and overthrow. Thus, the development of competent political leadership upon a foundation of moral legitimacy is a challenge the governments must meet to survive the growing international instability. Specifically, the challenge is to change perspectives and ensure that every policy, program, and political action contributes directly to the maintenance and enhancement of legitimate governance.

End-State Planning

The key to the implementation of a viable political stability strategy – and strategic clarity – is planning. This depends on a clear strategic vision, based on the new stability equation, from which to start. A viable strategy also depends on a management structure and resources to apply the vision on the basis of a realistic calculation of end, ways, meaning, and timing. This takes us to end-state planning.

End-state planning starts from the truism that conflict is a continuation of politics by other means, but with two qualifying arguments. First, military violence is required only when the conditions or changes sought cannot be achieved through political/diplomatic, socio/economic, or informational/psychological means. Second, end-state planning advocates synchronization of *all* national or international civilian and military instruments of power so as to gain the most synergism from the interaction of the variables selected for action.

The end-state planning argument concludes that, if the UN or the US or any other international player is going to succeed in the future conflicts in which they are most likely to become involved, civil and military forces must be structured and employed in ways that respond to the dynamic political, economic, social, as well as military centers of gravity of the various parties to the conflict. Additionally, there must be a clear definition of what ultimate success looks like.

End-state planning allows decisionmakers and policymakers to think logically, in synchronized small phases, about the conditions they seek to create. It also allows leaders and their staffs to consider the opportunities that may arise and obstacles that must be overcome. It is critical to realize which is which and what the implications for ultimate success might be. The key is to understand precisely what it is that must be achieved, to understand exactly what is required, and to make the decision whether or not to engage in a conflict or complex humanitarian emergency and start down a 'slippery slope' that may lead to some form of disaster.

Those efforts cannot be concerned only with the synergized use or movement of national and international instruments of power. They must also be concerned with the *long term* effects. It is not a matter of putting the proverbial cart before the horse. It is a matter of knowing where the horse is going and how it is going to get there. Decisionmakers, policymakers, and planners should never lose sight of that bigger picture.

Conclusions

Analysis of the problems of legitimate governance and stability with justice takes us beyond providing some form of humanitarian assistance or refugee assistance in cases of human misery and need. It takes us beyond traditional monitoring of bilateral agreements, or protecting a people from another group of people or from a government. It takes us beyond compelling one or more parties to a conflict to cease human rights violations and other morally repugnant activities, or repelling simple aggression. Analysis of the problems of governance and stability takes us back to where we began. The core strategic problem is responsible political leadership in the post-Cold War world. Foreign policy and military asset management must address this central issue.

The enormity and logic of the establishment of a durable and just peace demand a carefully thought-out, phased, long-term planning and implementation process for sustainable political, economic, and social development. Implementing this extraordinary set of challenges will not be easy. That will, however, be far less demanding and costly in political, social, military, and monetary terms than allowing the problems of irresponsible governance and political instability to continue to fester and generate crises that work to the detriment of all concerned.

The general rule would be that policymakers and decisionmakers must carefully calculate gains and losses, and when the case warrants, intervene earlier rather than later. If done earlier, this implies the initial and intense use of low-cost diplomatic and civilian resources and military support units to ensure legitimacy and stability. If done later, this normally implies the initial and intense use of high-cost military combat units to respond to a losing situation. Ultimately, however, the only test for involvement – whatever its form and level – is that of national self-interest. That is the only morality within the anarchy of world disorder.[4]

Some Final Thoughts on Lessons Learned from Peacekeeping Operations

The primary implications of this analysis are clear. The ability of failed, fragile, and menaced governments to control, protect, and enhance their stability and well-being is severely threatened in the contemporary international security environment. International organizations and individual states are increasingly called on to respond to injustices and instabilities generated by irresponsible governance. Furthermore, the international community is increasingly expected to provide the leverage to ensure that governance once regained remains with or is given to responsible, incorrupt, and competent political leadership that can and will address the root causes that created the crisis in the first place.

The conscious choices that the international community makes about how to conduct peace and stability operations and complex humanitarian emergencies now and in the future will define the processes of national reform, regeneration, well-being, and – thus – relative internal and international peace and security. In this connection, it must be remembered that an enforced peace can only provide the beginning environment from which to begin a political reconciliation and legitimization process.

Within the global security structure, the United States remains the world's only superpower. No other nation-state currently possesses the attributes needed for effective international and regional leverage – political clout, economic impact, cultural appeal, and military reach. Still, the US cannot do everything alone. There are those allies that can and will assist the US in creating a more peaceful and stable international security environment – given fully *committed* leadership. The special status of the US allows it the opportunity to facilitate positive change. By accepting this challenge, the United States can help to replace conflict with cooperation and to harvest the hope and fulfill the promise that peace operations offer.

NOTES

1. This and subsequent assertions are derived from statistical tests based on interviews with more than 300 civilian and military officials and scholars with direct experience in 69 *intrastate* conflicts. The effort was mandated by the Vice Chief of Staff of the US Army, Gen. Maxwell Thurman, during 1984–86. The model predicts at an impressive 88.37 per cent of the cases examined, and is statistically significant at the .001 level. The model, originally called SSI 1 and SSI 2, has also been called the SWORD model. The SWORD papers, although long out of print, are archived in their entirety by a private research organization, the National Security Archives, in Washington DC.
2. Boutros Boutros-Ghali, *An Agenda for Peace* (NY: UN 1992) pp.11, 32–4.
3. See: Max G. Manwaring and Ambassador Edwin G. Corr, 'Confronting the New World Disorder: A Legitimate Governance Theory of Engagement', in Max G. Manwaring and Wm. J. Olson (eds) *Managing Contemporary Conflict: Pillars of Success* (Boulder, CO: Westview Press 1996) pp.31–47.
4. George F. Kennan, 'Morality and Foreign Policy', *Foreign Affairs* (Winter 1985–86) pp.205–16.

Abstracts

An Interview with General John R. Galvin
MAX G. MANWARING

This introductory interview discusses the salient challenges and lessons of contemporary peace operations. In the context of the 'new world disorder', the spillover effects of intranational, national, and regional instability place demands on the international community to take control of a situation from those who have been profiting from chaos, establish law and order, feed and harbor the victims, and ensure an environment for the reestablishment of responsible civil authority. Increasingly, these international 'peacekeepers' are expected to support and protect that civil authority and a subsequent political reconciliation process. Thus, General Galvin establishes the driving concept found in our title, Toward Responsibility in the New World Disorder

Tragedy in the Balkans:
A Conflict Ended – Or Interrupted?
MICHAEL MOODIE

The author argues that while much of a positive nature has been 'accomplished in the former Yugoslavia, particularly Bosnia-Herzegovina, The influence of the international community has not been decisive in determining whether a lasting peace can or will be achieved. The fundamental issues that gave rise to the conflict in region – the dilemma between the pursuit of partition by some actors and the desire for integration by others – have not been resolved. Until such a resolution is achieved, the international community confronts the unattractive choice of leaving its military forces in place to maintain a fragile peace, or to depart in the knowledge that conflict is likely to erupt again.

From Peace Making to Peace Building in Central America:
The illusion versus the Reality of Peace
KIMBRA L. FISHEL

This study explores the tensions between the Central American peace process and the forms of conflict that are emerging. Positive signs in Central America include democratization, the continuing peace efforts, cooperation and integration, reform of the security and military forces, and macroeconomic growth. Nevertheless for every concrete procedure that signals advances in the peace process, an alternative reality underscores the illusion of peace. Long-term peace consolidation rests upon the legitimacy of the governments in question and that of outside supporting organizations. For legitimacy to endure, the peace building environment must be stabilized through reconciliation of two contradictory spheres: the reality and the illusion of peace.

The Challenge of Haiti's Future

DONALD E. SCHULZ

In this essay the author examines the prospects for the fostering and maintenance of political stability, socioeconomic development, and the rule of law in Haiti. The primary focus is on specific problems that need addressing, the role of the United States and the international community in providing assistance, and the prospects that the needed aid will be forthcoming. The author also discusses the impact of the recent political crisis, and presents a list of policy recommendations for overcoming that crisis and addressing some of the country's most pressing requirements.

Waiting for 'the Big One': Confronting Complex Humanitarian Emergencies and State Collapse in Central Africa

WALTER S. CLARKE

In 1994, the state-sponsored Hutu extremists in Rwanda attacked their Tutsi and moderate Hutu compatriots, causing hundreds of thousands of deaths. Two years later, a similar pogrom was launched against Hutu refugees in Zaire, with probably tens of thousands of killings. In both cases, the world appeared mesmerized by the magnitude of the crimes, providing no effective response. The author suggests that the world is witless in such situations because there are no effective procedures to respond to such emergencies. A comprehensive framework for designing and implementing an appropriate international response to state failure, complex emergencies, and peace operations is proposed.

Normative Implications of "The Savage Wars of Peace"

JOHN T. FISHEL

This analysis explores the Normative Implications of the results obtained from the author recent edited book, "The Savage Wars of Peace": Toward a New Paradigm of Peace Operations. *Several generalizations emerge. First, the operation must 'do no harm'. Second, the international organization most directly involved must determine an acceptable end state. Third, promotion of responsible democracy is a key ingredient of long term peace consolidation. Finally, the key to successful operations and establishing these three criteria is de jure and de facto legitimacy.*

Beyond the Logjam:
A Doctrine for Complex Emergencies
JOHN MACKINLAY

The author takes a deeply pessimistic view of the political and institutional volte-faces that would be required to develop a genuinely comprehensive peace support operations doctrine. Presently, peace support operations are unrealistically viewed as providing military solutions to military problems. In addressing the complex realities of a modern 'peacekeeping' crisis, such operations must be understood as an holistic process that relies on various civilian and military agencies and contingents working together in an integrated fashion to achieve a common political goal. Essentially, proposed doctrinal changes concern the need to recognize the real locus of power in a given operational area, and the relevant civilian and military resources and time stages needed to reach a truly successful conclusion of a given peace process.

Policing the New World Disorder:
Addressing Gaps in Public Security during Peace Operations
MICHAEL J. DZIEDZIC

Since the dynamics producing the 'New World Disorder' are unlikely to diminish any time soon, it behooves the US and the entire international community to refine the collective capacity to mount effective multinational responses to the problems of providing appropriate internal public security institutions – police, judges, and jailers. This analysis seeks to address the issue by identifying gaps in public security typically confronted during peace operations and recommending measures intended to increase international proficiency in coping with them.

The Future of Peace Support Operations
ROBERT H. DORFF

Rooted in growing challenges from failing states and increasing ungovernability, the small 'Uncomfortable Wars' of the recent past will persist as the dominant form of conflict in the international system. Choosing an appropriate response requires sound strategy, firmly anchored in an accurate understanding of these conflicts. Initial appearances to the contrary, they are not all the same, and objectives must be tailored accordingly. While overall strategy should be guided by the objectives of promoting 'legitimate governance', specific responses in the form of peace support operations must be built around a better understanding of the conflict and a sober assessment of what the international community can reasonably expect to accomplish.

Facing the Choice Among Bad Options
DAYTON L. MAXWELL

Because of the fear that the actions needed will cost too much, international decision-makers tend to avoid in-depth analyses of or long-term commitments to today's complex humanitarian interventions. Nevertheless, it is important that we learn from peacekeeping lessons since 1992, and humbly admit we might have done better in terms of results and costs had we faced the tough choices early on. As an example, addressing the root causes of continuing hostilities and experimenting with new approaches might have helped to avoid the various embarrassments experienced in Somalia, Bosnia, and Rwanda.

The 'Almost Obvious' Lessons of Peace Operations
MAX G. MANWARING and EDWIN C. CORR

The enormity and logic of the establishment of a durable and just peace demand a carefully thought-out, phased, long-term planning and implementation process for sustainable political, economic, and social development. Implementing this extraordinary set of challenges is not easy, but it can be done. It will be far less demanding and costly in political, social, military, and monetary terms than allowing the problems of irresponsible governance and the resultant political instability to continue to fester and regenerate crises that work to the detriment of all concerned.

About the Contributors

Dr **Max G. Manwaring** is an Adjunct Professor of Political Science at Dickinson College, an Adjunct Professor at the US Army Peacekeeping Institute, a political-military affairs consultant, and a retired US Army colonel. He received his PhD in political science from the University of Illinois. He has served in various civilian and military positions including the US Army War College, the US Southern Command's Small Wars Operations Research Directorate, the Defense Intelligence Agency, and the United States Southern Command's Directorate for Plans, Policy and Political-Military Affairs. Dr Manwaring is the author of several articles and reports dealing with political-military affairs and is editor of several books including *El Salvador at War*; *Uncomfortable Wars*; *Gray Area Phenomena*; and *Managing Contemporary Conflict: Pillars of Success*.

Mr **Michael Moodie** is President of the Chemical and Biological Arms Control Institute. In government, Mr Moodie served from March 1990 to January 1993 as Assistant Director for Multilateral Affairs at the US Arms Control and Disarmament Agency (ACDA) where he was responsible for such issues as chemical and biological weapons, conventional arms control, confidence building measures, and regional arms control. From 1983 to 1987, he was Special Assistant to the Ambassador and Assistant for Special Projects at the US Mission to NATO. In the policy research community, Mr Moodie has held senior positions at the Foreign Policy Research Institute, the Institute for Foreign Policy Analysis and the Center for Strategic and International Studies.

Ms **Kimbra L. Fishel** is a political scientist specializing in military and security issues. She received an MA in political science from the University of Oklahoma where she worked as a research assistant on El Salvador for Ambassador Edwin G. Corr. In the summer of 1997, she served on the support staff of a US team making a series of presentations to the College of High Strategic Studies in El Salvador. She teaches International Relations and American Government and has published numerous articles on US foreign policy, conflict and warfare under her previous name of Krueger. They include 'Internal Struggle Over US

Foreign Policy toward Central America: An Analysis of the Reagan Era', *Presidential Studies Quarterly* (Fall 1996). Her publications under the name of Fishel include Max G. Manwaring and Kimbra L. Fishel, 'Lessons That Should Have Been Learned: Toward a Theory of Engagement for the "Savage Wars of Peace"', John T. Fishel (ed.), *The Savage Wars of Peace: Toward a New Paradigm of Peace Operations* (Westview Press 1997). Kimbra Fishel is currently pursuing her PhD.

Dr **Donald E. Schulz** is a Professor of National Security Affairs at the Straegic Studies Institute, US Army War College. He is co-author of *Reconciling the Irreconcilable: The Troubled Outlook for US Policy Toward Haiti* and *The United States, Honduras and the Crisis in Central America*, and co-editor of *Mexico Faces the 21st Century, Revolution and Counterrevolution in Central America and the Caribbean, Cuba and the Future* and *Political Participation in Communist Systems*. His articles have appeared in *Foreign Policy, Orbis*, the *Journal of Interamerican Studies and World Affairs*, and *Small Wars and Insurgencies*, as well as such media outlets as *Newsweek, Washington Post, Miami Herald, Los Angeles Times*, and *Christian Science Monitor*.

Mr **Walter S. Clarke** is a retired US diplomat; Adjunct Professor of Peace Operations, US Army Peacekeeping Institute; frequent consultant to US armed services on peacekeeping and humanitarian exercises; former Deputy Director, US Liaison Office, Mogadishu, 1993. Co-editor (with Professor Jeffrey Herbst, Woodrow Wilson Center, Princeton University), *Learning from Somalia: Lessons: The Lessons of Armed Humanitarian Intervention* (Westview Press 1997), author of studies on peace operations and African political development issues in academic and professional military journals.

Dr **John T. Fishel** is Professor of National Security Policy at the Center for Hemispheric Defense studies of the National Defense University. Previous to taking this position, he was Professor of National Security Affairs at the US Army Command and General Staff College. He received his PhD in political science from Indiana University. As a reserve officer on active duty, Lt Colonel Fishel was assigned to the United States Southern Command where he was responsible for organizing civic action operations associated with exercises in Peru and Honduras, civic action seminars in Bolivia, conducting assessments in Peru, Bolivia, El Salvador, and organizing a major assessment of the El Salvadoran Armed Forces in combination with the Salvadorans. After Operation 'Just Cause', he was responsible for developing the post conflict civil-military operations plan for Panama and establishing and training the Panama National Police. Dr Fishel has authored numerous articles and book chapters on military and security issues. His publications include *The Fog of Peace: Planning and Executing the Restoration of Panama*; *Liberation, Occupation and Rescue: War Termination and DESERT STORM*; and *"The Savage Wars of Peace"*: *Toward a New Paradigm of Peace Operations*.

Dr **John Mackinlay** is a Senior Research Associate at the Centre for Defence Studies and Senior Lecturer of the War Studies Department, King's College, London. He began his career at the Royal Military Academy, Sandhurst, serving as an officer in the 6th Gurkhas in Borneo and Northern Ireland. In 1985, with a Defence Fellowship at Churchill College, Cambridge, he researched extensively through the Arab–Israeli war zones, including Beirut and South Lebanon. He completed his PhD at Kings College, London, in 1990. In 1991 at Brown University, Rhode Island, he directed 'Second Generation Multinational Operations', a research project on peacekeeping in the post-cold war era and edited the follow-on publication, 'A Guide to Peace Support Operations'. In 1994 he was UK Professor at the Marshall Center (US European Command, Garmisch). He is now a Senior Lecturer at the UK's Joint Services Command and Staff College (Bracknell).

Colonel **Michael J. Dziedzic** is presently a Senior Military Fellow at the US Institute for National Strategic Studies (INSS). His principal issue areas at INSS are peace operations (Team Leader) and security affairs in the Western Hemisphere. Previously, he was a member of the faculty at the National War College (NWC). Before arriving at NWC, he served as Air Attaché in El Salvador from 1992–94, during the implementation of the peace accords. Prior to that posting, he was a political-military planner in the Western Hemisphere Division of the Air Staff (1992), tenured Professor at the US Air Force Academy in the Department of Political Science (1988–91), and Visiting Fellow at the International Isntitute for Strategic Studies in London (1987–88). His scholarly works include *Policing the New World Disorder: Peace Operations and Public Security* (ed. with Ambassador Robert Oakley); *Mexico: Converging Challenges*; and various articles on Mexican defense policy, the transnational drug trade, hemispheric security matters, and current US peace operations.

Dr **Robert H. Dorff** is Professor of National Security Policy and Strategy at the US Army War College. From 1980 to 1997 he was a faculty member in the Department of Political Science and Public Administration at North Carolina State University. His ongoing research interests include European and especially German security policy, as well as democratization and global ungovernability. His research has been published in such journals as *European Security*, *Parameters*, *Journal of Politics*, *Publius*, *Comparative Political Studies*, and the *American Political Science Review*.

Mr **Dayton Maxwell** is a Senior Adviser, Complex Emergencies, for World Vision International, a large, multinational Non-Government Organization (NGO). He is a retired Senior Foreign Service Officer, Agency for International Development (USAID), where he served in Asia, Africa and Eastern Europe. As Deputy Director of the Office of Foreign Disaster Assistance (OFDA) from 1990–93, he led Disaster Assistance Response Teams (DART) to the Philippines (Baguio Earthquake), N. Iraq (Operation 'Provide Comfort' – Kurds), the Former Soviet Union (post-Gorbachev coup assessment, Operation 'Restore Hope'), the Republic of Georgia (Abkhazia) and Laos (drought/flood assessment).

Ambassador **Edwin G. Corr** is the Director of the Energy Institute of the Americas and the Associate Director of the International Programs Center at the University of Oklahoma. His diplomatic career under both Republican and Democratic administrations included ambassadorships to Bolivia, El Salvador, and Peru. He has served as the Deputy Assistant Secretary of State for International Narcotics Matters. Ambassador Corr has also served in Thailand, Mexico, and Ecuador, as a Peace Corps Director in Colombia, and as an infantry officer in the US Marine Corps. He received the BS degree from the University of Oklahoma and also holds Masters degrees from there and the University of Texas at Austin. Ambassador Corr is the recipient of several US and foreign awards, and has written and edited various articles and books including *Low-Intensity Conflict: Old Threats in a New World*.

Index

Aideed, Muhammed Farah 146
air power
  Balkans 19
  NATO 16–17, 20–1
Akashi, Yasushi 21
Albania 134, 183
Albright, Madeleine 25, 66, 84–5
Aleman, Arnoldo 34, 40
Alliance des Forces Démocratique pour la
  Libération du Congo-Zaire (AFDL) 79,
  80, 86
Angola 120, 121, 134, 138, 179, 184
ARENA party 34
Aristide, Jean-Bertrand 50, 59, 65, 68
Armenia 179
arms embargo, Muslims 19, 20
Arusha accord 76
Arzu Irigoyen, Alvaro 34, 37
Association of South East Asian Nations
  (ASEAN) 4
Atwood, Brian 165
Azerbaijan 179

Balconi, General Julio 39
Balkans, origins of conflict 12–14
Banyamulenge 78, 93
Baril, Lt-General Maurice 82
Belgium 75
Belize 40
Bihac 15
Bildt, Karl 26, 28–9
border disputes, Central America 40
Bosnia-Herzegovina 3, 5, 74, 93, 106, 120,
  121, 124, 138, 152, 153, 160, 165, 174,
  189, 195
  ceasefire 180
  conflict 13–14, 167, 184
  Dayton Accords 14, 20, 22–4, 93–4, 115,
    119, 138, 146, 161, 179, 180, 183
  NATO role 11–12, 14, 20–2, 110, 122,
    132, 185–6
  UN involvement 14, 15–18
Bosnian-Croat Federation 23
Boutros-Ghali, Boutros 16, 17, 22, 81, 160,
  165
Bukavu 79
Burundi 72, 78, 79, 80, 90, 93, 179

independence 75
refugees 77
Bush, George 160

Calderon Sol, Armando 34, 39, 45, 46
Cambodia 120, 121, 134, 138, 146, 151, 179,
  195
Cameroon 82
Canada 61, 139, 152
  military intervention in Zaire 82, 83, 87
Capitol Hill conference 51–64
Carnegie Endowment 37–8
Carter, General William G. 185–6
Catholics, Balkans 13
caudillo 64
Cédras, Raoul 50
Central Africa vii-viii, 72–5
Central America vii, 32–3
  democratization 33–6
  development 45
  macroeconomics 42–3
  peace making 33–43, 44–5
  regional integration 38–40
  security forces 40–2
Central American Common Market (CACM)
  39
Central American Democratic Security
  Treaty 39
Central American Integration 39
Chamorro, Violata Barrios de 34
Chapultepec Accords 40
children, faction fighters 126
Christian Democratic Party (PDC) 34
Christopher, Warren 82
Churkin, Vitaliy 20
civil disorder 145
civil society 60
  strengthening 154–5
civil war 45, 167
  El Salvador 33, 46
  Guatemala 32, 37
  Nicaragua 34
civilian targets, bombardment 15
civilians, deaths 181
CIVPOL (civil police of UN) 132, 135, 137,
  138, 147
  enforcement gap 144–9

multilateral cohesion 151–2
operation planning 142–3
relations with military forces 148–9
skills 140–1
Stand-by Force 139–40
training 141
see also police
Clarke, Walter S. vii–viii, 72
Clinton administration 16, 20, 26–7, 29, 38, 59, 62, 82
Clinton, Bill 19, 28, 38, 106
Cold War 1, 9, 10, 32, 74, 107, 114, 116, 138, 163–4, 184
complex humanitarian emergencies vii–viii, 5–6, 7, 9
military doctrine 126–9
military operations 3–4
nature of 115–16
operational problems 119–20
political responses 117–19
reconciliation 122–4
Zaire as 89–97
Comprehensive Campaign Plans 89–97
framework 97–8
conflict
costs 181, 187
post-Cold War 162–4
types of 167–8
Congo 10, 82, 195
Congo, Democratic Republic 75, 181–2
constabulary forces 143–4
Contact Group 18–20
conventional warfare 9, 126
Corr, Edwin G. viii, 107, 108, 167, 172, 173, 192
Costa Rica 36, 39, 43
crime 167
Central America 39, 41–2, 45–6
El Salvador 37
Haiti 58
international 134
organised 145
violent 147
criminal justice 153–4
Croatia 13, 25
Croatians 13, 22
Cuadra, General Joaquin 40
customs service, privatization 55, 62
Cyprus 10, 74, 107, 111, 118, 123

Dayton Accords 14, 20, 22–4, 93–4, 115, 119, 138, 146, 161, 179, 180
Debré, Bernard 81–2
debt, poor countries 115
defence forces
changing nature 116–17

state 121–2
see also military forces
defense gap 117
deforestation, Haiti 55
demobilization 120, 147–8
democracy 111, 162-3, 172
Haiti 55–8, 66
and market economies 106–7, 162
democratization 164
Central America 33–6
Denmark 117
deployment gap 137–44
development 107, 108
assistance 182–3
Central America 45
Haiti 52–5
relation to security 194
Devine, Michael 42
diplomacy
early warning systems 170–1
peace keeping 183–4
disarmament 91, 120, 121
Disaster Response Team (DART) 82
Dorff, Robert H. viii, 160
drug trafficking 35, 41, 45
Duarte, José, Napoleon 36
Dziedzic, Michael J. viii, 132

early warning systems 170–1
ECOMOG 122
economic development, Haiti 52–5
economic integration, Central America 39
ECOWAS 188
El Salvador 32, 39, 134, 138, 151
border disputes 40
crime 41
democratization 34, 37, 111
development 45
economic growth 43
poverty 37–8, 43
security forces 40
UN Mission 36–7
elections 121
Haiti 65
Nicaragua 34
end-state planning 189, 196–7
enforcement gap 144–9
environmental damage 69, 115
Eritrea 82
Ethiopia 82
ethnic cleansing 15, 124
ethnic minorities 13, 124, 129
European Community (EC), and Balkan conflict 14
exclusion zones 21
executive, separation of powers 155–6

Exit Strategy 151, 189

factions, criminalisation 125–6
family planning, aid 55
Farabundo Marti National Liberation Front
  (FMLN) 34
Fishel, John T. viii, 66–7, 102
Fishel, Kimbra vii, 32
Forces Armées du Rwanda 77, 79, 80, 86
Forces Armées du Zaïre 78
foreign aid, to Haiti 52, 59, 65
foreign investment, Haiti 53
France 18, 19, 27, 61, 152
  intervention in Rwanda 76
  Zaire crisis 81–2, 87

Galvin, General John R. vii, 1, 185
gang violence 120, 145
  El Salvador 35, 38, 41, 46
genocide, Rwanda 73, 76, 81, 85, 87, 88–9,
  94, 135
Germany 18, 187
globalization 114
Goma 76, 77, 79, 80, 84, 86, 87, 91
Gorazde 15, 19
governments
  incompetent 192, 194–5
  public order 150
Gow, James 184, 189
Greater Horn of Africa Initiative 186
Greece 111
Guatemala 32, 36, 39, 179
  border disputes 40
  crime 41–2
  peace process 37, 38
  security forces 41
Guatemala City 38
Guatemalan National Revolutionary Unity
  (URNG) 35, 37, 41
guerrillas 32, 36, 134
  former 37, 38, 40

Habyarimina, Juvenal 76
Haiti vii, 43, 50–1, 74, 106, 110, 132, 134,
  146, 147, 148, 149, 151, 152, 166, 174,
  179, 183, 189, 195
  Capitol Hill conference 51–64
  democracy and the rule of law 55–8
  political culture 50, 56, 64–6
  social and economic development 52–5
  structural adjustment 55, 60
Haitian National Police 51, 56, 57–8, 68–9
Hakim, Peter 51
Hamilton, John 42–3
Hammerskjöld, Dag 91, 104
High Commission for Human Rights 80

Holbrooke, Richard 23, 26–7
Honduran Public Security Force 41
Honduras 36, 39, 40
  security forces 41, 42
Horn, Abigail 51
human rights viii, 115, 165–6
  Guatemala 38, 42
  Haiti 56, 59–60, 69
  Zaire 80
humanitarian missions 3, 16
  blockade 15
  Central Africa 74, 79–80, 82, 84, 86, 87
Hutu 75–7, 80, 88–9, 93
Hutulands 82

Iceland 2
immigrants, illegal 46
Implementation Force (IFOR) 14, 20, 22,
  23–4, 110, 115, 138, 146, 185
institutional gap 150-6
insurgency 36
intercommunal violence 115, 117
Interhamwe 76, 77, 79, 80, 86
International Committee of the Red Cross
  79–80, 95
international community
  involvement in Haiti 59–63, 66–9
  peacekeeping 135
  response to emergencies 128
International Financial Institutions, Haiti
  development 54
international law 3
international organizations (IO) 6–7, 11
International Police Monitors 138
International Police Task Force (IPTF) 138,
  146, 149, 153
international system, tiered 166–7
intervention
  Central Africa 74
  costs 186–7
  failed and failing states 2–4
  investment, Haiti 53
Iraq 5, 183
Italy 2, 82
Izetbegovic, Alija 23

Japan 187
Jews, Balkans 13
judiciary 134, 150
  corrupt 41, 42
  Haiti 53, 57
  reform 153
  separation of powers 155–6
justice 150, 151

Kabila, Laurent 78–9, 80, 86, 90

Kagame, Paul 76, 88, 91
Kaplan, Robert 2, 73
Karadzic, Radovan 16, 26–8, 132
kidnapping 41–2
Kigali 76
Kinshasa 90, 94
Kisangani 80
Kivu 75, 76, 77, 78, 93, 94
Kurds 3, 183

land seizures, Haiti 58
land tenure, Guatemala 38
Lasswell, Harold 108
Last, David 104, 108
Lavalas Family 65
Lavalas Political Organization (OPL) 65
law enforcement 147
law and order 145, 150, 151
Lebanon 118
Legitimacy 104, 111, 172, 194–5
    Manwaring Paradigm 102, 103
    state 35, 37
Lemarchand, René, 80
Liberia 119, 120, 121, 125, 134, 179, 183, 184
Los Angeles 46

McCurry, Michael 83–4
Macedonia 183
Mackinlay, John viii, 114
McLarty, Thomas 38
macroeconomics, Central America 42–3
Maguire, Robert 51
Maingot, Anthony 64
major theater wars 160
Mali 82
Manwaring, Max viii, 1, 51, 66–7, 164, 172, 173, 192
Manwaring Paradigm 66–9
    dimensions 102–3
    see also "The Savage Wars of Peace"
Marcella, Gabriel 64
market economies, democracy and 106–7, 162
Maxwell, Dayton L. 179
Mbeki, Thabo 82
media 132, 137, 165, 166
Médicins sans Frontières 85
Metz, Steven 166, 167
Mexico 39
Middle East 10
Military Code, Nicaragua 40
military doctrine 102, 104, 105
    complex humanitarian emergencies 126–9
military forces
    Central America 39

civilian control 35–6
demobilization 119
El Salvador 40
Guatemala 41, 42
Honduras 41, 42
intervention 129
Nicaragua 40
peace enforcement 183
political control 4
rapid reaction mode 144–5
relations with CIVPOL 148–9
US, in Haiti 50
see also defence forces
military intervention
    Rwanda 76–7
    Zaire 81, 81–6
Military Observer Mission Ecuador/Peru (MOMEP) 109, 111
military operations 7, 11
    complex human emergencies 3–4, 116
    conventional 126
    dissidents, Zaire 76–7, 78–80, 86–7
    planning 89–92, 128–9
    public view of 169–70
    Zaire 73, 91
militias 166
Milosevic, Slobodan 13, 14, 22, 23, 26
Mladic, Ratko 16, 26
Mobutu Sese Seko 72, 77, 79, 88, 91, 94
Mogadishu 132, 161
Moodie, Michael vii, 12
Mozambique 120, 122, 134, 138
Mugunga 79, 80, 87
Multi-National Force 138, 146
murder, Central America 41
Muslims 13, 19, 22, 24, 138

Naim, Moises 37–8
Namibia 120, 122, 134
nation-states 40
    sovereignty 163
    stability 2–4
National Civil Police (PNC), El Salvador 40
National Civilian Police, Guatemala 41
National Concilation Party (PCN) 34
national identity, Balkans 13
National Opposition Union 34
National Security Strategy 106
national sovereignty, changing 4–5
nationalism, Balkans 25
Newbury, Catherine 85–6
Nicaragua 32, 36, 39, 134
    democratization 34, 37
    economic growth 43
    security forces 40
'no-fly zones' 15, 20–1

non-governmental organizations (NGOs) 4,
6–7, 11, 89, 95, 142, 152, 187, 188
Noriega, Manuel 138
North American Free Trade Association
(NAFTA) 54
North Atlantic Council 2
North Atlantic Treaty Organization (NATO)
vii, 4
IFOR 14, 20, 22, 23–4, 110, 115, 138, 146,
185
involvement in Balkans 11–12, 14, 20–2,
185–6
out-of-area concerns 1–2, 20
North Korea 10
Northern Ireland 10, 118, 123
Norway 139
Ntaryamira, Cyprien 76

Observer Mission in Central America
(ONUCA) 36
Observer Mission in El Salvador (ONUSAL)
36–7
Operation 'Desert Storm' 7
Operation 'Guardian Assistance' 85
Operation 'Maritime Guard' 20
Operation 'Maritime Monitor' 20
Operation 'Support Hope' 76–7
Opération Turqoise 76
Operation 'Uphold Democracy' 110
Organization of African Unity (OAU) 4, 188
Organization of American States (OAS) 4,
34, 188
Organization for Security and Cooperation in
Europe (OSCE) 4, 27–8
Ortega, General Humberto 40
Ortega Saavedra, Daniel 34, 35
Orthodox Christians 13
Ottoman Turks, rule in Balkans 13

Pale 22, 27
Panama 138, 195
paramilitary forces 41
peace
internal 112
sustainable 179
peace agreements, enforcement 145–6
peace building 107
peace enforcement, military forces 183
peace making
Central America 33–43, 44–5
integrated strategic framework 179–80
peace operations 104–5, 160–1
deployment gap 137–44
enforcement gap 144–9
institutional gap 150–6
as instrument of policy 106–10

lessons 198
new world disorder 134–7
policy 170–1
political context 105–6
support operations 102–3
peacekeeping vii, viii, 1, 74, 89, 192
integrated operation 6–8
mission statement 90–1
models 5–6
successes 10–11
UN in Yugoslavia 14, 15–18
penal system 150, 151
Perry, William 84
Persian Gulf War (1991) 7, 160
Peru 108
Plavsic, Biljana 27, 28
police 134
civil affairs 143–4
civilian control 35
demobilization 147–8
El Salvador 40, 41
Guatemala 41, 42
Haiti 51, 53, 56, 57–8, 68–9, 138
Honduras 41
indigenous 144, 150
interim forces 147
Nicaragua 40
reform 153
see also CIVPOL
political context, peace operations 105–6,
128
political culture 155
Haiti 50, 56, 64–6
political elites 156
political issues
Central Africa 94–5
complex humanitarian emergencies
117–19, 183–4, 193-4
political parties
El Salvador 34
Haiti 57
population increases 115
populations, displaced 123–4, 127–8
Port au Prince 132
poverty 115
El Salvador 37–8
Haiti 56
Predatory State 52, 56, 110
Prendergast, Jack 94
Préval, René 56, 59, 62, 65, 66
private voluntary organizations (PVOs) 4,
6–7, 11
privatization 43, 45
customs service 55, 62
Prototyping 108–9
Prunier, Gerard 76

public security 135, 141, 144
  follow-on assistance 152–3
  Haiti 56
  planning 142–3
  reform 157–8
  standards 153–4
  structural components 151
  sustainable 156–7
public service, ethos 151

Rapidly Deployable Mission Headquarters
  (RDMHQ) 140
raw materials, compeitioon for 115
reconciliation, peace process 122–4
Red Cross 79–80, 95
refugees viii, 3, 134
  Hutu 79
  Rwandan 73, 75, 80
  in Zaire 77–8, 86–8, 88, 90
Refugees International 82
regional integration, Central America 38–40
Reina Idiáquez, Carlos Roberto 41, 42
relief agencies 118
Republika Srpska 23, 27
Rhodesia 122
risks, complex emergencies 127–8
Roberts, Adam 15, 16
rule of law, Haiti 55–8
rules of engagement 83, 84, 138, 143, 169
Russia 18, 19–20, 27
  see also Soviet Union
Rwanda 5, 72, 78, 90, 91, 93, 95, 134, 166,
  181, 195
  genocide 73, 76, 81, 85, 87, 88–9, 94, 135
  independence 75

Saddam Hussein 9, 117
safe havens 15, 16, 18, 19
Salvador, El see El Salvador
sanctions 149
Sandinistas (FSLN) 34, 35
Sarajevo 15, 20, 21-2, 24, 25, 180
"Savage Wars of Peace", The viii, 102–12
  see also Manwaring Paradigm
Schulte, Gregory 22
Schulz, Donald vii, 50
security, failed and failing states 2–4
Security Council 3, 4, 15, 16, 17–18, 21, 75,
  79, 84–5, 87, 105, 184
security forces
  Central America 40–2
  civilian control 35–6
  demobilization 147–8
security risks 114
  new era 115–16
Senegal 82

separation of powers 155–6
Serbia 13
Serbs 13, 15, 24, 25, 138
  Bosnian 16, 18, 19, 20, 26, 27, 180
Shalikashvili, General John 83
Sierra Leone 179
Silva, Hector 34
Singer, Max 166
Slovenia 13
Smarth, Rosny 65
Smith, Gordon 82
social costs, IFI strategy 54
social development, Haiti 52–5
Somalia 3, 16, 74, 81, 96, 105–6, 110, 134,
  146, 147, 160, 165, 174, 183, 195
  UN operation 180
South Africa 82
South African Defence Forces 12, 120, 122
South Korea 10
sovereignty
  nation-states 115, 163
  national, changing 4–5
Soviet Union
  fall of Communism 13, 117
  former vii
  see also Russia
Spain 82, 139
Srebrenica 15, 18, 180
stability equation 195–6
Stabilization Force (SFOR) 20, 24–5, 28–9,
  110, 122, 132, 146, 152
Standing Joint Taks Force (SETAF) 85, 87
state, monopoly of power 120–2
states
  collapsing 115, 116
  failed vii–viii, 2–4, 135, 164–7, 169, 174
stove-pipe operations 184–5
strategic clarity 7–8
structural adjustment, Haiti 55, 60
SWAPO 120

Tajikistan 179
Taylor, Charles 119
terrorism 35, 45, 166
Third World 134
Tito (Josip Broz) 13
transnational corporations 4
Tudjman, Franjo 13, 23
Turkey 111
Tutsi(s) 73, 75–7, 88, 88–9

Uganda 77
  Tutsi exiles 75–6
Ulster see Northern Ireland
unemployment, Haiti 65
ungovernability 164–7, 169

United Kingdom 16, 18, 19
United Nations vii, 2, 192
  Charter 74
  Children's Fund (UNICEF) 79–80, 95
  Civil Police *see* CIVPOL
  Department of Peacekeeping Operations
    (DPKO) 139, 142, 152
  Development Program 152
  High Commission for Human Rights 80,
    95, 152
  High Commission for Refugees 77, 83, 95
  involvement in Bosnia 14, 15–18
  involvement in Haiti 60, 67–8
  military intervention in Zaire 81–2, 83
  Mission In Haiti 146
  Observer Mission in Central America
    (ONUCA) 36
  Observer Mission in El Salvador
    (ONUSAL) 36–7
  Protection Force *see* UNPROFOR
  role in Central America 33, 36–7, 44, 45,
    46
  role in humanitarian operations 92–3
  Security Council 3, 4, 15, 16, 17–18, 21,
    75, 79, 84–5, 87, 105, 184
  Somalia operation 180
  strengthening 7
  Transitional Authority in Cambodia
    (UNTAC) 138
United States 192
  civil war 163
  CIVPOL personnel 139
  defense policy 117
  gang violence 46
  Haitian reform 54, 59–63, 66–9
  ICITAP 153
  military operations 50, 61, 76–7, 132–4
  Military Support Group 61, 69
  National Security Strategy 106
  Panama operation 138
  peace operations 170–1
  peace support strategy 160–1, 168–70,
    193–4
  role in Balkan conflict 18–19, 25–7, 29,
    185–6
  role in Central America 33, 36, 38, 42–3,
    44, 45
  Somalia operations 180
  as superpower 198

uncomfortable wars 8–10
  Zaire crisis 72–3, 81, 82–5
Unity of Effort, Manwaring Paradigm 102,
    103, 107
UNOSOM II 105–6, 146
UNPROFOR 15, 16, 17, 20, 21, 22, 23, 110,
    180
UNTAC 138, 146, 151
US Information Agency 66
USAID 37, 153, 165, 185, 186
  Disaster Response Team (DART) 82
USEUCOM 85
Uvira 79

Van den Broek, Hans 26
Vance-Owen Plan 184
Vicos Project 108
Vietnam War 9

war criminals 24, 26–8, 30, 121, 125–6, 129
warlords 3, 96, 116, 118, 120, 121, 166, 167
wars
  conventional 9, 126
  internal 109
  intra-state 9, 134
  post-Cold War 80–1
  uncomfortable 8–10
Westendorp, Carlos 26
Westphalian system 163
Wildavsky, Aaron 166
World Bank 182, 186
World War II 123, 187

Yugoslavia vii, 3, 5, 12, 110, 134, 167, 184,
    189
  ethnic groups 13
  strategic ambiguity 7

Zaire 134
  conflict 78–80, 81
  crisis 72–4
  military intervention 81, 81–6
  potential CCP 90–2
  refugees 77–8
  see also Congo, Democratic Republic
ZANLA 122
Zepa 15, 18, 19, 22
Zimbabwe 122
ZIPRA 122